Medieval Literature and Postcolonial Studies

Postcolonial Literary Studies

Series Editors: David Johnson, The Open University and Ania Loomba, University of Pennsylvania

Published titles:
Medieval Literature and Postcolonial Studies, Lisa Lampert-Weissig
Eighteenth-century British Literature and Postcolonial Studies,
Suvir Kaul
Victorian Literature and Postcolonial Studies, Patrick Brantlinger

Forthcoming titles:
Renaissance Literature and Postcolonial Studies, Shankar Raman
Romantic Literature and Postcolonial Studies, Elizabeth A. Bohls
Modernist Literature and Postcolonial Studies, Rajeev Patke
Postwar British Literature and Postcolonial Studies, Graham MacPhee

Medieval Literature and Postcolonial Studies

Lisa Lampert-Weissig

Edinburgh University Press

For Helge

© Lisa Lampert-Weissig, 2010

Edinburgh University Press Ltd
22 George Square, Edinburgh

www.euppublishing.com

Typeset in 10.5/13 Sabon
by Servis Filmsetting Ltd, Stockport, Cheshire, and
printed and bound in Great Britain by
CPI Antony Rowe, Chippenham and Eastbourne

A CIP record for this book is available from the British Library

ISBN 978 0 7486 3717 1 (hardback)
ISBN 978 0 7486 3718 8 (paperback)

The right of Lisa Lampert-Weissig
to be identified as author of this work
has been asserted in accordance with
the Copyright, Designs and Patents Act 1988.

Contents

Series Editors' Preface

Postcolonial Literary Studies foregrounds the colonial and neo-colonial contexts of literary and cultural texts, and demonstrates how these texts help to understand past and present histories of empires. The books in the series relate key literary and cultural texts both to their historical and geographical moments, and to contemporary issues of neo-colonialism and global inequality. In addition to introducing the diverse body of postcolonial criticism, theory and scholarship in literary studies, the series engages with relevant debates on postcolonialism in other disciplines – history, geography, critical theory, political studies, economics and philosophy. The books in the series exemplify how post-colonial studies can re-configure the major periods and areas of literary studies. Each book provides a comprehensive survey of the existing field of scholarship and debate with a timeline, a literature survey, discussion of key critical, theoretical, historical and political debates, case studies providing exemplary critical readings of key literary texts, and guides to further reading. At the same time, each book is also an original critical intervention in its own right. In much the same way that feminism has re-defined how all literary texts are analysed, our ultimate aim is that this series will contribute to all texts in literary studies being read with an awareness of their colonial and neo-colonial resonances.

D. J. and A. L.

List of Illustrations

Acknowledgments

It is a pleasure to conclude the writing of this work by thinking about all of the people who helped me to create it. I am very grateful to Ania Loomba and David Johnson for all of their support and astute advice and for their faith in me. Many other friends and colleagues have generously shared their work, advice and expertise. I would like especially to thank Laurel Amtower, Nadia Altschul, Anthony Bale, Siobhain Bly Calkin, Jonathan Boyarin, Marshall Brown, Matti Bunzl, Brian Catlos, Nesrine Chahine, Kathleen Davis, Barbara Fuchs, Rosemary George, Michelle Hamilton, Geraldine Heng, Sharon Kinoshita, Kathy Lavezzo, Seth Lerer, Louis Montrose, Nancy Nenno, Maura Nolan, Ghada Osman, Esra Özyürek, Michael Provence, Leslie Sconduto, Yasemin Yildiz and Nina Zhiri.

I also benefitted greatly from discussions with students in my undergraduate 'Crusade, Conquest, and Conversion' and 'Parzival and the Grail' courses as well from my graduate seminar on 'Race in Early English Literature'. Kedar Kulkarni, Ingrid Murillo and Leslie Quintanilla were important discussion partners. Ana Grinberg not only researched the dates for the timeline, but also got me thinking about monsters in new ways and generously shared her knowledge of Spanish language and literature. Caralyn Bialo was an important and trusted reader as I finished up the project.

UCSD's Literature Department staff have provided invaluable help and support. I thank especially Nancy Ho-Wu, Debbie Morrow, Heather Fowler Zion, Lucinda Rubio-Barrick, Dawn Blessman, Thom Hill and Nancy Daly. Grants from the UCSD Academic Senate funded research assistants; Michelle Null's advice was invaluable during the application process. UCSD Humanities librarian Rob Melton was, as always, extremely knowledgeable and helpful. I am also very thankful for the work of the outstanding staff of the Geisel Library ILL department.

At Edinburgh University Press, Jackie Jones, Edward Clark, James Dale, Rebecca Mackenzie, Sarah Burnett, Eliza Wright and Máiréad McElligott have been extremely helpful.

Portions of Chapters 2 and 3 appeared in an earlier form as 'Race, Periodicity and the (Neo-) Middle Ages' in *Modern Language Quarterly* 65:3 (2004): 391–422 and appears here with permission. Steve Wiggins of Gorgias Press generously provided permission to include the poem by al Ama at-Tutuli.

I am also very grateful to the colleagues, friends and family who have helped me by providing both hospitality and insights. Milica Spremić's invitation to a memorable conference in Belgrade, Serbia in 2005 has been very important to me. Edith Wenzel invited me to participate in a stimulating 2007 conference on Occidentalism at the Humboldt University in Berlin. This experience and the work I heard there have had a deep and lasting influence on my thinking, as did memorable discussions with her and with her husband, Horst. That same summer, Anthony Bale's conference 'Antisemitism and English Culture' at Birkbeck College, London, afforded me the opportunity to push my thinking in new directions as did discussions with Adam Sutcliffe. Zsuzsanna Lipták and Ferdinando Cicalese and their daughters, Réka and Noëmi were wonderful hosts who took me on an eye-opening tour of Salerno. My in-laws, Ingrid and Rainer Weißig, made me feel at home in the Black Forest. Discussions and excursions with them got me thinking about borders and about Germany and Europe in new ways.

On the home front, family and friends have been enormously supportive. Bree Dietze and Sandra Huzenlaub gave me precious time to work. My mother, Frances Lampert, has been, as always, fiercely supportive and wickedly funny. My stepchildren Eva, Julian and Bryn have inspired me with their questions and their laughter. My son, Sasha, gave me some very firm deadlines and countless joyful reasons to meet them. My most heartfelt thanks go to my husband, Helge. He not only schlepped stacks of books, and solved computer and translation problems at all hours, but also gave me the love, support and encouragement I needed to meet goals and make dreams come true all at the same time.

Timeline

The idea of the 'Middle Ages' can be traced back to Petrarch and is a conception of historical periodisation focused on Europe. Simply translating the label 'medieval' to other regions of the world can be seen as inappropriate and Eurocentric. In this timeline, however, I have chosen to include some events from around the globe in order to provide a broader and more inclusive frame of reference. A few select 'post-medieval' references related to this project are also included in what can only be seen as a 'speculum timeline' of medievalism and Medieval Studies, a continuing stream of events and works.

Date	Historical Events	Literary and Other Publications
c. 150	Mochica culture in northern Perù	
c. 164	The oldest surviving Mayan monuments constructed in Mesoamerica	
c. 270	Zapotec culture begins to flourish in southwest México	
284–305	Diocletian is Emperor of Rome	
306–37	Constantine changes system of the Roman Empire	
355	Franks and Saxons expand along the Rhine	
386–557	Northern Wei dynasty in China	

401	Visigoth King Alaric attacks Italy
410	Sack of Rome
413	Burgundian settlements in Trier, Speyer and Mainz
415	Visigoths invade Iberian peninsula
c. 425	Beginning of Anglo-Saxon incursions in England
442	Huns cross Danube into Balkans
476	Fall of Rome (traditional)
479–502	Southern Ch'I Imperial dynasty in China
481–511	Clovis I is king of the Franks
493–526	Theodoric is king of Italy
502–57	Southern Liang Imperial dynasty in China
507	Franks defeat Visigoths at Vouillé
511–26	Iberian Peninsula under Ostrogothic protectorate
534–93	Peak of Mayan building
536–45	Franks campaign in Provence
565	Saint Columba founds monastery in Iona, Scotland
568	Lombard conquest of Italy
570–636	Isidore of Seville
c. 570–632	Muhammad
581–618	Sui Imperial dynasty in China
589	Visigoths convert to Christianity at the Third Council of Toledo
590–604	Pope Gregory I establishes the basis for Roman papacy
593–4	Bishop Gregory of Tours' *Ten Books of Histories* on the Merovingian kingdoms

596–7	Missionaries sent to Kent by Pope Gregory I	
612	Visigothic King Sisebut of Spain inaugurates a policy of forcible conversion of all Jews in the kingdom	
618–907	T'ang Imperial dynasty in China	
622	Muhammad's hijra from Mecca to Medina. Start of Islamic calendar	
628	Dagobert I expels Jews from Frankish kingdom	
c. 630	The Maya devise a 260-day calendar	
632	Heraclius, Byzantine emperor, decrees forced baptism of all Jews in Byzantine empire	
636		Isidore of Seville's *Etymologiae*
694–711	All Jews under Visigothic rule in Spain declared slaves, their possessions confiscated and Jewish religion outlawed	
c. 700	Monte Albán, sacred capital of Zapotecs, reaches a population of 20,000	
711	Muslim forces lead by Tariq ibn Ziyad defeat Roderic at battle of Guadalete	
717–20	Caliph Omar II introduces series of discriminatory regulations against Christians and Jews	
731	Mayan Jaguar Paw dynasty reinstated	Bede's *Historia ecclesiastica gentis Anglorum*
732	Battle of Tours	

739	Alfonso I, king of León and Asturias, conquers all Galicia and recaptures most of León
c. 750	Pueblo period in southwest North America begins
756	Abd al-Rahman I emir in Córdoba
	The ruling Umayyad dynasty in Damascus gives way to the Abbasids from Baghdad
768–814	Reign of Charlemagne
778	Franks defeated at Roncesvalles; death of Roland
800	Charlemagne crowned Holy Roman Emperor
c. 800	Oxkintok and Sayil, in northern Mayan lowlands, are established and become major urban centres
	Mochica culture in Perù declines
	Jewish and Muslim merchants bring slaves to al-Andalus
	Mixtec culture develops in southwest México
	Charlemagne takes Barcelona
800–909	Aghlabid dynasty in Tunisia
c. 800–1000	Andalusi cities are important markets for slaves from the Slavic regions and northern Spain
850–950	Abandonment of many Mayan centres in Guatemala and México
868–905	Tulunid dynasty in Egypt
c. 900	*Beowulf*

905	Sancho I creates the independent Basque kingdom in Navarra
907–1125	Liao dynasty in Khitan
909–1171	Fatimid caliphate dynasty in Maghrib and Egypt
c. 910	Second Pueblo period
917–71	Southern Han dynasty in Kwangtung
c. 920	Mixtecs fight their way into the Zapotec valley, occupying Monte Albán
929	Abd al-Rahman III proclaimed caliph in Córdoba
c. 930	Seibal undergoes a decline
932	Fernán González declares himself first king of Castilla
934–65	Later Shu dynasty in Szechuan
935–69	Ikhshidid dynasty in Egypt
936–47	Later Chin Imperial dynasty in China
947–51	Later Han Imperial dynasty in China
960–1127	Northern Sung Imperial dynasty in China
987	Kukulcán invades Mayan sites in southern México
1000	Christianity established in Iceland Svein of Denmark conquers Norway Ethelred ravages Cumberland and the Isle of Man Andean empires of Wari and Tiwanaku collapse
c. 1000	Zenith of Inca Empire Virtual disappearance of Slavic slaves and Jewish slave traders from Muslim Spain

	Considerable part of Aragón captured from the Muslims by Sancho III, king of Navarra
	Mayan city of Chichén-Itzá becomes a Toltec colonial capital
1002	Venetian fleet defeats Muslims besieging Greeks in Bari
1003	Muslims devastate León
	Leif Eriksson's voyage to North America
1007	Kakuyid dynasty of Isfahan, Persia, founded
1009	Muslims settle in northwest India
	Danes attack London
1010	Foundation of Ly dynasty in north Vietnam
1011	Ethelred invades South Wales
	Muslim forces sack Pisa
1012	Prosecutions of heresy in Germany
1013	King Svein I of Denmark defeats Ethelred II of England
1014	Battle of Clontarf between Irish and a Viking confederation
1015	Muslims of Spain conquer Sardinia
1016	Normans invade and settle in southern Italy
	Moroccan Hammudid dynasty reaches power in Córdoba
1018	Byzantine army defeats south Italian rebels at Cannae

1021	Byzantine army attacks Benevento, in southern Italy
1022	Burning of heretics becomes an established policy
1024	Sung rule established in Szechwan, China
1025	South Indian Chola attack against Sumatra and Malaya
1027	Umayyad dynasty in power in Córdoba
1028	Sancho III of Navarra unites Castilla to his kingdom
1029	Cholas expelled from Ceylon
1030	Sancho III makes his son, Fernando I, king of Castilla
1032–1227	Western Hsia dynasty in Tangut
1033	Creation of the kingdom of Castilla
1035	Establishment of Christian kingdom of Aragón
1037	Christian kingdom of Castilla-León is founded after the battle of Tamarón Seljuk Turks established in Khurasan, after emigrating from central Asia
1039	Gruffudd ap Llywelyn defeats an English invading force in Wales
1040	Seljuk Turks conquer Ghazanvid territories in Persia
1044	Aniruddha becomes king of Pagan (in Burma)
1045	Seljuk Turks raid Armenia for the first time
1046	Henry III crowned Holy Roman Emperor

1047	Duke William puts down internal rebellions in Normandy
	Greeks defeat a Seljuk force near Erzurum
1051	Cathars executed at Goslar
1054	Schism between Byzantine and Western churches
1055	Gruffudd ap Llywelyn conquers South Wales
	Seljuk Turks take Baghdad, ending Bawayhid rule
1056	Gruffydd ap Llywelyn raids into England
	Fernando proclaims himself emperor of Spain, initiating the Reconquest
1056–1147	Almoravid dynasty in Morocco
1059	Robert Guiscard invested as duke of Apulia and Calabria, and count of Sicily
	Seljuk raid into the Byzantine empire
1061	Robert Guiscard begins the Norman conquest of Sicily
1063	Harold of Wessex begins to conquer Wales
1064	Seljuk sultan Alp Arslan conquers Armenia
1065	Seljuk Turks conquer Transoxiana and Syria
1066	Battle of Hastings
1068	Ly Thanh-Tong of Dai Viet, captures Rudravarman III of Champa, annexing his northern provinces
1069	Mutamid becomes king of Sevilla and takes Córdoba

1070	At Valpelage, Alfonso VI of León defeats Sancho II of Castilla
1071	Seljuks conquer Armenia, Anatolia, and begin conquering Syria
1072	Robert Guiscard captures Palermo
1073	Seljuks begin the systematic conquest of Asia Minor
1075	Seljuk Turks take Damascus
1076	Berbers destroy Ghana, capital of the Madingo Empire of Ghana (Western Sudan)
1077	End of Pagan dynasty in Burma
1080	William I ravages Northumbria and invades Scotland
1081	Alfonso VI of Castilla exiles Rodrigo Díaz de Vivar (El Cid)
1082	Robert Guiscard takes Durazzo and Corfu, recovered by the Byzantines the next year
1084	Guiscard expels the Germans from Rome and his Normans sack the city
1085	Alfonso VI of Castilla and León takes Toledo, the old Visigoth capital, and defeats the Muslim kings of Valencia Seljuks take Ankara and Antioch from the Byzantines
1086	Defeat of Alfonso VI of Castilla at Sagrajas against Almoravids and Sevillans

1086–7		*Domesday Book*
1086–1145	Judah ben Samuel ha-Levi	
1087	A Genovese-Pisan fleet takes Mahdiyah, in Barbary	
1089	The Fatimids recover Ascalon, Tyre and Acre from the Seljuks Urban negotiates with Alexius a crusade against the Turks, at the Council of Melfi	
1090	Founding of the Almoravid dynasty in Granada Roger Guiscard takes Malta Al-Hasan ibn-al-Sabbah, founder of the Assassins, establishes himself in Alamut, Iraq	
1091	Yusuf ibn-Tashfin destroys, and unites, the Muslim kingdoms of Andalusia Roger Guiscard completes the conquest of Sicily Baghdad becomes the Seljuk capital	
1092	William II seizes northern Cumberland and Westmorland from the Scots	
c. 1092–1156	Peter the Venerable	
1093	Alfonso VI seizes Santarém, Lisboa and Cintra Malcolm III Canmore, king of Scotland, killed while invading England	
1094	The Welsh expel the Normans from northwest Wales	
c. 1095		*Chanson de Roland*
1095–1102	First Crusade	

1096	Pogroms by Crusaders in Werelinghofen, Germany
	Normans complete their conquest of South Wales and recover Anglesey
	Russian princes unite against the Cumans
1098	The Fatimids recover Jerusalem from the Seljuk Turks
	Magnus of Norway conquers the Orkneys, the Shetlands and the Isle of Man
1099	Crusaders take Jerusalem
	Death of El Cid
1101	Crusader armies are defeated by Turks
1102	Almoravids take Valencia
1103	Unsuccessful Norwegian invasion of Ireland
1110	Emperor Henry V starts an expedition against Italy
	Baldwin I is crowned first Latin king of Jerusalem
1111	Russian forces defeat the Cumans in today's Ukraine
1115–1234	Chin dynasty in Jürched
1118	Alfonso I of Aragón captures Zaragoza from its Muslim ruler
	Roger II, count of Sicily, attempts to conquer Tunis
1120	Alfonso I of Aragón defeats Islamic forces at Cutanda and Daroca
	Foundation of the Knights Templar
1122	Concordat of Worms
	David III of Georgia takes the last surviving Muslim stronghold in Caucasia

1124	The Fatimids surrender Tyre to Baldwin II of Jerusalem Lothar, king of Saxony, penetrates the lands of the pagan Slavs	
1125	The Jürched take Peking	
1126	Alfonso I of Aragón defeats the Muslims at Arinsol, near Lucena The Jürched take Kaifeng, the Sung capital	
1126–98	Averroës (Ibn Rushd)	
1127–1279	Southern Sung Imperial dynasty in China	
1130	Sicily becomes a kingdom under Roger II	
1135–9		Geoffrey of Monmouth's *Historia regum Britannie*
1139–1204	Maimonides	
c. 1140		*Poema de Mío Cid*
1143	Alfonso Enríquez is recognised as the king of Portugal by Alfonso VII	
1144	Zangi takes Edessa, massacring the Franks First recorded blood libel at Norwich, England	
1146	Roger of Sicily takes Tripoli, in north Africa Anti-Jewish riots in Rhineland by the Crusaders of the Second Crusade	
c. 1146–c. 1223	Gerald of Wales	
1147–9	Second Crusade	
1155	Frederick crowned Holy Roman Emperor Pope Adrian IV grants Ireland to Henry II	
c. 1155	Death of Geoffrey of Monmouth	

1158	Henry II campaigns against the Welsh	
1159–73	Travels of Benjamin of Tudela	
1160		*Letter of Prester John* begins to circulate
	Loss of all conquests by the king of Sicily in north Africa	
	Taira Kiyomori, leader of the Japanese 'feudal' confederacy, wins control of the imperial government	
1160–1215		Marie de France's *Lais*, *Fables*, and *Espurgatoire seint Patriz*
1164	Malcolm IV of Scotland defeats Norse and Celtic rebels	
	Muslims in Spain recapture Córdoba and Almería	
1165	Henry II makes his last, unsuccessful attempt to subjugate the Welsh princes of Snowdonia	
1167	Saladin, commanding the Syrian garrison of Alexandria, surrenders to Amalric of Jerusalem and his Fatimid allies	
1167–1227	Genghis Khan	
1168	Amalric attempts to invade Egypt, finally abandoning the siege of Damietta in 1169	
	The Toltec empire destroyed by tribes from northern México	
1170	Murder of Archbishop Thomas of Becket	

c. 1170–8		Chrétien de Troyes writes *Erec et Enide, Cliges, Yvain,* and *Lancelot*
1171	Henry II lands in Ireland Yusuf abu Ya'qub is the supreme Muslim ruler in Spain	
1173–1240	Llywelyn ap Iorwerth	
1174	William of Scotland is captured while invading Northumbria Saladin takes over Damascus	
1175	Muhammad of Ghur begins his invasion of India	
1177	A naval expedition sent by Yusuf, emperor of Morocco, fails to take Lisboa	
c. 1180	Evidence of men and women from Sardinia, North Africa and Malta traded as slaves in Genoa	
1182	Saladin takes Edessa and Nisibis King Philip Augustus of France decrees the expulsion of the Jews from his kingdom and the confiscation of their real estate	
1183	Saladin takes Aleppo and makes Damascus his capital	
1186	Muhammad of Ghur destroys the Ghaznavid kingdom of the Punjab and takes Lahore	
1187	Saladin takes Jerusalem in the Battle of Hattin	
1188	Saladin Tithe in England	
1189–92	Third Crusade	

1190	Massacres of Jews at York and other cities in England
1192	Muhammad, Sultan of Ghur, conquers northern India
1192–1313	Kamakura Shogunate in Japan
1193	Delhi becomes the Muslim capital in India; Muslims take the great Buddhist centre of Bihar
1194	Henry VI recognises Amalric as king of Cyprus
1198	Frederick II is crowned king of Sicily
1199–1216	King John reigns in England
c. 1200	The México/Aztecs make their way southward into the Valley of México Incas dominate Cuzco valley; Manco Capac is ruler of the Inca in Cuzco, Hurin dynasty Spanish Muslim slaves widely available in Christian Mediterranean cities, especially in Cataluña, Provence and northern Italy Third Pueblo period
	Nibelungenlied
1201	John grants a charter to the Jews in England
1202	Muhammad of Ghur completes his conquest of upper India; Ikhtiyar al-Din's forces seize Bengal
1202–4	Fourth Crusade
1203	Jayavarman VII of Cambodia conquers and annexes Champa

1203–4	Philip Augustus conquers Normandy and Anjou
1204	Crusaders sack Constantinople
1205	The Seljuk Turks take Kayseri, the Danishmend capital in Anatolia Ikhtiyar, the Muslim ruler of Bengal, fails in an attempt to invade Assam
1206–1368	Yuan (Mongol Great Khans) Imperial dynasty in China; Temujin, the Mongol prince, takes the title Genghis Khan after uniting Mongolia as empire
1208	Llywelyn seizes Powys
1209	John invades Scotland Thamar, queen of Georgia, takes Kars in a victorious campaign against the Turks
1210	John makes an expedition to Ireland, enforcing his authority there
c. 1210	Wolfram von Eschenbach's *Parzival* Gottfried von Strassburg's *Tristan und Isolt*
1210–29	Albigensian Wars
1211	Genghis Khan destroys the Kara-Khitai empire in east Turkestan and invades China
1215	Fourth Lateran council Paris's *universitas* is recognised, evolving later into the University of Paris The *Magna Carta*

	Genghis Khan takes Peking; the Chin then make Kaifeng their capital
1216	Leo of Armenia takes Antioch from Bohemond IV
1217	Alfonso of Portugal defeats the Muslims at Alcácer do Sal
1217–29	Fifth Crusade
1220	Jaya Parameshvaravarman II becomes King of Champa on the withdrawal of the Khmers (of Cambodia)
1221	Jokyu Disturbance in Japan
1222	A Mongol army defeats the Russians and Cumans of the Kalka, near the sea of Azov
1225	Jalal-ad-Din liberates Persia from the Mongols Tran Thai-tong becomes sole emperor of Dai Viet, founding the Tran dynasty
1227	Death of Genghis Khan, his empire is divided The Almohad Abu-l-'Ala' Idris (al-Ma'mum) declares himself the Muslim ruler of Spain
1227–74	Thomas Aquinas
1228–1574	Hafsid dynasty in Tunisia
1229	The Inquisition is established in Toulouse
1230	Fernando III of Castilla succeeds Alfonso IX of León, thus uniting the two kingdoms Bang Klang T'ao becomes King of Sukhodaya, the first Thai (Siamese) state to free itself from Cambodia

c. 1230	Sinchi Roca, of the Hurin dynasty, is ruler of the Inca It becomes routine to note slaves' homelands in sale contracts in southern France and Cartagena
1231	The Mongols begin their campaigns to conquer Korea Gregory IX appoints inquisitors against heresy in Germany
1232	Muhammad ibn-Yusuf of Granada proclaims himself king in Spain Almohad emperor al-Ma'mun dies, succeeded by 'Abd-al-Wahid
1232/3–1315/6	Ramon Llull
1233	Richard the Marshal, Earl of Pembroke, in alliance with Llywelyn, begins his revolt against Henry III Gregory IX organises the Holy Office (Inquisition)
1234	The Mongols take Kaifeng and destroy the Chin dynasty
1235	Blood libel at Fulda, Germany
1236	Fernando of Castilla and León takes Córdoba The Teutonic Knights complete their conquest of the Pomezanians, of west Prussia A Mongol army led by Batu (grandson of Genghis Khan) conquers the Volga Bulgars

	Georgia conquered by the Mongols
1237	Batu's Mongol army destroys the city and principality of Riazan, Russia
1238	Jaime I of Aragón takes Valencia
	Batu destroys Moscow and other central Russian cities
1239	King Theobald of Navarra arrives at Acre, beginning a new crusade together with Richard of Cornwall
1242	The Mongols evacuate central Europe
1243	The Mongols defeat Kaykhusraw II of Rum and his Greek allies, near Erzinjan
1244	The Christians are finally expelled from Jerusalem
1245	John de Plano Carpinis travels to the court of the Great Khan
1248	The Genoese conquer Rhodes from the Greeks
1250	Louis IX is defeated and captured by the Egyptians while withdrawing from Mansurah
	The Ayyubid, an-Nasir, of Aleppo, take Damascus
1250–1390	Bahri Mamluk sultanate in Egypt
1251–84	Tokimune rules in Japan
1253	Hulagu, grandson of Genghis Khan, begins his conquest of the Islamic Empire
1253–5	William of Rubruck travels to China and Mongolia

1254	Henry III accepts the throne of Sicily
	Louis IX expels the Jews from France
1257	The Mongols raid the Punjab
1258	Mongol sack of Baghdad
	Kublai Khan invades China
c. 1260	Pueblo culture expands into Verde Valley, Tonto Basin, upper Salt River Basin, and present-day southwest Arizona
c. 1265–1321	Dante Alighieri
1271–95	Marco Polo in China
1274	A fleet sent by Kublai Khan to conquer Japan repulsed by Hakata Bay and sub-sequently destroyed by a storm
1276–7	First Welsh War
1279	Kublai Khan completes the Mongol conquest of China; the southern Sung dynasty is extinguished
1282	Sicilian Vespers uprising
1290	Edward I expels the Jews from England
1291	Mamluks take last Latin states in the Holy Land
	Edward I is Scotland's overlord
1292	Mongols invading Muslim India are repulsed at Sunam
	Kublai Khan sends a fleet to conquer Java, which is repulsed the next year
1294	Welsh revolt against Edward

1297	Wallace leads a Scottish rising against Edward, defeating English forces at Stirling Bridge
	'Ala'-ad-Din conquers the Hindu kingdom of Gujarat
1298	Battle of Falkirk
1298–9	Massacre of thousands of Jews in 146 localities in southern and central Germany led by the German knight Rindfleisch
1299	New wave of Turks ('Ottoman'), driven westward by Mongols, are in occupation of western Anatolia
1300	Edward takes Caerlaverock Castle, in southwest Scotland
1300	The Shans in Burma defeat a punitive Mongol expedition from China
c. 1300	Quinatzin is ruler in Texcoco, central México
1303	Mongols unsuccessfully besiege Delhi
1304	The Scots submit to Edward in a parliament at St Andrews
1304–74	Francesco Petrarca (Petrarch)
1306	Philip IV expels the Jews from France
	Robert Bruce, Earl of Carrick, is crowned as king of Scotland. English forces defeat him at Methven, then at Dalry
	A Mongol invasion of India defeated on the Indus

1306–9	Ethiopian embassy to Papacy	
c. 1308–21		*Divina Commedia*
1312	The Knights Templar order is suppressed	
1313	The Scots expel the English garrison from Perth; also they recover the Isle of Man	
1313–75	Giovanni Boccaccio	
1314	Bruce repulses English forces attempting to relieve Stirling Castle; defeats Edward at Bannockburn, completing the expulsion of the English from Scotland	
1315	Edward, brother of Robert of Scotland, invades Ireland	
1320	First Franciscan mission to India	
	Capac Yupanqui is ruler of the Inca	
	Declaration of Arbroath, earls and barons of Scotland reject the English rule	
1325	The México/Aztecs found the city of Tenochtitlán	
	Crusade against the Mongols and Lithuanians in Poland	
1325–49	Travels of Ibn Battutah	
1326	Ottomans capture Bursa and make it their capital	
1328	In the Treaty of Edinburgh, Edward III makes peace with Scotland, recognising Bruce as king	
1330–1521	Dominion of Aztec Empire over most ancient México	
1333	The King of Granada takes Gibraltar from Castilla	

1336	Mubarak Shah rebels against Muhammad of Delhi and makes East Bengal independent	
1337–1453	Hundred Years War begins	
1338–1537	Ashikaga Shogunate in Japan	
1344	Lewis of Hungary expels Mongols from Transylvania	
	Crusade to the Canary Islands planned	
1346	Black Death outbreak in Georgia	
	Syria, Mesopotamia and Palestine infected by Black Death	
	Mirza, in revolt against Muhammad, founds the Muslim kingdom of Kashmir	
1347	First record of Black Death in Sicily	
	Black Death outbreaks in Constantinople, Naples, Genoa and southern France	
	Calais surrenders to Edward, who expels its citizens and establishes an English colony	
	Black Death in Italy, Spain, Marseilles, Provence, Paris and southern England	
1348–53		Composition of *Decameron*
1352	The Ottoman Turks take Gallipolli, making this their base for conquests in Europe	

1353	Fa Ngum, a Thai prince who had conquered the Upper Mekong Valley, proclaimed King of Lan Ch'ang (Laos)
1355	The Scots take Berwick-upon-Tweed
1361–2	Second outbreak of Black Death in western Europe
1366	Murad establishes the Ottoman capital in Adrianople
1367	Timur becomes effective ruler of the Asiatic Mongols
1368	Chu Yuan-chang expels the Mongols from China and founds Ming Imperial dynasty
1375	Catalan Atlas Acamapichtli, the first historical ruler of the México/ Aztecs, is elected *tlatoani* in Tenochtitlán
1378	Great Schism of Western Christianity
c. 1380	Yáhuar Huaca is ruler of the Inca
1381	English Peasants' revolt
1382–1517	Burji Mamluk sultanate in Egypt
1384	The Scots destroy Lochmaben Castle and raid Cumberland; an English expedition invades Scotland as far as Edinburgh
1385	The Turks take Sofia Timur partially conquers Azerbaijan
1386	Murad takes Nis and compels Lazar, Prince of Serbia, to become tributary

1380–1400		Likely composition dates for Geoffrey Chaucer's *The Canterbury Tales*
1389	Serbs defeated by Ottomans at Kosovo polje	
1389	Massacre of the Prague (Bohemia) Jewish community	
c. 1390		British Library, MS Cotton Nero A.X (*Sir Gawain and the Green Knight, Pearl, Patience, Cleanness*)
1398	Timur invades the Punjab	
1400	Henry IV campaigns in Scotland; then in North Wales Owain Glyn Dwr begins his revolt	
1401	Henry's second Welsh campaign fails to crush the revolt	
1402	Glyn Dwr defeats and captures Edmund Mortimer in Maelienydd	
1413–14	Disputation of Tortosa (Spain)	
1415	Battle of Agincourt	
1420–33	Hussite Wars	
1425	Portugal begins attacks on the Canary Islands	
1428	Le Loi, having defeated the Chinese, declares himself Emperor of Dai Viet, establishing the Le dynasty	
c. 1430		Borgia Map
1437	A Portuguese expedition led by Prince Henry the Navigator fails to take Tangier	

1438	Inca Empire embarks on a course of expansion from the present-day north Ecuador to central Chile; Pachacuti Inca Yupanqui is the emperor
1441	Start of European slave trading in Africa. The Portuguese captains Antão Gonçalves and Nuno Tristão capture twelve Africans in Cabo Branco (modern Mauritania) and take them to Portugal as slaves
1442	First report of Roma in Europe (Barcelona)
1444	Lançarote de Freitas, a tax-collector from the Portuguese town of Lagos, forms a company to trade with Africa, and brings first large group of African slaves to Europe
1446	Muhammad X recovers Granada
1448	The Inca invade Araucania in present-day south Chile Outbreak of war between England and Scotland
1449	Cheng-t'ung, the Chinese Emperor, is defeated and captured while attacking the Oirats (western Mongols)
1452	Start of the 'sugar-slave complex'. Sugar is first planted in the Portuguese island of Madeira and, for the first time, African slaves are put to work on the sugar plantations

1455	Beginning of the War of the Roses
	Pope Nicholas V issues *Romanus Pontifex*
1459	Turkish conquest of Serbia
1460	The Turks take the Greek principality of Morea
1460–70	Inca conquest of the Chimús in Perú
1461	The first of the Portuguese trading forts, the castle at Arguin (modern Mauritania), is completed
1462	Portuguese found colony on the Cape Verde Islands
	Henry of Castilla takes Gibraltar
1468	Sunni Ali, ruler of Gao (on the middle-Niger), takes Timbuktu; founds African empire of Gao
1469	Marriage of Isabella I of Castilla and Fernando V of Aragón
1470	The Turks capture Negroponte from Venice
c. 1470	Despite Papal opposition, Spanish merchants begin to trade in large numbers of slaves in the 1470s
1471	The Portuguese conquer Tangier
1472–1549	Wattasid dynasty in Morocco
1476	Carlos de Valera of Castilla in Spain brings back 400 slaves from Africa
1477	Isabella and Fernando establish the Inquisition in Castilla

Completion of *Le Morte D'Arthur* by Thomas Malory (appears alongside c. 1470)

1480	The Turks begin to besiege Rhodes, repulsed by the Knights Hospitallers. The Turks take Otranto
1482	Boabdil rebels against his father, Abu-al-Hasan, and seizes Granada Diego Cão, a Portuguese mariner, reaches the Congo. The Portuguese make a settlement on the Gold Coast
1483	Torquemada appointed inquisitor general of Castilla and Aragón Expulsion of Jews from Warsaw
1485	End of the War of the Roses; Henry Tudor becomes King Henry VII of England
1486	Portuguese settle the West African island of São Tomé
1486–1502	Ahuizotl reigns as *tlatoani* of the Aztec Empire
1488	Bartolomeu Dias rounds the Cape of Storms (renamed later of Good Hope) and explores the Indian Ocean and the East African coast
1492	Columbus's first voyage Fall of last Muslim stronghold in Iberia, Granada. Edict of Expulsion signed, forcing Muslims and Jews in Spain to convert or emigrate
1581	Tasso's *La Gerusalemme liberata*
1786	Sir William Jones lectures on Sanskrit to Asiatic Society

1819	Gesellschaft für ältere deutsche Geschichtskunde founded	Walter Scott's *Ivanhoe*
1835	Macaulay's 'Minutes' on Indian education	
1847		Disraeli's *Tancred*; Petar Njegoš's *The Mountain Wreath*
1851	Crystal Palace exhibits feature 'medieval' and 'primitive' villages	
1864	Early English Text Society is founded	
1869–76	Richard Wagner's *Der Ring des Nibelungen*	
1870		Gaston Paris's 'La Chanson de Roland et la nationalité française'
1872		Journal *Romania* founded
1875		León Gautier's edition of *La Chanson de Roland*
1882		Richard Wagner's *Parsifal*
1899		Kaiser Wilhelm visits Saladin's tomb in Damascus
1989	Slobodan Milošević assembly at Kosovo polje	
1995		Goytisolo's *El Sitio de los sitios*
1996	Front National celebrates 1500 year anniversary of baptism of Clovis	
1998	Bin Laden's 'Declaration of the World Islamic Front for Jihad against the Jews and the Crusaders'	
2006	Pope Benedict XVI's address on 'Faith, Reason and the University'	

Prologue

Ah, the dead, the unended, endlessly ending dead: how long, how rich is their story. We, the living, must find what space we can alongside them; the giant dead whom we cannot tie down, though we grasp at their hair, though we rope them while they sleep. (Rushdie 1995: 136)

The long, rich story of the Middle Ages is one that scholars and artists were writing even before the fourteenth-century poet Petrarch referred to a 'middle time' between the glory of Rome and a better time that he saw as yet to come. Such engagement with the medieval past has occurred, of course, into the present day.[1] One might assume, though, that these engagements with the Middle Ages would have little or no intersection with contexts and concepts that are of concern in postcolonial studies, a discipline that would appear to be concerned primarily, or even exclusively, with the much more recent past. Such an assumption, however, can obscure significant historical connections. Just one example of such a connection is how the development of the discipline of medieval studies occurred alongside and sometimes in direct relation to the rise of European nationalism and colonialism.

In this book, I approach the layered connections between the disciplines of medieval studies and postcolonial studies in three main ways. Chapter One provides an overview of the current field of postcolonial medieval studies. I examine how postcolonial theory has influenced the reading of medieval texts and contexts, and also, just as significantly, how medievalists have provided important critiques of key terms and concepts in postcolonial studies, including Orientalism, colonialism and nationalism. The chapter also attempts to illuminate the historical connections between postcolonial studies and medieval studies by examining the development of medieval studies in the context of the rise of European nationalism and colonialism.

Chapter 2 presents readings of medieval texts and contexts from the perspective of postcolonial studies. Texts examined include a love poem written in Arabic and early Spanish from medieval Iberia; an Old French romance about werewolves, *Guillaume de Palerne*; the Middle High German romance *Parzival* which features a noble knight whose skin is speckled black and white 'like a magpie'; and the medieval 'bestselling' travel narrative, *The Travels of Sir John Mandeville*, which includes descriptions of fabulous encounters all around the globe. These readings attempt not only to provide new insights into these texts themselves, but also to reconsider concepts important to postcolonial studies, such as hybridity and race, from a longer historical perspective. Chapter 3 examines contemporary medievalisms in current discourse about 'Islam and the West', specifically in relation to the question of 'Islam in Europe', which has been an increasing focus of debates in the new millennium. I will look at the use of medievalisms in debates about the identity of Europe and European identity as they play out through specific locations and situations, as in controversies over the construction of mosques and minarets that have recently developed across Europe. The chapter ends with readings of contemporary novels by Juan Goytisolo, Salman Rushdie, Tariq Ali and Amitav Ghosh that engage with the question of 'Islam and the West' through the legacy of the Middle Ages.

This book attempts to make postcolonial medieval studies accessible to non-specialists. An important intended audience is those who study later historical periods from a postcolonial perspective. Because postcolonial studies so often neglects premodern texts and contexts, this project aims to demonstrate the vital importance of early contexts to key concepts such as 'race' and 'hybridity' and the relevance of medievalisms in contemporary politics and literature. For those already familiar with postcolonial medieval studies, this book also attempts to offer something new by encouraging further comparatist work, by examining, for example, certain developments in nineteenth-century medievalisms as pan-European phenomena and by introducing readings of literatures that have received less attention in postcolonial medieval studies, such as those from the Middle High German corpus. The project also seeks to draw increased attention to areas such as al-Andalus and Norman Sicily, which are only now beginning to receive the focus they deserve in Anglophone literary scholarship.

Scholars of the Middle Ages are increasingly embracing a global context, seeking historical connections between different parts of the world that have long been obscured by the constricting boundaries of nation and period. This volume hopes to encourage this continuing project and to invite students of later periods to take advantage of the new findings and perspectives it affords.

Note

1. See Dagenais and Greer 2000.

Chapter 1

The Future of the Past

Various contributors to a recent forum entitled 'The End of Postcolonial Theory?' pointed to elements within the field of postcolonial studies that they considered to be problematic. These included a perceived narrow focus on English empire and the Anglophone tradition, and a sense that postcolonial studies has become a 'niche' subject trapped within a labyrinth of arcane postmodernist rhetoric. Most importantly, the critics expressed anguish over a sense of the inadequacy of postcolonial studies to address ever-increasing neocolonialism and imperialism after 9/11. By way of a corrective, one forum participant, Fernando Coronil, urged a turn to history, 'A view of colonialism as starting from the fifteenth century would offer a different understanding of modern colonialism and colonial modernity' (Agnani et al. 2007: 637). I agree wholeheartedly with Coronil's suggestion: we must look to the longer history of colonialism. But, if looking back as far as the fifteenth century provides new insights, what happens if we lengthen our view even further, into the medieval period? A more thoughtful examination of a truly longer view of the history and ideologies of colonialism is necessary not only to help us understand medieval literature and culture differently, but also to help us understand the histories, ideologies and literatures of postcolonialism through new lenses as well. As Robert Bartlett has demonstrated in *The Making of Europe*, European nation-states were themselves consolidated through a form of colonial expansionism (1993). By acknowledging this longer history of colonialism, one that exists across cultures, we can see how medieval history, culture and literature are fundamental to our understandings of the processes of colonialism, processes which have conventionally only been examined in relation to later historical periods.

The point here is not simply to move the periodisation line back by a century or two so that medievalists can 'catch up' with the Renaissance or early modern period, as Margreta de Grazia has put it:

There can be no denying that the modern divide has been hard on medi-evalists, and they cannot be blamed for trying (like a third world country) to catch up, often by stretching the starting point of the modern back a century or more so that the Middle Ages is no longer a middle of any kind, but rather a beginning *avant le* [sic] *lettre*, an earlier early modern or premodern. (2007: 457)

De Grazia's remarks and her linking of medievalists and 'the third world' call attention to an issue central to this book. The privileges afforded to those who are labelled (or label themselves) 'modern' are considerable. One important privilege is the seeming ability to determine who or what is not modern, and if and how those others will ever be able to 'catch up' to the 'modern world'.

The human stakes of such privileging within academia are relatively low. The relative prestige of historical fields such as the 'Renaissance' and the 'modern period' is likely to have consequences for the funding of research, faculty positions and library resources. But it is outside the university where this privileging of 'modern' has the greatest impact. If one compares the 'first world' and the 'third', the stakes in attempts to 'reach parity', to be considered part of the modern club, are enormous. As Enrique Dussel has convincingly argued, the creation of 'moder-nity' has been a Eurocentric project: 'Modernity appears when Europe affirms itself as the "center" of a *World* History that it inaugurates; the "periphery" that surrounds this center is consequently part of its self-definition' (1993: 65). This self-definition of 'modern Europe' has been shaped in part by a particular view of medieval Europe, a medieval Europe that is commensurate with Christendom and from which certain demons, such as the history of the Muslim presence on the Iberian Peninsula from 711 to 1492, have been exorcised.

Who gets to determine the boundaries between modern and premod-ern, central and peripheral, first world and third world, European and non-European, and what are the stakes of these determinations? What is occluded by the traditional ways of seeing these boundaries, and what is the impact of these formulations not just intellectually, but politically? A central premise of this book will be that the ideological groundwork for colonialism was being laid well before 1492. Both the medieval founda-tions of colonialism and later interpretations of these foundations – that is, both scholarly medieval studies and the popular medievalisms found in all kinds of cultural production – have been essential to the vision of Europe as a progressive and enlightened global centre, a centre that is defined in large part through contrast to non-Europeans.

The process of defining European modernity, one inextricable from the histories and ideologies of colonialism and imperialism, also draws upon a narrative of history in which secularism triumphs over religion. In this narrative, an enlightened modern Europe emerges from the grip of the Church and from a narrowness or even backwardness of thought and superstitious belief that is assumed to accompany cultures in which religion holds such power in both institutions and the popular imagination. As has become evident in recent years, however, the 'triumph of secularism' has not, in point of fact, actually occurred for large portions of the world's population. Furthermore, 'secularism', as it has come to be defined, is not a neutral doctrine that exists beyond religion, but a particular way of seeing the relationships among politics, religion and ethics that derives from Christianity (Asad 2003: 1–66). This particular formulation of secular modernity is also based on a historical narrative that includes a specific vision of medieval Europe as Christendom and as untainted by Judaism and Islam. As I will examine in the final chapter of this book, this particular vision of the past is still in play in contemporary debates over what constitutes 'Europe' and 'European civilization', including discussions of how European countries are to 'deal' with their increased Muslim population, a population that often is directly connected to Europe's colonial past. In these debates, representations of the Middle Ages are not merely academic.

In this first chapter, I want to look at other examples of why postcolonial medieval studies is more than just a 'me too' gesture on the part of medievalists. Looking back further into the past, in ways that are historically informed rather than merely schematic, substantially alters one's field of vision, not only providing new readings of medieval texts, but also generating important critiques of fundamental concepts in postcolonial studies. I will first provide an overview of the field of postcolonial medieval studies, demonstrating how it has influenced medieval literary scholarship. I will then discuss critiques by medievalists of concepts important to postcolonialism, including Orientalism, nationalism and colonialism. Despite the mutual benefits of bringing medieval studies and postcolonial studies together, the combination has aroused controversy. I will briefly discuss debates surrounding postcolonial medieval studies and then go on to examine the historical context for the development of medieval studies and medievalisms in the nineteenth century and crucial links in this development to formative elements in European nationalism and colonialism.

Navigating the Field: Postcolonial Medieval Literary Studies

Postcolonial studies challenges Eurocentric geographic and temporal paradigms and also critiques cultural hegemonies and inequalities.

Engagement by medievalists with postcolonial studies has led to approaches that broaden and shift regional frames, question normative formulations of European Christendom, and take on constructions of periodisation. These broadenings of perspective are not limited to those scholars who explicitly engage with postcolonial theory, although arguably, it is the recent engagement with postcolonialism that has greatly expanded interest in global topics and in the question of Europe and its 'Others' within medieval studies. The new approaches and broadened interests have also brought new attention to non-canonical texts and introduced fresh perspectives on the canon. Medievalists have not simply applied modern theory to medieval texts, but have also produced important critiques of postcolonial studies from perspectives made possible by their study of the past.

Challenging Periodisation

Perhaps the most important of the new perspectives that postcolonial medieval studies affords is a challenge to traditional periodisations, specifically a challenge to schemes which privilege the modern or attempt to locate the 'birth of modernity'. Without much searching at all, one can easily find studies that claim for the modern or 'early modern' the birth of subjectivity, the nation, capitalism, the concept of race and racism. These concepts, among others, are seen as coming into being in the modern period and sometimes are also, tautologically, seen as defining what is modern. These divisions between premodern and modern have also frequently been used to classify cultures, with the West depicted as the birthplace and standard-bearer of modernity and other 'backwards', 'primitive', or 'developing' cultures lagging behind as their geographic and cultural differences come to be represented as temporal, denying these cultures and peoples their coevalness and their equality.[1] As we will see, this placement of the 'Other' back in time is not new and not merely academic, but was part of the ideologies of colonialism, as the colonised peoples of places such as India were compared by European colonisers with their own medieval ancestors.

Periodisation schemes that mark stark contrasts between the premodern and the modern are usually teleological, relying on notions of progress and privileging the modern, but not always. As we will see in the next chapter's discussion of Amitav Ghosh's *In an Antique Land*, depictions of a stark division between modern and premodern forms of slavery can form a nostalgic vision of the past that can create its own kinds of distortions.

As we examine the shape of the field of postcolonial medieval studies below, we will see that analyses and critiques of periodisation schemes emerge in much of the work. Rethinking temporality is central, for example, to the work of Jeffrey Jerome Cohen, whose edited collection *The Postcolonial Middle Ages* (2000) can be seen as marking the emergence of postcolonial medieval studies as a field. Kathleen Davis's 'Time behind the Veil: The Media, the Middle Ages, and Orientalism Now', part of that volume, made a powerful statement of how time can be made to become place. Examining presentations in the US media, Davis showed how Afghanistan was depicted as locked in a backward era characterised as medieval, an analysis that became even more relevant after 9/11. Davis's *Periodization and Sovereignty: How Ideas of Feudalism and Secularization Govern the Politics of Time* (2008) continues to challenge problematic temporalisations. Building on her influential earlier work, Davis shows how the typical periodisation scheme, which figures a 'religious, "pre-political"' Middle Ages as transcended by the developments of the Renaissance and the Enlightenment, was part of an apparatus developed alongside political theory that justified both slavery and imperialist subjugation. Beginning in the sixteenth century, jurists used medieval documents and the concept of the 'feudal' itself in order to create a vision of feudalism within Europe that was distinct from the 'modern' slavery being practised in European colonial possessions. Building on her earlier analysis of the US media, Davis concludes by remarking upon the relevance of such loaded terms as 'feudalism' in contemporary accounts of Pakistan in relation to the US-led 'war on terror'. She demonstrates how representations of medieval and modern sovereignty are still deployed in order to justify political aims that are anything but 'enlightened' (2008: 132–4).

Rethinking Borders and Boundaries

As representations of the Muslim world as not only geographically but also temporally different show, the new 'Dark Continent' is often figured more as a time than as a place. Place and space, however, still play central roles in postcolonial medieval studies. One of the most striking developments of the influence of postcolonial studies on medieval literary studies has been a new emphasis on 'place'. Recent studies have both shifted attention to new areas and generally broadened the geographic scope of the field. We can see, for example, a new attention to border regions. This work demonstrates the crucial interrelationships among conceptions of space and place and conceptions of time. By shifting our gaze on the map, looking beyond Europe, or by recognising the importance of different regions and locations, such as the Mediterranean or al-Andalus, we can reveal new paths across time. Illuminating connections between places in fresh ways generates analysis that not only is relevant to medieval texts, but which also illuminates the implications of these texts for later historical developments, including colonialism. Each of these studies demonstrates the importance of border geography to the construction of communal myth, national identities and religious identities, and challenges at its fabled roots the notion of a homogenous English identity so important to later formations of English nationalism and imperialism.

Borderlands

Michelle Warren's *History on the Edge: Excalibur and the Borders of Britain, 1100–1300* (2000) focuses on what she terms 'border writing'. She examines literary relationships between regions of the British Isles and also extends her analysis across the channel to examine the relationship between English and French versions of Arthurian legend. She begins with the seminal writings of Geoffrey of Monmouth (died c. 1155), himself a border figure, and continues her analysis of Arthurian literature into the Old French Grail cycles. Reading Arthurian romance through the 'cultural trauma' of the Norman Conquest, Warren argues that the creation of Arthurian myth is significant not only within a medieval context, but within a later colonial frame, as the 'ghosts of colonized Britons haunt subsequent formulations of imperial Britain' (2000: xi, ix).[2]

Patricia Clare Ingham's study of 'national fantasy' in Arthurian legend, *Sovereign Fantasies: Arthurian Romance and the Making of Britain* (2001), also draws attention to the importance of place and region to postcolonial paradigms, providing further insights into the significance of relationships between the regions of Britain, especially Wales and England. These relationships, once again, are central to the creation of myths of an English community and nation that shape later forms of English imperialism. Likewise, Jeffrey Jerome Cohen's *Hybridity, Identity and Monstrosity in Medieval Britain: On Difficult Middles* (2006) examines Gerald of Wales (c. 1146–c. 1223), whose writings on both Wales and Ireland Cohen sees as deeply influenced by the hybrid nature of his Cambrian-Norman identity. Cohen also reflects upon how the Norman presence shaped the medieval town of Norwich and both its Christian and Jewish communities, tying the Norman Conquest to the 1144 accusation of Jewish ritual murder in Norwich, the first recorded occurrence of such an event.

Sharon Kinoshita's *Medieval Boundaries: Rethinking Difference in Old French Literature* (2006a) also asks us to look past the boundaries that often constrain thinking about medieval literature, specifically national borders, which were actually created long after the medieval period. Kinoshita proposes instead examining Old French literature within the broader regional frame of the Mediterranean, taking into consideration the influence of trade routes and other points of intercultural contact on medieval literary production. Kinoshita's call for 'Mediterranean studies' also helps to bring into focus medieval Iberia, a region often neglected in studies of English and French medieval literatures, which still dominate postcolonial medieval studies. Inclusion of al-Andalus, as medieval Iberia was referred to in Arabic, brings into view the role of both Arabic and Hebrew literatures in medieval culture. Examination of the Iberian corpus fills an important lacuna in one of the seminal works of postcolonialism, Said's 1978 *Orientalism* (Hamilton 2007). Making connections across traditional regional divides can lead to new and striking theories, such as Michelle Reichert's thesis that the romances of Chrétien de Troyes were influenced by Iberian texts (2006). Al-Andalus, its relative neglect in postcolonial medieval scholarship and its vital importance to medieval literary production will be taken up as the subject of a case study in the next chapter.

A Global Vision

In addition to intensified study of border regions and of broader relations between regions, postcolonial studies also has influenced an overall broadening in the geographic scope of medieval literary studies. This more global focus is exemplified by the Global Middle Ages Project (G-MAP), founded by Geraldine Heng and now being developed by Heng, Susan Noakes and a number of international collaborators. With a global scope, the project uses web-based technology 'to teach university communities and the general public to see what an interconnected world looks like in deep time: a thousand years of culture, history, technology, ideas, and civilization, from about 500 to 1500'.[3] We see a similar attention to connections between and across time and space in David Wallace's *Premodern Places: Calais to Surinam, Chaucer to Aphra Behn* (2004). Wallace draws upon Roland Barthes's concept of 'the *punctum*: a sign or detail in a visual field provoking some deep – yet highly subjective – sense of connectedness with people in the past' to weave a narrative that brings together Calais, Flanders, Somerset, Genoa, the Canary Islands, Surinam, and Guyana through attention to significant moments of cultural hybridity, including linguistic hybridity (2004: 2). Wallace, whose work has long challenged traditional periodisation schemes, here draws upon Dipesh Chakrabarty's critique of historicist teleology in *Provincializing Europe* (2000) to argue for a historically informed methodology that can connect time and space. Wallace demonstrates, for example, how the English presence in Calais 'in some ways adumbrates later English colonial experiments', a point from which we can see early traces of ideas such as 'nation,' 'frontier,' and 'race' (2004: 3).

Kofi Campbell's *Literature and Culture in the Black Atlantic: From Pre- to Postcolonial* (2006) also makes global connections across time and space, deploying the concept of 'temporally synchronous hybridity' to trace movements across 'the black Atlantic, from England to Africa to the Caribbean . . . and back again' (2006: 6). His study encompasses a much longer historical frame than Paul Gilroy's concept of the 'Black Atlantic', which usually begins with the Middle Passage (Gilroy 1993). Focusing on Middle English literature, Campbell demonstrates how a negative view of Africa and Africans developed far earlier than the transatlantic slave trade. These earlier cultural and political views laid the groundwork for justifying the later exploitation of Africans and are therefore essential for understanding the Black Atlantic both in the past and in the present, as Campbell demonstrates through readings of contemporary Caribbean authors such as Derek Walcott and Paul Keens-Douglas.

Wallace and Campbell ask us to reconsider the position of medieval English literature within a complex web of global interconnections that function both spatially and temporally. In *Angels on the Edge of the World: Geography, Literature, and English Community, 1000–1534* (2006), Kathy Lavezzo, while also asking us to take a broad, global perspective, shifts our focus from interconnectivity to positionality. Lavezzo explores the development of the idea of 'nation' that later became so important to English imperialism, which figured England as the centre of a global empire. Lavezzo calls attention to medieval English writers' embrace of England's global marginality, its location on the world's edge, arguing that a sense of English community developed in contrast to Christendom's traditional centre of power, Rome. Lavezzo also points to the intimate relationship between conceptions of time and place in early English texts, and uses a focus on location as a means to break through traditional periodisation barriers, taking her analysis of the development of English identity into the Reformation period.

Each of these studies highlights the ways in which postcolonial medieval studies affords new perspectives on place and space and their connection to one another both within medieval texts and contexts and also on a theoretical level. Another locus for what we might call a new globalism in medieval studies is the fourteenth-century *Travels of Sir John Mandeville*, which will be discussed in the context of cartography and exploration as a case study in the next chapter. The descriptions of the so-called monstrous races in *Mandeville's Travels,* as well as in texts such as Gerald of Wales's *Topographia Hibernica* (History and Topography of Ireland) and the fallacious but extremely popular 'Letter of Prester John', reportedly authored by an incredibly rich and powerful Christian king in India, have also been the subject of new work, such as Michael Uebel's *Ecstatic Transformations* (2005). Both Mandeville's *Travels* and the figure of Prester John – the search for whom was part of European exploration, such as the voyages of Vasco da Gama – demonstrate the global implications of narratives and myths that may seem at first glance to be limited to European contexts alone.[4]

This overall broader scope and emphasis on interconnection is not limited to these recent works. In her important response to world systems theory, *Before European Hegemony* (1989), Janet Abu-Lughod argues for the importance of a premodern, specifically thirteenth-century, cultural and economic network of cities and regions across Africa, Europe and Asia. These early networks fundamentally shaped later political and economic developments, including the much touted sixteenth-century 'rise of the West'. Like the studies by Wallace and Campbell, Abu-Lughod's research provides fundamental correctives both to Eurocentrism and to histories of 'globalization' in which 'periodisation of the "modern" . . . relies on nothing but the tautological assertion of itself' (Lang 2006: 905). We find again here one of the most important new developments of postcolonial medieval studies, that is, the rethinking of how perceptions of time and place are interconnected, and the subsequent insights afforded by thinking more broadly about place and more deeply about time.

This broadening of the scope of medieval studies is not limited to the work of scholars who are directly engaged with postcolonial studies, particularly among historians. Indeed, as the work of Charles Verlinden and Janet Abu-Lughod and others shows, historians have been demonstrating the global connections of European history and its connection to later questions for decades now, although this broader emphasis is just now becoming more standard in literary scholarship. A recent example of such work is Paul Freedman's *Out of the East: Spices and the Medieval Imagination* (2008) an important history for those interested in questions of cultural contact and trade in the Middle Ages, and one can see it as part of a broadening of scope in medieval studies that intersects with postcolonial medieval studies, but does not necessarily engage it explicitly. Freedman's book carefully traces the importance of the spice trade in the medieval period and demonstrates its foundational role in helping to create the material conditions that led to the 'Age of Discovery' and beyond into the beginnings of transatlantic colonialism. Freedman does not reference postcolonialism and indeed, in a prominent essay co-authored with Gabrielle Spiegel, seems to have strong methodological reservations about approaches to medieval texts informed by contemporary theory (Freedman 2008; Freedman and Spiegel 1998). Nevertheless, work such as Freedman's provides the historical contextualisation that is essential to postcolonial medieval studies and, I would argue, is part of a trend away from Eurocentrism in medieval studies scholarship. This development can be seen not only in the context of postcolonial studies or postcolonialism, but also globalisation.

Decentring Christianity/Rethinking Race

Along with an increased global emphasis, there has been, in the past two decades, important growth in the examination of representations of both Jews and Muslims in medieval texts and a subsequent decentring of Christianity as the normative frame of reference for medieval studies. Once again, scholars interested in postcolonial medieval studies can see this range of studies as interconnected, with those that engage most directly with postcolonialism often developing explicit strategies for decentring the Christian, just as the globalist medieval projects often feature explicit engagement with revision of traditional temporal and spatial frames.

The amount of scholarship on Jewish-Christian relations in medieval Europe in the last two decades is very large.[5] Literary studies of representations of Jews have often drawn most explicitly on postcolonial and critical race theory, attempting to decentre normative constructions of Christian identity and to see the representations of Jews in relationship to other outsiders.[6] This work engages with the Jew as 'Other', but also, more importantly, I think, it demonstrates how the figure of the Jew was used to create normative visions of Christendom and Christian identity, visions that arguably shaped the way that all other types of 'outsiders' or 'Others' were created both in the medieval period and subsequent periods.[7]

As historian John Tolan points out in the introduction to *Saracens: Islam in the Medieval European Imagination* (2002), with the exceptions of work by Norman Daniel ([1960] 1997) and R. W. Southern

(1962), until quite recently there were noticeably fewer general studies of medieval European Christian representations of Muslims than there were about comparable representations of Jews (2002: xvi). Tolan sees his own work as explicitly engaged with correcting Said's distorting view of the Middle Ages as the 'adolescence' of Orientalism. He invites us to see this work as a taking-up of Kathleen Biddick's invitation to medievalists to engage with postcolonial theory, and, in turn, he issues his own invitation to those working on colonialism and imperialism in later periods to deepen their historical knowledge (Tolan 2002: 280–1; Biddick 2000a: 36, 46). Literary scholar Suzanne Conklin Akbari is even more explicit in her engagement with postcolonial theory in her studies of medieval Christian representations of Muslims and Islam. She not only uses postcolonial studies to illuminate depictions of connections of Muslims with idolatry and the Antichrist, for example, but, also, as we will see below, uses medieval texts and contexts to critique contemporary discussions of Orientalism and race.[8] In *Empire of Magic* (2003), Geraldine Heng argues that the very basis of the genre of romance in English literature is the memory of the trauma of the historical encounter between Christians and Muslims in the Crusades, extending this important insight across a variety of texts to argue for a medieval beginning for the concept of race.

As we can begin to see here, it is not simply that medieval studies has been influenced by postcolonial studies, but that medievalists have used a longer historical view to provide new critiques of concepts critical to postcolonialism. Work such as Heng's and the special issue of the *Journal of Medieval and Early Modern Studies* edited by Thomas Hahn in 2001 have led to historically informed reconceptualisations of the concept of 'race'.[9] Studies such as Campbell's also add new perspectives to concepts such as the 'Black Atlantic', and medievalists have provided important critiques of other critical concepts, such as Orientalism, nation and colonialism.

Rethinking Theoretical Perspectives on Orientalism, Nationalism and Colonialism

Orientalism

In his landmark *Orientalism* ([1978] 1994), Edward Said suggests that thinkers in Western Europe have attempted to understand and define the 'Orient' or the 'East' as a construct defined in opposition to the 'Occident' or the 'West'. Orientalism is a way of studying the East, and more generally a way of conceptualising it in opposition to the West. Through Orientalism, the 'Orient' came to be understood as, among other things, irrational, backward, sexualised and feminised, as opposed to the rational, developed, civilised and masculine West. Orientalism has an academic, institutional component through which scholars and others, including intellectuals, bureaucrats and colonial administrators, have sought to 'know' the Orient, a perspective on intellectual inquiry that seeks not simply to understand, but also, arguably, to control or contain. Orientalism also has an 'imaginative meaning' as writers, artists, intellectuals and politicians constructed a vision of the Orient that was integrally connected to the academic approaches as the two types of intellectual work developed together. Finally Orientalism, Said argues, as a mode of attempting to know and define the Orient, has also aided the attempt to control non-Western peoples: 'Orientalism can be discussed and analyzed as the corporate institution for dealing with the Orient – dealing with it by making statements about it, authorizing views of it . . . in short, Orientalism as a Western style for dominating, restructuring, and having authority over the Orient' (Said [1978] 1994: 3). Said's analysis of Orientalism, which draws upon the thought of Michel Foucault for its understandings of discourse and the relationship between knowledge and power, 'can be said to inaugurate a new kind of study of colonialism' (Loomba 1998a: 44). While Said's overall work has very broad implications, *Orientalism* focuses primarily on textual evidence from modern France and England. At the same time, however, Said argues for Orientalism's existence going as far back as Aeschylus and, notably for our purposes, its presence in the work of Dante.

Medievalists have engaged with Said's work in a variety of ways. Orientalism has, of course, influenced readings of medieval texts, but medievalists have also offered significant critiques of Said's work on historical, textual and theoretical grounds, pointing especially to a limiting reliance on binarisms in his analysis. In her introduction to a cluster of articles responding to *Orientalism*, Lucy Pick points out, for example, that Said's attempt to trace academic Orientalism back to the medieval period (using Southern 1962) does not work because the chairs founded in languages such as Arabic and Hebrew in fourteenth-century medieval universities ultimately did not endure. She argues that 'the failure of these language chairs to take hold marks not a beginning, but the end of a two-century-long surge in academic Orientalism characterized by the translation of a large number of texts into Latin and Arabic' (1999: 266). Pick's observation draws attention to an important historical critique of the binary structure of Orientalism as posited by

Said. The translation projects of al-Andalus mark an example of cultural interchange that cannot be reduced to a one-sided attempt by Western European thinkers to understand or control the East, as Said describes modern Orientalism; the medieval situation was more complex and could even be seen as symbiotic.

In places such as medieval Iberia or Norman Sicily, where Muslims, Christians and Jews co-existed, we find the development of complex hybrid cultures that do not fit into the mechanisms of Orientalist discourse as Said sets them forth. As Maria Georgopoulou points out, medieval Crusader states are another location of hybrid cultures that call the Orientalist model into question. Using an art-historical approach, Georgopoulou focuses on two glass beakers, which while apparently made by Muslim artisans, portray Christian images. Georgopoulou uses these artifacts as the jumping-off point to critique medieval scholarship that has itself been influenced by binarist Orientalist thought and which has therefore been unable to imagine a world of interfaith and interethnic cultural exchange. Georgopoulou argues for the importance of the marketplace in Crusader states as a place of exchange, where division of labour was based on craft rather than ethnicity and where the lives of 'locals' or 'Oriental Christians' challenged any notions of clear divisions between East and West (1999). As Pick notes, a focus on the visual arts and material artifacts, which do not really figure in Said's analysis, can yield new findings (1999: 269). Another example of the fruitfulness of such as an approach is Suzanne Akbari's observations about early medieval maps, which typically divide the world not into two parts, East and West, but into three: Asia, Africa and Europe. This insight allows her to argue for the origins of a binary model of 'East' and 'West' in the late fourteenth century, thereby historicising what, in the analysis of Said and numerous other thinkers, seems like an almost eternal division (2000).

Medievalists have also critiqued the most prominent discussion of a medieval text in *Orientalism*: Said's analysis of Dante's *Commedia*. Said finds Dante's portrayals of Mohammed and Ali in the *Inferno*, in which Dante depicts them as riven in twain, to be 'peculiarly disgusting' (1994: 68–9). Despite his analysis of the more positive portrayals of Avicenna, Averroës and Saladin in Limbo, who stand alongside figures such as Socrates, Plato and Aristotle, Said nevertheless finds in the *Inferno* a reductive Orientalist view. He argues that Dante can only understand these Muslim figures within a 'fixed' Christian cosmology, a 'closed system' which reduces them to their adversarial roles in relation to Dante's own belief system (1994: 69–70). As numerous medievalists have shown, however, Dante's views of Islam are more complex and ambivalent than Said's analysis acknowledges. Dante's representations appear to derive from some considerable understanding of theology and culture that is not entirely surprising, given his geographic position and the proximity of both Norman Sicily and al-Andalus (Akbari 2000). While Miguel Asín Palacios's reading of Dante's positive embrace of Muslim culture has not found wide acceptance, Dante's treatment of Muslims is also not an outright rejection of them (Asín Palacios 1943). Nor does Dante's depiction of Mohammed stand out as particularly gruesome in an *Inferno* littered with the suffering figures of the damned (Coggeshall 2007: 137–8).

These critiques of Said's treatment of Dante in *Orientalism* demonstrate how reductive or schematic readings of early texts can end up distorting findings and theories. How might the analysis of *Orientalism* be changed by including more detailed examinations of early Muslim-Christian points of contact, such as those found in Crusader kingdoms or medieval Iberia, and how might findings of different kinds of intercultural contact impact current ideas about tensions between 'civilisations'? In the next two chapters we will take up these questions, particularly the importance of including medieval Iberia and other neglected European regions for studies of the Middle Ages, and also for contemporary political discourse.

On a more general theoretical level, focusing on issues of temporality, medievalists have demonstrated that, in relation to his reading of Dante, it appears that Said's own vision of the medieval is itself as 'boxed in' and 'imprisoned' in its own schematic as Said argues Dante's to be.[10] Focusing on temporality, these critics have shown how Said's temporal scheme fixes the Middle Ages as a kind of historical 'adolescence' (Biddick 2000a: 36). Kathleen Davis argues that Said posits medieval Orientalism as the basis for later forms and yet simultaneously also argues that this basis had no grounding in reality. This conception divorces Orientalist knowledge from the cultural interaction of which al-Andalus, Norman Sicily and the Crusader states are obvious examples. Said's omission of certain historical contexts, combined with his conflation of disparate premodern historical moments, ends up figuring the Middle Ages as a site of historical origin but also as a moment that exists before 'the movement of history' (2000: 112). As Davis argues, the implications of this portrayal go beyond simple distortion:

> Said's dichotomy . . . instates a core 'reality' that privileges and solidifies the very discourse he critiques. If we grant with Said that medieval Europe's

system of representing Islam is purely antiempirical, based not on any experience with Islam but only on a fully closed, self-generated tradition, then we privilege Europe as an absolutely self-constituting object. (Davis 2000: 113, qtd in Kinoshita 2007: 78)

In this way we could see *Orientalism* generating a form of Eurocentrism much in the way that Dussel posits the development of Eurocentrism more generally (Dussel 1993). Such representations also lead to the occlusion of other historical developments, such as the close connection between nineteenth-century Orientalisms and medievalisms, both of which are important components of nineteenth-century colonial and imperial ideologies, as we will see below.[11]

The ways in which the Middle Ages is often bracketed off or oversimplified in order to create or justify a particular view of modernity can end up distorting understandings of both the medieval and the modern. The stakes in these discussions can sometimes be very high. Suzanne Akbari's exploration of the close connection between representations of Jews and Muslims in the Middle Ages has important implications for contemporary Orientalism. It reveals the historical grounds for Said's statement that 'The transference of a popular anti-Semitic animus from a Jewish to an Arab target was made smoothly, since the figure was essentially the same' (Said 1994: 286). In doing so, Akbari's work opens new paths for the study of Orientalism, antisemitism and Islamophobia. In the current political climate, the need for fuller understandings of the connections between antisemitism and Islamophobia is great (Akbari 2005: 32). Bracketing off certain eras or regions as either 'fixed' or 'unknowable' seriously impedes our ability to understand the historical roots of contemporary conflicts and cultural formations.

Nation and Nationalism

The concepts of nation and nationalism have played an important role in postcolonial studies, and numerous influential studies have presented the concept of the nation as a distinctly modern one.[12] Medievalists have challenged this thinking on historical and theoretical grounds. Studies stretching back over decades have demonstrated that we can indeed identify conceptions of nation in medieval thought.[13] Historian Susan Reynolds speaks of medieval 'regnal communities' and argues against separating the related, but distinct, notions of the modern nation-state from 'the medieval idea of a kingdom as comprising a people with a similarly permanent and objective reality' (Reynolds 1997: 252). The

kingdom, she argues, is a significant and recognisable political formation even if not all medieval kingdoms survived to become recognisable
nation-states in the modern era (Reynolds 1997: 250–2). Other scholars
have attempted to make a specific case for England as a medieval nation-
state, including the notable contribution of Thorlac Turville-Petre,
who argues for an English national self-definition through the English
language and English language literary production between 1290 and
1340, the years prior to the Hundred Years War (1996).

These studies have implications beyond the simple acknowledgement that the concept of nation may be older than usually assumed.
Periodisation and historicisation affect how concepts such as nation
and nationalism are conceived and help to determine their impact.
Rees Davies points out that current definitions of nation and nationalism emphasise 'political' and 'civic' criteria while underplaying elements of the 'ethnic', the 'cultural', and the 'genealogical-mythical' in
national thinking (2004: 568). Indeed, Davies argues the approach in
definition can be so narrow in its focus on mass media and literacy,
following Benedict Anderson, that it can be seen as excluding all but
the most recent times and even perhaps 'many contemporary countries which are currently members of the United Nations' (2004: 569).
Noting that medieval communities are surely excluded by the terms
through which nations are defined, despite being 'termed *nationes* by
contemporaries', Davies calls for an attempt to understand premodern societies on their own terms (Davies 2004: 569). This plea for
understanding societies across time has important implications for
understanding them across spaces as well. As Partha Chatterjee has
shown, many theories of nationalism have posited Western European
countries as setting the pace in the development of nation-states, with
the rest of the world playing catch-up ([1986] 1993). Chatterjee's
study demonstrates, however, that the development of anti-colonial
nationalism in regions such as India and Africa is not simply a matter
of imitation, but also involves distinct modes of cultural resistance.
If traditional Western understandings of the nation and nationalism
took a longer history of Western nationalism into account, further
insight into both similarities and differences across global nationalisms would be possible.

Historians such as Reynolds and Davies similarly strongly object to
the ways in which most theories of the development and nature of the
nation-state follow teleological models, an objection that is also found
in the more theoretically oriented discussions. Kathleen Davis (1998)
critiques both Bhabha's and Anderson's treatments of the medieval

period, asserting that their arguments frame the Middle Ages as a site of absolute alterity. Tracing Bhabha's formulations back through Anderson to Walter Benjamin, Carolyn Dinshaw points out how Bhabha and Anderson, each in his own way, make assumptions about medieval notions of time and languages that distort understandings of the medieval period. On a more general level, Dinshaw also argues that

> [i]n some very influential theoretical and critical work developing out of postmodernism, the Middle Ages is still made the dense, unvarying, and eminently obvious monolith against which modernity and postmodernity groovily emerge. It is important to assert medieval indeterminacy because such postmodern interventions are hampered by their binary blind spots; the point is not simply to claim that the medieval is postmodern *avant la lettre* but to argue that a more patient consideration of the Middle Ages would extend the range of their interventions and . . . clarify their politics. (1999: 15–16)

Patricia Ingham also challenges representations of the Middle Ages as a monolith constrained by tight periodisation boundaries, and her discussion of the nation emphasises the 'oppositions, the heterogeneities, and the overlapping cultures legible in the difficult middle spaces' produced through the relationship between England and its once and future colony, Wales (2001:12). Ingham's focus on conflict and heterogeneity leads not only to new formulations of the medieval past of Britain, but also to recalibrations of later British nationalisms, especially those expressed through the Arthurian tradition, which still has an impact into the present day. Overall then, we find that postcolonial medieval studies not only shows the empirical limitations of periodisation, which constricts thinking about nation and nationalism to the modern period, but also demonstrates the larger theoretical pitfalls of these limits.

Colony and Colonisation

As with the terms 'nation' and 'nationalism,' the terms 'colony,' 'colonisation', and 'colonialism', as well as the closely related terms 'frontier' and 'empire', have all been deployed and debated by medievalists. As in the case of debates over 'nation' and 'nationalism', much of the discussion has taken place without specific reference to postcolonial theory, although postcolonialism is an important subtext of most discussions. Historians have debated the concept of the colony in relation to the

Norman Conquest, the Crusades, and what Robert Bartlett has called the 'Europeanization of Europe' (1993). The debates often focus on the utility of these terms for medieval contexts: are they too vague? Are they anachronistic impositions of nineteenth- and twentieth-century concepts that end up distorting or politicising earlier histories? Among historians there is no consensus on these questions, a situation that I think not only reflects scholarly differences, but the vexed nature of these questions politically even in the present day.[14]

Some historians see strong historical continuities. Charles Verlinden contends that the 'techniques of colonization which spread across the Atlantic world originated' in the medieval period (1970: 3). He points out that the sugar cultivation and trade that became so important to colonisation and the slave trade beginning in the seventeenth century had their roots in the sugar plantations developed by Italian city-states in the Holy Land at the time of the First Crusade. He therefore argues for continuities between the early 'colonial techniques' of the Mediterranean and those later ones of the Atlantic.

Another identifiable locus in the debates about 'medieval colonialism' is the work of Joshua Prawer, whose *Latin Kingdom of Jerusalem: European Colonialism in the Middle Ages* (1973) explicitly applies the terms 'colony' and 'colonialism' and even 'apartheid' to what he sees as the relations between the lords of the Crusader states and the native population, relations that are characterised by a striking lack of integration between the parties (1973: 524). Prawer's work has been the subject of intense debate. His thesis has been attacked as anachronistic and because it seemed to be critical of the relationship between Israelis and Palestinians. The statement with which he ends *Latin Kingdom*, for example, that 'Apotheosis of the past and the link with tradition, important at a certain rate of growth in a new society, turn into a dead weight of anachronistic postulates' (1973: 533), can be parsed as a critique of developments in the modern Israeli state. Conversely, because of Prawer's status as an Israeli academic, his work has also become part of bitter international debates over Zionism and anti-Zionism.[15] Prawer, born in 1917 in Polish Silesia, emigrated to Palestine in 1936, where he completed his studies at the newly founded Hebrew University. In addition to his work as an historian, he also played an important role in the development of institutions of higher learning in Israel (Constable et al. 1991: 727–9). His work, and the work of many of his students, seems ripe for a balanced and detailed analysis that would take into account both his scholarship and its political contexts from the point of view of postcolonial medieval studies.

Postcolonial Medieval Studies: How is the Field Viewed?

In light of the significant interventions into critical terms discussed above and the new directions in research that postcolonial medieval studies has opened, one might think that the field is now safely well established. Indeed, postcolonial medieval studies is now an acknowledged part of medieval literary scholarship, especially in the United States. The status of postcolonial medieval studies is not, however, universally accepted across medieval studies, nor, perhaps more significantly, is it generally referenced in the broader field of postcolonial studies. Those working on postcolonialism in later periods tend either to instrumentalise the medieval period or to ignore it altogether.

Take, for example, *Empire: A Very Short Introduction*, in which Stephen Howe singles out an example from recent scholarship in medieval studies to critique what he sees as problematic uses of the term 'postcolonial' in literary studies more generally:

> A recent book of literary studies is rather mind-bendingly entitled *The Postcolonial Middle Ages*, whilst another literary scholar suggests (admittedly with tongue slightly in cheek) that '*Beowulf*' and Chaucer's *Canterbury Tales* could be read as postcolonial texts. (2002: 26)

That even a 'very short' discussion of empire has space to dismiss attempts to bring postcolonial studies and medieval literature together well demonstrates that the combination of fields is still viewed with scepticism by non-medievalists. Within medieval studies, the most influential critique of the field comes from the respected historian Gabrielle Spiegel, who argues against 'superimposing' contemporary theories, including postcolonial theory, 'on periods and persons for which they were never designed and to which they simply do not apply' (2000: 249–50). She objects not only to the general problem of the anachronistic application of modern theory to premodern texts, but focuses specifically on the use of postcolonial theory, which she sees as developing within and for the purposes of analysing specific historical conditions which, in her view, simply cannot translate to medieval contexts (2000: 246).[16]

Spiegel's concern over anachronism is an important one. Attempts to simply 'apply' the insights of postcolonial theory to any context, medieval or modern without careful attention to historical, cultural, and political specificities can lead to distortion and obfuscation. This issue is widely acknowledged among scholars working in the field of postcolonial medievalism and, indeed, one of the more important contributions of the field is, I believe, to bring the perspective of earlier historical contexts not only to the study of medieval texts, but to post-colonial studies more broadly. Postcolonial studies and medieval studies have interrelated genealogies. In an important essay, Bruce Holsinger examines the importance of medieval scholarship to the development of postcolonial studies, showing that theories too have their own histories (2002). Holsinger demonstrates how members of the Subaltern Studies school of postcolonial South Asian history drew upon work by medieval historians of the *Annales* school such as George Duby, Jacques Le Goff and Marc Bloch to develop their historical and theoretical paradigms. The study of precapitalist Europe, he shows, proved important to these historians' attempt to understand non-Western societies. Holsinger's careful genealogy of the relationship between medieval studies and post-colonial studies provides a thorough and perceptive debunking of the idea that medieval studies can only absorb theoretical perspectives, not generate them.

Work such as Holsinger's has done much to settle debates over the status and legitimacy of postcolonial medieval studies, but it is fair to say that those engaged with postcolonial inquiries into later periods still usually ignore the Middle Ages, positing a *de facto* irrelevance to events prior to the fifteenth century. Ignoring the Middle Ages, however, obscures an important element in the development of ideologies of colonialism and imperialism, that is, the close intertwining of the early field of medieval studies with Orientalism and with nationalisms across Europe in the nineteenth century.

Nineteenth-century Roots of Medieval Studies

Medieval studies as a discipline has its origins in the late eighteenth and nineteenth centuries. While its development was influenced by European nationalism, colonialism and imperialism, it also had a reciprocal influence on these developments and their accompanying ideologies. The vision of the East so central to Orientalism, for example, has, in a variety of critical ways, been central to the representation of Europe's medieval past. These representations of medieval Europe, in turn, were central to the creation of dominant representations of modern Europe and of the 'West,' more generally.[17] Medievalists have recently begun to unearth the political roots of the academic study of medieval literature, but because the academy still remains divided into the 'national' divisions created in the nineteenth century, these developments have not been brought together in an attempt to create a more pan-European perspective, revealing similarities in situations across Europe that nation-centred disciplinary boundaries often obscure. In this section I will provide an overview of the development of medieval studies in relation to a range of European nationalisms and colonialisms, demonstrating how the fields of postcolonial studies and medieval studies, which might on the surface seem to be worlds apart, share important roots, roots that powerfully attest to the viability and the potential of postcolonial medieval studies.

The study of medieval history, languages and literatures has deep roots in the German tradition, specifically in the German nationalism that developed in the wake of the unrest of the French Revolution and the challenges of the Napoleonic Wars. An important component of this emerging nationalism was a 'longing for myth', a search for the *Vorzeit,* or 'pre-time', of Germanic culture.[18] Early 'cultural nationalists' like Johann Gottfried Herder (1744–1803) were searching for the authentic voice of the *Volk* (folk or people), although Herder's investigations were not limited to the Germanic, nor was his thinking explicitly linked to a political agenda. Likewise, Joseph Görres (1776–1848) proposed a cross-cultural theory of myth, arguing that German art reached its zenith when it was influenced by Eastern art during the Crusades (Williamson 2004: 80). August Wilhelm Schlegel (1767–1845), another noted Orientalist, wrote of a *Rittermythologie* (knightly mythology) in the German past, asserting that 'Those giant shadows, which appear to us through a fog, must again acquire firm outlines, and the image of the *Vorzeit* must once more be animated by its own unique soul.'[19] Jakob Grimm (1785–1863) presented what he saw as evidence of a pre-Christian Germanic essence in works such as his *Wörterbuch* (Dictionary) (1852) and *Kinder und Hausmärchen* (1812–15). Much of the source material for Grimm's folklore has now been discredited as doctored and purposively misleading, shaped in a way to promote 'cruelty, violence, anti-Semitism, and, above all, submission to the authority of the state' (Frantzen 1990: 69). The development of scholarship on the distant German past was, then, very much tied to the philosophical and political ideologies that grew along with a new German national consciousness (Williamson 2004; Frantzen 1990). As we can see, this important and internationally influential intellectual production had deep connections to the German political context.

Thinkers such as Johann Gottlieb Fichte (1762–1814) and Freiherr vom Stein (1757–1831) engaged the work of 'cultural nationalists' for explicitly nationalist ends. We can see Grimm's work reflected in the work of Fichte's more influential ideas on nation and its relation to language (Peck 1996: 137). In addition to undertaking studies of specific texts, German scholars also developed institutions that were to become objects of national pride. In 1819 Stein founded the Gesellschaft für ältere deutsche Geschichtskunde (Society for Older German Historical Knowledge) which had ties to illustrious cultural figures such as Goethe (1749–1832) and the Grimm brothers, and which took on the task of creating the *Monumenta Germaniae Historica* (Historical Documents of Germany), a multi-volume series of early German texts and documents that is still used today. The goal of these volumes was to bring together the key texts of the Germanic past (Geary 2002: 23–7).

We can see the influence of these nationalist currents in nineteenth-century scholarship on specific medieval literary texts, texts now considered the crown jewels in the Middle High German canon. The *Nibelungenlied*, a German poem composed around 1200, became the focus of intense scholarly discussions in Berlin in the first decades of the nineteenth century, as figures such as Schlegel and Grimm debated its origins and its relationship to the German mythic past. The debate over the poem was eventually 'solved' by Karl Lachmann (1793–1851), whose genealogically inspired methods of textual editing, known as 'stemmatics', became enormously influential within medieval studies. Stemmatics posited that medieval texts derived from archetypal or '*Ur*' texts, a way of viewing textual origins and transmission that remained influential in medieval studies and classics for decades (Williamson 2004: 84–92; Frantzen 1990: 62–71).

The connections between these earlier searches for a true Germanic past and contemporary politics become even clearer after German unification in 1871. The appointment of Wilhelm Scherer (1841–86) to a professorship in Strassburg, a territory disputed with France, was hailed as a move to bolster 'the German spirit against France . . . as fortification of German imperialism' (Peck 1996: 139). Scherer came to see his presence in this disputed territory as 'colonising' and even Bismarck weighed in against a possible move by Scherer to Berlin, stressing the importance of the professor's work to 'the lands of the empire'.[20] Although figures such as Grimm and Scherer remained at a certain distance from politics, they 'romanticized, on the one hand, the legendary past and the mythical world of the Middle Ages, and on the other, the glorious future of political, economic, or colonial successes, literally in exotic, other worlds like Africa, or the South Seas' (Peck 1996: 139).

Connections between Orientalism, nationalism and medieval studies in Germany can be found, then, before Germany became a colonial power or even a unified nation-state. An emblematic case is the study of Wolfram von Eschenbach's thirteenth-century romance *Parzival*, which, Todd Kontje argues, demonstrates how a 'prenational writer with an "Oriental" imagination gradually became the author of a modern *Bildungsroman* whose "typically German" hero combines martial valor, dreamy introspection, and racial purity' (2004: 117). For the influential Lachmann, *Parzival* constituted an early example of the *Bildungsroman* form, considered by some to be the quintessentially German form of the novel. From this premise, nineteenth-century German medievalists came to figure Parzival as a hero who represented a German national spirit, a spirit that transcended both the Oriental and French-influenced themes and details so important to Wolfram's medieval text. This anachronistic interpretation also reorganised literary history. By figuring Parzival as a hero in the modern mould, German scholars such as August Friedrich Vilmar (1800–68) were able to argue for a thirteenth-century German 'golden age' of literature that predated those of rival traditions from England, Spain and France. Viewed in this way, German literature not only becomes part of a European tradition that transcends any 'Oriental' elements lurking in its past, but is also elevated as a singular tradition that is 'modern' prior to any other (Kontje 2004: 115).

Not surprisingly, Germans were not alone in championing their national literary tradition. Rival national traditions presented competing histories of medieval literature, as one can see clearly in the development of medieval studies in France. As R. Howard Bloch has noted, 'At a time when nation-states were deciding militarily whether Alsace or Lorraine – that is Strasbourg – were to be French or German, specialists debated passionately whether Europe's earliest literary monuments were of French or German origin' (1994: 6). Gaston Paris (1839–1903), a foundational figure in the field of French medieval studies, was motivated in part by nationalist concerns, a motivation of which he was himself aware. In 1870, as France was under attack by Prussian forces, he delivered a lecture, '*La Chanson de Roland et la nationalité française*' that figures the poem *Roland* as 'a repository of precocious national sentiment', arguing that the French fatherland (*la patrie*) came into existence in this epic (Kinoshita 2006b: 270).[21] Paris, who had studied in Germany, was deeply influenced by Lachmann's editorial methods and railed against the French educational system, which he saw as falling far behind that of Germany, especially with respect to the study of French texts. Scholars have indeed spoken of a 'philological arms race' between French and German scholars during this time (Graham 1996: 75). As part of this frenzy to build academic prestige, Paris, along with Paul Meyer (1840–1917), began the journal *Romania* in 1872, intending for the journal to rival the *Jahrbuch für romanische und englische Literatur*. The Société des Anciens Textes Français was founded in 1875.

Just as the *Nibelungenlied* and *Parzival* found an honoured place in the German canon, *Roland* came to be viewed as the national epic of France. It is probably not coincidental that the 'three most important editions of the poem published by French scholars prior to 1950' each appeared during conflicts between France and Germany: the Franco-Prussian War, World War I and World War II. *Roland* was seen not only as a source of national pride, but as a sign of French superiority over other Europeans because, they argued, of their role as the originators of a 'national consciousness' (Duggan 1989: 99). The scholar Vitel asserted that, in contrast to the French, who created *Roland*, other Europeans, specifically the Prussians, were savage primitives, 'Mohicans and Redskins' (Duggan 1989: 101). This analogy of the 'Other' highlights the nationalism that imbued *Roland* scholarship and its relationship to nascent imperialism as well (Duggan 1989: 100).

Paris's famous 1870 address about the fatherland, which stresses the principles of 'unity and expansion' that characterise French national sentiment, was delivered at a key moment in struggles between France and Germany and a turning point in the history of French colonialism: the 1870 annexation of Algeria, which had already been under French military rule since 1830 (Kinoshita 2006b: 271). The formal annexation was connected to political instability in France and to the French loss of the Alsace-Lorraine region to the Germans. In 1871, Algerian tribal lands were seized and given to French colonists, including some of those displaced by the loss of Alsace-Lorraine (Kinoshita 2001: 81). The occupation was understood as a later Crusade and compared to the attack on Tunis by St Louis in 1270 (Riley-Smith 2003: 156). Drawing upon nationalistic scholarship, such as Joseph François Michaud's *Histoire des croisades,* representations of the Crusades and France's colonial incursions became blended together, as perhaps best exemplified by the Salles des Croisades in the Palace of Versailles. These rooms contained more than 120 paintings of crusading scenes; the timing of their creation is linked by scholars to the intensification of French colonialism in North Africa (Riley-Smith 2003: 155–6).

Against such a background, it seems clear that readings which emphasise both the 'French essence' of *Roland* and those portions of the poem that figure the inferiority of Muslims, have at least as much to do with nineteenth- and twentieth-century receptions of the poem and the political contexts from which they emerge as with the contents of the poem itself. Its depictions of Muslims are, in fact, more nuanced and ambivalent than the classic modern readings suggest, in spite of that key phrase in *Roland*, '*Paien unt tort e crestiens unt dreit*' ('Pagans are wrong and

Christians are right') (Kinoshita 2001; 2006a). In any case, *Roland* as medieval national epic became a standard part of the French school curriculum in 1880, a canonisation that influenced students not only in France, but in its colonial possessions as well.

The importance of France's colonies to medieval studies is evident in the biography of another founding French medievalist, Joseph Bédier (1864–1938), who spent his childhood in the French colony of La Réunion. Bédier was the successor to Paris's chair at the Collège de France and he shared Paris's fervent nationalism. Scholars have questioned whether Bédier's vehement opposition to Lachmannian editorial methods and their influence in France was motivated by nationalism. Bédier's thesis, which argued for the exclusively French origins of *Roland*, has also been seen as part of the 'heady climate immediately before the outbreak of WWI' (Nykrog 1996: 289, 286–307). Scholars have also explored potential nationalist influences in his rejection of Oriental influences in the medieval genre of the fabliaux and in his efforts to restore *Tristan* to its role as a major French work in light of the flurry of attention given to German versions of the text in the wake of Richard Wagner's popular opera. Examining the impact of the childhood that this ardent French nationalist experienced on La Réunion, Michelle Warren argues compellingly that Bédier's creation of a 'pure and continuous French identity all the way back to the eleventh century' reflects a complex attempt 'to heal the social and psychological ruptures of a colonial identity split between two homelands' (2005: 205, 22). By bringing together each of these likely influences on Bédier's approaches, we can see another important example of the interplay between nationalism and colonialism in the creation of medieval studies.[22]

While the establishment of institutional medieval studies appears to have benefitted a great deal from what has been called the nineteenth-century German 'academic machine' and from French attempts to match it, the work of Englishman Sir William Jones (1746–94) is regarded by many as the theory that launched 1,000 philological studies (Graham 1996: 69). In a 1786 lecture at the Asiatic Society, Jones argued that Greek, Latin and Sanskrit were all related, a thesis that Jones proposed after only a short time studying Sanskrit (Olender 2002: 6–7). After this, Sanskrit came to supplant Hebrew as the 'fashionable subject' of a new hypothesis about the origin of language itself. Scholars threw themselves with renewed energy into the study of ancient tongues, hoping to unlock the secrets of the distant past and locate the dawn of civilisation (Olender 2002: 1–20). The scholarly frenzy extended beyond philology: 'All the human sciences, from history to mythology, and soon to include "racial science," were affected by the discovery of a tongue that was known not only as Indo-European but also as Aryan' (Olender 2002: 7). This growth in philological inquiry, in England as in France and Germany, developed alongside nationalism and imperialism.[23]

English Anglo-Saxon studies can be dated back to the Society of Antiquaries founded in 1586 (Frantzen 1996: 48). The study of Anglo-Saxon culture was subject to a variety of approaches and attitudes beginning in the early modern period, but the work of John Mitchell Kemble (1807–57) is a crucial turning point in the history of the discipline. Kemble's work marks the moment when Anglo-Saxon studies became influenced by the perspective of '*Wissenschaft*', the German word for science that also in this case signifies a systematised or 'scientific' method that elevates the inquiry above the realm of the merely amateurish or antiquarian (Frantzen 1996: 57). Just as scholars such as Mary Louise Pratt have shown that the natural and biological sciences could be used to service imperialist ideologies, so too can we see the 'science' of philology in England shaped by politics and ideology, as it was in France and Germany (Pratt [1992] 2008: 15–36; Loomba 1998a: 57–69).[24] There are important parallels between what Williamson has called the 'longing for myth' in Germany and the 'desire for origins' from which Frantzen takes the title of his study of the development of medieval studies, especially Anglo-Saxon studies, in English. Anglo-Saxonists were also seeking to unearth the English past and reveal English national character. As was the case in France, the influence of German methods on English scholars was not a matter of a simple transfer; the nature of Anglo-Saxon studies was the subject of dispute as the quest for a national identity and history, so crucial to the ideologies of English imperialism and colonialism, was negotiated.[25]

We can see, for example, political concerns affecting the development of the study of later medieval English literature as well as Anglo-Saxon. F. J. Furnivall (1825–1910), who founded the Early English Text Society (EETS) in 1864, held some progressive views regarding the education of the working class and women.[26] At the same time, however, the Society, which produced editions of medieval English texts, was clear in its goal of using the English literary canon instrumentally for imperial ends. In an 1869 report, the EETS members declared, 'We are banded together to trace out the springs, and note the course, of a language that shall one day be the ruling tongue of the world, which is now the speech of most of its free men' (qtd in Biddick 1998: 93). An 1877 report from the Society proclaims that its texts will be made available to 'every student and boy in the British Empire' (qtd in Biddick 1998: 93). Ironically, the study of the English literary past was a part of colonial school curricula well before it became a standard part of English educational institutions (Biddick 1998b: 95–6, citing Viswanathan 1989: 3). The EETS volumes were distributed not only in England and the US, but also in India, noting that the study of English literature became a component in the Indian Civil Service examinations, instituted in 1855 (Biddick 1998b: 231 n. 31). Biddick observes that English-authored studies on Indian languages and cultures were shelved in colonial libraries next to editions of medieval English literature, arguing convincingly that this unusual juxtaposition is emblematic of the complex relationship between nineteenth-century nationalism and imperialism and medievalist and Orientalist scholarship (1998b: 96).

Indeed one could say that both Orientalism and medievalism had shaping roles in British educational mandates in colonial India. Thomas Babbington Macaulay's 'Minute of the 2nd of February 1835' demonstrates this clearly. In this document, Macaulay (1800–59) addresses a controversy between two factions in the fight over Indian education in the 'General Committee on Public Instruction'. The 'Orientalists' wanted to continue to provide stipends for the study of Arabic and Sanskrit, while the 'Anglicists' wanted this funding shifted to English instruction. Macaulay sided with the Anglicists and used as part of his argument what he considered the indisputable 'intrinsic superiority of Western literature' (Macaulay 1972: 241). He argued that an infusion of English would have the same 'elevating' effect on Indian literature and learning as Greek and Latin had on Anglo-Saxon and Anglo-Norman cultures, equating contemporary Indians with the medieval English in a familiar trope.[27] Macaulay's goal is a colony that is 'Indian in blood and colour, but English in taste, in opinion, in morals, and in intellect' (Macaulay 1972: 249). Macaulay viewed contemporary 'natives' as lagging several centuries behind their European counterparts, just as 'contemporary medievals' are described by numerous nineteenth-century English writers in England, as well as those from France, Germany and Spain. This formulation was literally staged in nineteenth-century international exhibitions, which often juxtaposed re-creations of both medieval and 'primitive' communities (Ganim 2005).

In Spain it was not the acquisition and maintenance of colonies, but their loss and a sense of overall national decline that inspired nationalistic soul searching among the intellectuals and scholars of the 'Generation of '98', including medievalist Ramón Menéndez Pidal (1869–1968), whose work sought to find 'the essential qualities of Spanish literature' (Gerli 2001: 119).[28] The notions of Spanish identity developed by the

Generation of '98 contributed to the exclusion of literature written in Muslim-controlled portions of Spain between 710 and 1492. These texts and their complex status in relation to notions of Spanish identity will be explored in more detail in the section on al-Andalus in the next chapter. The negotiation between Orientalism and nationalism that the controversy over the status of al-Andalus represents is a crucial element of the historical development of the discipline of medieval studies, not only in relation to Spanish literature, but more broadly as well.

This negotiation between Orientalism and nationalism can also be found in Italian scholarship. The scholarship of Michele Amari (1806–89), a scholar of medieval Sicily, cannot be separated from his early life as a revolutionary in the Sicilian separatist movement, a role later reflected in his foundational work on the 1282 'Sicilian Vespers' uprising and his later stance as an ardent supporter of Italian unification (Mallette 2005a). Comparing Amari and his friend and fellow scholar Ernst Renan (1823–92), known for his influential 1882 address, 'Qu'est-ce qu'une nation?' ('What is a Nation?'), Karla Mallette demonstrates how historical and political contexts can influence intellectual direction. Amari, she argues, is fighting for a future Sicilian nation; Renan takes the existence of the French nation as a given. Renan's view of the Orient is shaped by France's role as a colonial power in Arab lands. At that time, Italy had no such possessions. Instead, Amari came to address the relationship between Sicily and Italy and to understand both of their roles as the 'backward South' of a larger Europe in the terms of colonialism. This may account for the different Orientalisms and nationalisms of the two thinkers (Mallette 2005b). The intersections between scholarship and politics shown in Amari's work demonstrate not only currents in European Orientalism and imperialism that are directed outside the European continent, but also those that are focused within Europe, at the European 'South', specifically Italy and Spain. This tension between North and South still marks European politics and thought even in the era of the European Union, with southern European countries considered lesser members of the European club (Dainotto 2007).

With this overview I have attempted to call attention to important intersections between the rise of European colonialism and the development of medieval studies, a set of connections that will surely continue to benefit from further exploration into Scandinavia (Bjork 1997; Kennedy 2007) and Europe's Eastern and Slavic regions, which Jan Piskorski reminds readers are sometimes called the 'Third Europe' or 'Black Europe'. The relationship between colonialisms and medievalisms are also very relevant to discussions of Europe's internal colonies, notably Ireland (Piskorski: 2002). As Davis and Altschul put it, 'to an important degree the idea of the Middle Ages issued from the same colonial imaginary that subsumed both territory and time to the sphere of its real and desired control' (2009: 2). Nadia Altschul has demonstrated how the writings of Venezuelan scholar Andrès Bello, working in the early nineteenth century in London, provided an alternate view of the Spanish 'national epic', the *Cid*, that saw it in relation to French sources, a view that until very recently has been overlooked in the *Cid* scholarship predominated by the theories of Pidal and the Generation of '98. Bello's perspective as a Latin American *criollo* enabled a new view of medieval literature that challenges the view of the Spanish metropole (Altschul 2009). Further work on the development of medieval studies from a postcolonial perspective will clearly continue to add to our understanding of the interconnections between the fields of medieval studies and postcolonial studies, demonstrating that the alleged historical incompatibility between the two fields ignores how disciplines, too, have layered histories that are infused with complex political and ideological influences.

Notes

1. The original discussion of the 'denial of coevalness' comes from Fabian ([1983] 2008).
2. Earlier myths of the creation of empire as progress also underlay later accounts of empire, both in the shaping force of Virgil's *Aeneid* on a text such as Geoffrey of Monmouth's and in later accounts of warfare and 'civilisation building', including the Vietnam War and contemporary schemes for global development, such as those put forth by the United Nations (Waswo 1997).
3. See web addresses in 'Further Reading' under 'Web Resources'.
4. On Prester John and European exploration, see Freedman 2008.
5. Among the most important works in the field are Anna Abulafia (1995), Jeremy Cohen (1982; 1996; 1999; 2006; 2007), Robert Chazan (1987; 1989; 1997; 2000), Denise Despres (1994), Gavin Langmuir (1990a; 1990b), and Kenneth Stow (1992; 2007).
6. As evidenced in studies by, among others, Bale (2006), Biddick (2003), Chism (2002), Delany (1999), Kruger (2006), Lampert (2004) and Tomasch (1998; 2000).
7. See Lampert (2004).
8. See, for example, Akbari (2000; 2004; 2005a). See 'Further Reading' for Akbari's important new work, *Idols of the East* (2009), which appeared too late to be discussed here.
9. See also the discussion of 'race' in the next chapter.
10. Said [1978] 1994: 70. See Kathleen Biddick (2000a; 2000b), Kathleen Davis (2000) and Sharon Kinoshita (2007).
11. See Ganim (2000; 2005).

12. Such as Benedict Anderson ([1983] 2006) and Homi Bhabha (1990).
13. See discussions of Galbraith (1941), Strayer (1963; 1970), Huizinga (1959) and others in Ingham (2001: 8–9) and Lavezzo (2004: vii–xxxiv).
14. On these arguments, see Smith (1999) and West (1999).
15. See Kedar (1992: 341–66) and Bartal (2001).
16. For an additional summary of Spiegel's argument and her critique of Biddick, see Campbell (2006: 12–14) and Altschul (2008: 589–90).
17. See Ganim (2005).
18. I take the phrase 'the longing for myth' from George S. Williamson's *The Longing for Myth in Germany*. My discussion of German medievalism draws on Williamson (2004: esp. 72–120), Frantzen (1990), Peck (1996) and Geary (2002).
19. 'Jene riesenhaften Schatten, die uns wie durch einen Nebel erscheinen, müssen wieder feste Umrisse bekommen, dem Bilde der Vorzeit muß seine eigenthümliche Seele wieder eingehaucht werden', Schlegel (1812: 34; cited in translation in Williamson 2004: 78).
20. Bismarck refers to the importance of '*seiner Arbeit im Reichslande*' (Sternsdorff 1979: 178, cited in translation in Peck 1996: 139).
21. See also Hult (1996: 195).
22. This section draws upon Gumbrecht (1986), Nichols (1996), Hult (1996), Nykrog (1996) and Warren (2005).
23. This Europe-wide search for national literary origins was arguably inspired by a forgery, Scot James Macpherson's *Poems of Ossian* (1765). Macpherson's text can be read as a reaction to the destruction of traditional Highland language and culture, a situation for which postcolonial analysis seems highly relevant. See Hall (2007) and Leerssen (2004).
24. On the 'science' of philology, see also Bernal (1987).
25. For an excellent in-depth discussion of the development of Anglo-Saxon studies, see Frantzen (1990, especially 62–95).
26. See Ganim (2005: 33–4).
27. On Macaulay, see Franzten (1990: 28–35) and Kabir (2006: 84–5). On the equation of non-European peoples with medieval Europeans, see Davis (2000 and 2008), Ganim (2000), Kabir (2006) and Goh (2007).
28. Menéndez Pidal's work is widely acclaimed, but has come under scrutiny since his death in 1968. For critiques and debate, see Alonso (1969), Brown (1995), Linehan (1996), Gerli (2001), Armistead (2001) and Warren (2003: 31–2).

Chapter 2

Medieval Intersections

The Case of al-Andalus

How al-Andalus is viewed and how or even whether it is included in literary histories of Europe has a profound influence on how European literature and, indeed, Europe itself are conceived. In the last chapter we saw how the history of al-Andalus is a contested one, sometimes figured as a world of harmonious interactions between Muslims, Christians and Jews, and sometimes as a disastrous period from which a Christian population had to fight to recover. As we will see in the next chapter, these two points of view continue to play a role today not only in scholarship, but in public discourse more generally. Despite its importance, however, al-Andalus is only beginning to receive its fair share of attention in postcolonial medieval studies. This case study will attempt to provide essential background to this important and emerging site of issues in the field.

During the period between 711 and 756 Iberia was ruled through a viceroyalty from North Africa, after which the Umayyad dynasty (756–1030) was established by Abd-al-Rahman I, who had escaped the slaughter of the Umayyads by the Abbasids in Damascus in 750. Under the Umayyad caliphate, Córdoba became an unparalleled cultural centre. The years from 1030 to 1090 are sometimes known as the period of 'petty kings', a time of continued cultural efflorescence and of political decay. The year 1090 ushered in the so-called Moorish period, when Iberia was ruled by two different groups from North Africa: the al-Murabitun, or Almorávides, who ruled between 1090 and 1146, and the Muwahhidun, or Almóhades, who had control between 1127 and 1248.[1] The 'Reconquista', or Christian 'Reconquest', began and continued throughout the Moorish period; this period saw a further flourishing of cultural production, especially in the areas of philosophy and of translation. The Grenada period (1230–1492) ended with the Christian capture of Grenada, the last Muslim stronghold and the subsequent expulsions of Jews and Muslims from Iberia.[2]

In al-Andalus, impressive innovations in many fields were introduced by figures such as Ibn Gabirol (c. 1021–70), Ibn Hazm (994–1064), Petrus Alfonso (1062–1135), Ibn Tufayl (1110–85), Ibn Rushd (known in Latin as Averroës, 1126–98), Ghazzali (d. 1111), and Maimonides (1135–1204), just to name a few (Lasater 1974: 15–34; Menocal [1987] 2004). Their cultural achievements ranged across philosophy, science, translation, architecture, music and, of most interest to us, literature. This was a multilingual society, functioning in classical and colloquial Arabic, Latin and four distinct dialects of Romance or early Spanish – Castilian, Catalan, Galician, and Portuguese – in addition to Hebrew, which was

الأعمى التطيلي

١ دَمْعٌ مَسْفُوحٌ و ضُلُوعٌ حِرارْ   ماءٌ و نارْ   ما اجْتَمَعَا إلاّ لأمْرٍ كُبَارْ

٢ بئْسَ لَعَمْري ما أرادَ العَذولْ   عُمْرٌ قَصيرٌ و عناءٌ طَويلْ

٣ يا زَفَراتٍ نَطَقَتْ عن غَليلْ   و يا دُموعاً قد أعانَتْ مَسيلْ

٤ إمْتَنَعَ النَّومُ و شَطَّ المَزارْ   و لا قَرارْ   طِرْتُ و لكِن لم أعِدْه مَطارْ

٥ يا كعبةً حجّتْ إليها القُلوبْ   بَيْنَ هوىً داعٍ و شَوْقٍ مُجيبْ

٦ حَنَّةَ أوّاهٍ إليها مُنيبْ   لَبَّيْكَ لا ألْو لِقَوْلِ الرَّقيبْ

٧ جُدْ لي بحَجٍّ عندها و أعْتِمارْ   و لا أعْتِذارْ   قَلْبي هَدْيٌ و دُموعي جِمارْ

٨ أهْلاً و إنْ عرضَ بي للمَنونْ   بِمائسِ الأعْطافِ ساجي الجُفونْ

٩ يا قَسْوةً يَحْسِبُها الصَّبُّ لينْ   عَلَّمْتِني كيفَ تَسوءُ الظُّنونْ

١٠ مُذْ بانَ عن تلك اللّيالي القِصارْ   نَوْمي غِزارْ   كأنَّما بَيْنَ جُفوني غِرارْ

١١ حَكَّمْتُ مَوْلىً جارَ في حُكْمِهِ   أكْني به لا مُفْصِحاً بِاسْمِهِ

١٢ فأعْجَبْ لإنْصافي على ظُلْمِهِ   و أسْألُهُ عن وَصْلي و عن حُرْمِهِ

١٣ ألْوى بحَقّي عن هوىً و أخْتِيارْ   طَوعَ النِّفارْ   فكلُّ أنْسٍ بَعْدَهُ بالخِيارْ

١٤ لا بُدَّ لي مِنه على كلِّ حالْ   مَوْلىً تَجَنَّى و جَفَا و أسْتَطالْ

١٥ غادَرَني رَهْنَ أسىً و أعْتِلالْ   ثُمَّ شَدَا بَيْنَ الهَوى و الدَّلالْ:

١٦ مَوْ الْحَبيبْ أنْفرمُ ذي مَوْ أمَرْ،   كَنَ دَشْتَرْ،   نُفّيسْ أميبْ كَسَدِ نُوليغَرْ

By permission of Gorgias Press

primarily used as a written language (López-Morillas 2000: 43; and Lasater 1974: 27–8). Mozarabic, the form of Hispano-Romance spoken in Muslim-controlled regions, is also referred to as *romance andalusí*.[3]

Poetry was considered the highest literary form, with poets from Muslim, Christian and Jewish backgrounds composing in Arabic, and, in the case of Jewish poets, also in Hebrew. Andalusians produced unique innovations of classical Arabic forms, the *muwashshah* (pl. *muwashshahat*), dating back to 900, and its offshoot form, the somewhat less complex *zajal*, which appeared before 1100 (Lasater 1974: 35–6). Some of these forms combined classical and colloquial Arabic. Certain critics, foremost among them María Rosa Menocal, see the *muwashshahat*, which feature unique combinations of linguistic registers, as emblematic of the hybrid culture of al-Andalus itself (Rosen 2000: 185; and Lasater 1974: 14). The reasons for this characterisation become clear, I think, in a beautiful example of the form by al-Ama at-Tutuli, the 'blind poet of Toledo' (d. 1126):

> Tears that are shed and a breast that is burned
> > Water and fire!
> Things never joined save for matters of moment!
> > > By my life, it is harsh, what the censor has said,
> > > For life is but short while love's toils are long.
> > > O, for the sighs that betray one who loves!
> > > And O, for the tears that flow like a stream!
> Sleep is taboo, visitation is far;
> > No peace and quiet!
> I would fly, yet I find no place to take flight!
> > > O Ka'ba to which all hearts journey forth
> > > Torn by passion that calls and answering love,
> > > You called on a sinner returning to you;
> > > Here I am! I heed not the words of the spy!
> Allow me to travel and worship therein;
> > Make no excuse!
> My heart is the gift and my tears are the stones.
> > > Welcome is he, though he expose me to death;
> > > One supple of waist and languid of eye.
> > > O hardness of heart which love sees as soft,
> > > You have caused me to learn that thoughts can think ill!
> Since he made off from those nights which were short
> > My tears gush forth
> As though in my lids were sharp-pointed swords!
> > > I've chosen a lord who unjustly condemns;
> > > To him I allude not revealing his name;

> My justice is wondrous in view of his wrong!
> Him you may ask for the tryst and refusal.
> He tore from a passion well proven my share
>   Of obedience,
> Though shunned. Joy after him may choose whom it wills.
>   I cannot resist him on any condition;
>   A lord who accuses, treats harshly, delays;
>   Who left me in pledge to despair and disease,
>   Then sang with an air between boldness and love:
> 'Meu l-habib enfermo de meu amar.
>   ¿Que no ha d'estar?
> ¿Non ves a mibe que s'ha de no llegar?' (Monroe [1974] 2004: 248–51)

The main body of the poem is written in Arabic and the *kharja*, or 'exit', the lyric's final lines, are composed in Romance with some Arabic words mixed in. *Al-habib* means 'lover' in Arabic and is one of several terms, such as *mamma* [mother], that frequently appear in romance *kharjas* (Rosen 2000: 169). James Monroe translates these final lines as 'My beloved is sick for love of me. / How can he not be so? / Do you not see that he is not allowed near me?' ([1974] 2004: 251).

This poem, intricate in rhyme and prosody, is structured around oppositions, a characteristic feature of Arabic love poetry, beginning with the water and fire in the opening lines (Mallette 2003: 688). We can see echoes of this opening opposition evoked in the ironies expressed in the poem: the assertions that life is short, but that the toils of love are long and that the speaker would flee, but can find no way to do so. The speaker is clearly in a state of extreme suffering, as is made most vivid through the violent image of tears gushing from his eyes as though his eyelids contained sharp swords. Such suffering is also described in Ibn Hazm's (994–1064) *Tawq al-Hamama* (The Dove's Neckring), in which love is connected to suffering and compared to illness. This characterisation of love is an essential part of the Andalusian poetic tradition.

The Ka'ba, the centre of the Hajj pilgrimage, is invoked, Karla Mallette argues, as a witness and a sign of spiritual presence (2003: 689). It also seems possible that the object of the speaker's love is being compared to the Ka'ba, with the beloved's presence drawing the speaker just as the Ka'ba draws pilgrims, a reading supported by the reference to the 'spy', another frequent feature in these poems, who seems bent on keeping the lovers apart. The speaker asks to be allowed to come and worship and figures his heart and tears as elements of the pilgrimage. His heart becomes the gift, the sacrifice of an animal and his tears the stones that are thrown at Mina in the medieval version of the Hajj.[4]

An alternate reading of the last line of the poem is offered by Sola-Solé, who translates it into modern Castilian as: '*Que venga a mí que cura mi acercamiento*' [May he come to me and be cured by proximity to me] (1990: 102–3, quoted in Mallette 2003: 689). The transcriptions/ translations of both Monroe and Sola-Solé emphasise the power of proximity to a numinous presence, making the poem's final lines hark back to the image of the Ka'ba and the reference to a pilgrimage to a holy space that is woven through the poem's early lines. These references and the circular link they create between the poem's early stanza and its closing *kharja* stress the powerful connection between the sacred and the erotic in the poem, conjoining them just as the lyric mingles together both different languages and formal and colloquial linguistic registers. One can indeed see such a poem as an emblem of cultural hybridity, and also discern within it central elements in what is usually considered the 'Western' tradition of poetic love: for example, the poem's focus on suffering, its sharply contrasting images, and its blend of the erotic and the sacred. Scholars such as Menocal have advocated wider recognition of the importance of the Arabic literary tradition to European literatures, but this perspective has been largely neglected both inside and outside of academia until very recently (Menocal [1987] 2004).

The *kharjas* appeared in modern editions put together by German scholars around a century ago, but it was not until Samuel Stern published his path-breaking study showing that some of the *kharjas* contained words in Romance that they began to receive wider attention (1948). Stern's article proved to be the dawn of '*kharja* studies', and scholars have since presented numerous theories about the nature and origins of the *kharjas*. Were they, as a contemporary observer implied, the basis upon which the rest of the poem was built? Did Arabic poetry influence Romance forms or did the opposite influence occur? Or, is this perhaps a case of mutual influence? The speakers of the Romance *kharjas* are often female. Can we see the Romance tradition as a feminine one, as opposed to a masculinised classical Arabic poetic tradition? These and many other questions remain unresolved, as do the transcriptions and interpretations of the poems themselves, which manuscript and linguistic complications make extremely challenging.[5]

To some extent technical challenges do account for the extremely contentious nature of *kharja* studies, but by no means entirely. When one learns that the field has been marred by some vituperative rhetoric, one might guess that the controversies stemmed from offended religious sensibilities or perhaps from the fact that the *kharjas* sometimes contain suggestive or even vulgar material. The battles in the field, however, appear primarily shaped by disciplinary turf battles, battles which, in this case, are also connected to the debates about Spanish identity and the role of the period of al-Andalus in Spanish history. At the core of the disputes is a concern over which tradition these poems rightly belong to, which tradition is the dominant or originary one, and which specialists are truly qualified to study the poems. One might think that Stern's initial work on the *kharjas* would have sparked interdisciplinary cooperation, with Arabists and Romanists working together to untangle the poems' complex and layered meanings. While there has been some collaboration, Arabists and Romanists have also spent several decades arguing vigorously for the primacy of their own specialisation in journals such as *Al-Andalus* and *La Corónica*.

More is at stake in these debates, however, than simple disciplinary propriety. Just beneath the surface flow the undercurrents of a larger debate over the nature of al-Andalus and its role in Spanish history and culture. For example, Anthony Espósito examines the ways in which the *kharjas* have been anthologised as fragments in survey texts of medieval Spanish literature. He argues that, by wresting the *kharjas* away from their larger lyric context, without reference to the Arabic and Hebrew poems of which they are part, many anthologies support the notion of a popular 'Spanish' voice, a concept which draws upon Romantic conceptions of nation and *Volk*. Such an approach creates a notion of a particular Spanish-language tradition that exists separately from the Arabic- and Hebrew-language poetry of al-Andalus, and has survived through a period of 'foreign' influence. Further, the way that the *kharjas* are translated and presented often erases their homoerotic content, also insuring that they do not provide a challenge to (hetero)normative national ideals (Espósito 1995; 2000). Of course, from another perspective the inclusion of the *kharjas*, even in a fragmented form, seems to represent a step toward inclusiveness, as earlier anthologies of Spanish literature typically would not mention Andalusian writings at all, beginning instead with the twelfth-century Spanish 'national epic', *Poema de Mío Cid*.

The Contested History of al-Andalus

Just as Iberia was (and to some extent still is) a contested territory, its history has also been the subject of fierce dispute as tensions over the legacies of Muslim and Christian rule play themselves out in scholarship about medieval Spain. The modern historiographical debate is exemplified by the exchange between Américo Castro and Claudio Sánchez-Albornoz. In *España en su historia: cristianos, moros y judios*

([1948] 1983]), published while Castro lived in exile from fascist Spain, he described the culture of medieval Iberia as one comprised of 'three castes': Christians, Muslims and Jews. Castro developed the idea of '*convivencia*', an idealistic vision of interactions between the three castes, in which 'the sense of self possessed by members of each caste was generated through the experience *[vividura]* of opposing the other two' (Glick 1992: 2). In this context, *convivencia* means more than simply 'coexistence'; it is an inextricable and binding set of interrelationships among the three groups, each of which contributes to the culture of the other two as well as to a collective Iberian culture.

Sánchez-Albornoz vehemently opposed this relatively positive view of a hybrid Iberian culture. His *España, un enigma historico* (1956) views the Muslim conquest of 711 as a disaster for the pre-existing Christian culture, an event that did just the opposite of creating cultural vibrancy. Sánchez-Albornoz emphasises the resulting conflicts between Christians and Muslims, arguing that these struggles drained Spain's resources, leaving it impoverished and underdeveloped in comparison with the rest of Europe. Despite the often bitter tone of this academic debate, Castro and Sánchez-Albornoz are both searching to define the nature of Spanish literature and, by extension, the national character of Spain itself (Herr 1958). This quest was also undertaken most prominently by Ramón Menéndez Pidal, (Castro's teacher), a member of the Generation of '98, who, as we noted in the previous chapter, wished to reveal and elevate a sense of Spanish identity in the face of a sense of Spanish political and economic decline.[6]

In more recent scholarship, the notion of *convivencia* remains contested. It was celebrated in various exhibits and works in 1992, the 500th anniversary of Columbus's voyage and also in works by scholars such as María Rosa Menocal, whose *The Ornament of the World: How Muslims, Jews, and Christians Created a Culture of Tolerance in Medieval Spain* lauds a multicultural medieval Iberia as a 'first-rate' place (2002: 15). Working from a different perspective, historians such as David Nirenberg have called for closer scrutiny of the conflictual nature of intercultural relationships on the peninsula as revealed through archival research (1998). Brian Catlos, also stressing an archival approach, has argued that the complex relationships in medieval Iberia are best understood by examining questions of mutual interest and structural compatibility between groups, arguing wittily that '*conveniencia*' is a better-suited term than the overarching idealism implied by '*convivencia*' (2001).

Scholars do seem to be moving beyond the acrimony that characterised the exchanges of Castro and Sanchez-Albornoz. However, the issue at the centre of their debates – the conflicting views of the role of Muslim, or more broadly 'Semitic', influence in Spain between 711 and 1492 – has figured critically in national debates around the question '¿que es España?' [what is Spain?], the search for the nature of the Spanish national character. In the periods during which Spain coped with the loss of its colonies, during the Franco regime, during the rise of immigration after Spain's entry into the European Union in 1986, and, most recently, in the aftermath of the 11 March 2004 Madrid bombings, the question of Spain's historical relationship with Northern Africa and with Muslim cultures has come to the fore (Aidi 2006; Tofiño-Quesada 2003).

These issues, both in their medieval and modern contexts, have not received much attention in postcolonial medieval studies (Kinoshita 2007: 12), and those who write about Iberia frequently reference the way it has been marginalised both within academia and beyond (Blackmore and Hutcheson 1999; Hamilton 2007b). Although, for example, Spain has played important political roles in institutions such as the European Union, discussions of 'Western Europe' and even of Europe in general still often seem to follow the maxim attributed to Alexandre Dumas: '*L'Afrique commence aux Pyrénées*' [Africa begins at the Pyrenees]. Scholars offer numerous reasons for Spain's marginalised status, all of which seem to point back to the Middle Ages, when much of Iberia was under Muslim control. There is also the so-called Black Legend, the idea that Spanish conquest in the New World was especially brutal, in part because of the exclusionist practices Spanish Christians developed to deal with the region's Muslims and Jews, practices which led to forced conversions, the Inquisition, the notorious blood laws, the *limpieza de sangre*, and finally to the Spanish (and Portuguese) expulsion of Jews and Moors (Greer, Mignolo and Quilligan 2007: 2).

Even as some scholars and cultural figures in modern Spain have deployed Orientalist notions, Iberia has also been itself marginalised by a type of Orientalism, the idea that it is somehow more 'Eastern' than 'Western' owing to its mixed background. This argument reveals how much ideas of what constitutes 'Europe' can depend on notions of 'Christendom' (Tofiño-Quesada 2003). Spain's very marginalisation and the historical and ideological reasons behind it, however, make Iberia central to any postcolonial exploration of medieval cultures and literatures. In the centuries between the beginning of Muslim rule in 711 and the expulsions of 1492, Iberia arguably became the most culturally complex region in Europe, and in the subsequent years of Spanish conquest in the 'New World', Spain also became one of the most important actors in colonialism.

What is Lost by Ignoring al-Andalus?

Or, put another way, what is gained by paying greater attention to al-Andalus in the context of postcolonial medieval studies? The most prominent thinker on this issue is Menocal, who has spent her career demonstrating the importance of medieval Iberia to a wide range of questions. Her arguments are forcefully and persuasively presented in *The Arabic Role in Medieval Literary History* ([1987] 2004) in which she challenges regnant views of the origins of European literature. She argues that 'European scholarship has an a priori view of, and a set of assumptions about, its medieval past that is far from conducive to viewing its Semitic components as formative and central' ([1987] 2004: xiii). While Menocal concurs that medieval European Christians had a strongly negative (and distorted) view of Islam, the same was not the case, she argues, for the culture of al-Andalus and for Arabic influences more broadly ([1987] 2004: 37). Focusing on the controversial 'Arabist thesis' of the origins of troubadour poetry, she demonstrates clearly that while these origins may be complex and a case of mutual rather than one-way influences, the Arabist influence in Provençal poetry cannot be denied. Even a cursory reading of al-Ama at-Tutuli's lyric poem, above, reveals a focus on paradox and a connection between the erotic and the spiritual that should be familiar to any student of Western poetry; it seems possible, for example, to trace its thematic and stylistic connections to seventeenth-century English verse such as that of John Donne.

Menocal demonstrates the viability of the theory of Arabist influence, showing the historical possibility of multicultural interaction through figures such as William IX, Duke of Aquitaine (1071–1126) who had direct contact with the languages and cultures of al-Andalus, and his granddaughter, Eleanor of Aquitaine (1122–1204) who had ties to the courts of Sicily and Spain ([1987] 2004: 27–51). Historians have been readier to acknowledge the influence of al-Andalus than literary specialists have, and Menocal builds on this work to show the influence of translations, particularly those of Aristotle and of medical and scientific work, to thinkers in Paris and in Italy; she then argues for the influence of these thinkers on writers such as Dante, who seems to be reacting *against* the Arabist learning embraced by many in his time. The question of influence, however, whether negative or positive, is undeniable.

As Menocal observes, this Arab influence in Western thought and literature was taken as a given through the eighteenth century. But in the nineteenth century, just as Europe was gaining colonial subjects in the Arab world, figures such as Madame de Staël, Chauteaubriand and

Schlegel directed the focus of the search for European literary sources to the Latin, Romance and Christian traditions, to the exclusion of 'Eastern' traditions. Christianity and Christian heresies, Ovid and folklore were established as the only roots of the medieval 'Romance' tradition (Menocal [1987] (2004): 81–2; Dainotto 2007). Until recently, the focus in Spanish literary studies has also bypassed 'Semitic' influences. As Tofiño-Quesada puts it, 'In 1492, *Catholic* and *Spanish* became synonyms and have remained so for the majority of Spaniards, despite some modern efforts to see the Moorish presence in the Peninsula not as a foreign invasion, but as part of the very fabric of the Spanish state' (2003: 141). The canon of medieval Spanish literature played a role in this sense of Spanish identity. This is evidenced in the development of study of the *Poema de Mio Cid*, an epic that became the centrepiece of Spanish medieval literature and that was read as a text of the Reconquista. Until recently, with the inclusion of the literature of al-Andalus in anthologies as noted above, it was the Spain of the *Cid* that was presented as the model of an 'authentic' Spanish literary heritage.[7]

In critiquing this model of Spanish literature and of European literature more broadly, Menocal points out 'the very use of the title "Spaniard" is implicitly defined in racial and religious terms. The Cid is a Spaniard, but Ibn Hazm and Maimonides are not; they are an Arab and a Jew respectively' ([1987] 2004: 23 n. 17). What is at stake in the question of al-Andalus is a new way of looking at (medieval) Europe and at the Western tradition. The vaunted 'Renaissance' of the twelfth century, for example, drew much knowledge and inspiration from the cultural milieu of medieval Iberia. Recognition of this tradition is critical to shaping understandings of Europe and the 'West', understandings which, as we will discuss in the next chapter, have become central to contemporary global politics post 9/11. These debates are on-going in the scholarly world. For example, Sylvain Gouguenheim's *Aristote au Mont-Saint-Michel les racines grecques de l'Europe chrétienne*, takes on theories of Muslim influence on European culture (2008). Gouguenheim argues against the notion that it was the medieval Muslim world that kept alive the traditions of ancient Greece during the Middle Ages, which he sees as part of a reverse ethnocentrism that depicts an enlightened Islamic culture in contrast to a barbaric Christian one (15–16). Gouguenheim argues that the Greek tradition was preserved through translations by Christians, including Arab Christians. Gouguenheim's examination of translation projects by Christians, which sheds light on centres such as Mont St Michel, is also shaped by polemic, as indicated by an appendix that attacks the German Orientalist Sigrid Hunke (1913–1999) as a friend of the infamous Nazi Heinrich Himmler (1900–45) (2008: 203–6). The tenor of Gouguenheim's book is indicative of how heated these debates can become and demonstrates how even quite specific historical arguments can be viewed as having global ramifications.

Evidence of interconnections between cultures is, however, undeniable. Alice Lasater opens *Spain to England: A Comparative Study of Arabic, European, and English Literature of the Middle Ages* (1974) with a very concrete example. She relates the story of a remarkable artifact of the English St Cuthbert, who was buried in a cloak of 'purple silk brocade, bearing the fish design of Persian royalty. Embroidered into it, in gold thread, in Kufic (a stylized Arabic) script was the *kalmia* or saying "There is no god except The [one] God"' (1974: 3). When discovered in 1827 the garment's origin was unidentified; in 1931 it was determined to be part of an exchange of gifts between Charlemagne (742–814) and the Abbasid caliph in Baghdad, Harun al-Rashid (763–807), at the turn of the ninth century. The cloak eventually found its way to the Durham monastery where Cuthbert was laid to rest, bestowed on the saint as a symbol of wealth and status without knowledge of its connections to Islam (Lasater 1974: 3–4). It is often physical artifacts that demonstrate most strikingly the relationships between cultures in the medieval European past, revealing cultural contact that is only recently being reexamined. Such examples provide a historical channel for understanding the relationship between East and West in ways beyond conflict or 'clash'. It is to another example – a literary one – of such connections that we now turn.

Norman Frontiers and the Twelfth-century Werewolf Renaissance

Playing wittily on the idea of a twelfth-century Renaissance, Caroline Walker Bynum has referred to a 'werewolf renaissance of the twelfth century' to describe the proliferation of werewolf tales she has encountered while studying twelfth-century explorations of metamorphosis and the concept of change (2001: 94). Bynum suggests numerous explanations for the appearance of tales of werewolves, vampires and other supernatural creatures, pointing to significant changes in economic, social and cultural life, including 'colonial wars and missionary activities that brought European Christians into contact with radically different mores' (2001: 26).

The werewolves in these tales differ markedly from Greek and Roman depictions of vicious, cruel, bestial figures. They are, in contrast, sympathetic – humans trapped in animals' bodies (Bynum 2001: 94). The most extended depiction of such a figure occurs in a twelfth-century romance in the Old French dialect of Picard, *Guillaume de Palerne*, which is thought to have been composed sometime between 1188 and 1200 (Sconduto 2004: 4). I want to explore *Guillaume* in relation to Norman conquest and the hybrid cultures that developed in its wake, reading this lesser-known tale in the light of recent work on border writings, hybridity and monstrosity in the works Geoffrey of Monmouth, Marie de France, and Gerald of Wales. Scholars have been engaged in tracing the literary impact of the Norman Conquest of England in the literature of the British Isles, demonstrating the ways in which post-Norman literature can be understood through and can also expand understandings of postcolonial theoretical tools like the concept of hybridity. *Guillaume* extends the geographical reach of these discussions, as the romance is set in Sicily, which Karla Mallette has called a 'hybrid culture' of Norman and Muslim influences (2005a: 4). While the reasons for the 'werewolf renaissance' are complex, in this case study I will suggest that this literary trend may have been in part a reaction to Norman expansion, a theory supported by the setting of *Guillaume de Palerne*, the most elaborate and extended of these werewolf tales, in Norman-ruled Sicily.

The Normans

The Normans (*Nortmanni* or Northmen) were originally Scandinavian raiders, pagans who were very active in their attacks on France in the late ninth century and who eventually came to settle there. An agreement between one of their leaders, Rollo, and the Frankish king Charles the Simple in 911, in which Charles ceded land to the Normans around Rouen, is traditionally seen as marking the beginning of a broad Norman European expansion through conquest and subsequent settlement. Because of the extent of the territory ruled by Normans, John Le Patourel has even spoken of the 'Norman Empire', although the Normans themselves did not conceive of their expansion as the spread of an empire, nor did they create imperial titles for themselves (Le Patourel 1976).

The Normans eventually became Christians, and indeed, when Normans settled a conquered territory they had a tendency to integrate and adopt numerous aspects of the cultures they had vanquished, even as they dominated their new territories through military, monetary and technological advances. The most significant of these conquests is that of England in 1066 by William, Duke of Normandy, who became England's king. The conquest of England is now by far the most famous of the Normans' victories, but the overall Norman expansion was much broader than this and extended into southern Italy and Sicily, 'The Kingdom of the Two Sicilies', the setting of *Guillaume de Palerne*.

As historian Alex Metcalfe has remarked, one cannot accurately refer to a 'Norman conquest' of Sicily (2003). Norman incursions in this region occurred over decades, taking advantage of the internal strife that plagued southern Italy. In 1038 the Normans arrived in Sicily to assist Christians struggling against Muslim rulers who had controlled the island for nearly two centuries. This Norman participation was viewed as fighting in a holy war. In 1072, Robert Guiscard and Roger de Hauteville took Palermo, and Roger and his descendants, William I and William II, ruled Sicily until 1189, after which their family's control disintegrated. In 1198 control fell to the young Frederick II. William I and William II never knew Normandy and while one can still legitimately speak of the idea of a 'Norman period' and 'Norman kingship', the nature of life in Sicily during this era should not be conflated with the cultures that developed in the aftermath of the Norman Conquest of England.[8]

The Norman Conquest of England: Postcolonial Readings

As I will outline below, the majority of postcolonial readings of Norman influence have so far focused on the aftermath of the English conquest. Figuring importantly in these studies is Geoffrey of Monmouth, whose *Historia Regum Britannie* (History of the Kings of Britain c. 1130) is without a doubt one of the key source texts of the literatures of medieval Europe. Included in its vast scope are seminal formulations of the 'matter of Britain', including the introduction of the story of King Arthur. Geoffrey creates a genealogy for the English that derives from the Trojans, and he describes an England that weathers cycles of good and bad rulers and waves of invasion and conquest by Romans and Saxons. The Normans are not referenced in the text directly, but as numerous scholars have demonstrated, their coming rule over Britain, a present reality for Geoffrey, is clearly implied.

Monmouth is a town on the Welsh border, or 'marches', but despite his Welsh origins, Geoffrey had powerful Norman patrons, and scholars are divided on the question of his political loyalties. Some focus on the importance of Geoffrey's patronage, arguing for a text that ultimately supports and justifies Norman rule.[9] Others emphasise the ambiguity of the *Historia*.[10] Michelle Warren views Geoffrey as a 'border intellectual', reading in his text both support for and subversion of Norman rule (2000). Patricia Ingham also stresses the ambiguous nature of Geoffrey's text, arguing that its immense influence derived in large part from the way that it could be usefully claimed by both Welsh and Anglo-Norman readers (2001). The arguments on both sides are compelling. A definitive stance on Geoffrey's intentions and allegiances, however, is less important than the understanding shared by critics that this foundational text presents a complex reaction to a medieval example of colonisation and its aftermath, an example which, through the story of Arthur and its subsequent literary legacy, became a central component of the creation of 'Englishness' and the idea of English empire.

The late twelfth-century *Lais* of Marie de France seem worlds away from Geoffrey's epic scope, but they too reflect the consequences of Norman conquest. Noting in the *lais* 'Yonec' and 'Milun' the unusual presence of illegitimate offspring, who are usually absent from medieval tales of adulterous love, Sharon Kinoshita looks to the tales' settings in southern Wales, an area of intense border conflict after the Norman invasion. In each of these *lais* an adulterous union produces a son who later goes on to 'vindicate' his parents' love (2006a: 105). Kinoshita interprets the tales' Welsh setting through Mary-Louise Pratt's important concept of the 'contact zone': 'social spaces where disparate cultures meet, clash, and grapple with each other, often in highly asymmetrical relations of domination and subordination – such as colonialism and slavery, or their aftermaths as they are lived out across the globe today' (Pratt [1992] 2008: 7). Kinoshita argues that the *lais'* presentation of these sons is part of their negotiation of two radically different cultures, Welsh and Norman (2006a: 105). When the Normans arrived in Wales, they were confronted with very different cultural practices, such the Welsh custom of treating illegitimate offspring as the equals of siblings born in wedlock. Welsh methods of warfare and clerical practices were also the subject of Norman critique. The Welsh territories took the Normans nearly 200 years to subdue, although during this time there was also extensive intermarriage, creating a complex, hybrid Cambro-Norman culture.[11] Kinoshita argues that 'Yonec' and 'Milun' ultimately provide 'alternating visions of the colonial encounter' (2006a: 106). 'Yonec' presents an 'erotic fantasy and an allegory of native resistance to colonial rule', while 'Milun' imagines a more utopian world in which the boundaries between 'colonizer and colonized are erased' (2006a: 106). Like Warren and Ingham in their readings of Geoffrey of Monmouth, Kinoshita sees in Marie's texts a subtle and complex negotiation of cultural hybridity within the Anglo-Norman colonial context.

A third focus of recent postcolonial readings of Anglo-Norman culture are the writings of a member of the Cambro-Norman elite, Gerald of Wales (c. 1146–1223, also known as Giraldus Cambrensis or Gerald de Barri), whose works on Wales and Ireland, the *Descriptio Kambriae* (Description of Wales), the *Expugnatio Hibernica* (The Conquest of Ireland), and the *Topographia Hibernica* (History and Topography of Ireland), impacted later representations of these regions. Kathy Lavezzo focuses on the importance of the relationship between geography and identity to Gerald, noting that writings by the 'prime apologist for the invasion of Ireland' (2006: 53) also include moments that appear to critique the brutalities of the colonial situation.

Other critics have seen Gerald's views as less ambivalent. Jeffrey Jerome Cohen reads Gerald himself as a type of hybrid who continually confronts his own mixed Welsh-Norman heritage in his writings. Cohen assesses Gerald's overall treatment of difference, particularly Irish difference, as dehumanising (2006: 77–108). Rhonda Knight, examining illustrations in manuscripts of Gerald's *Topographia Hibernica*, argues that these depictions of love between humans and animals and of hybrid bodies, such as those of werewolves and the Oxman of Wicklow, construct Irish bodies as monstrous and yet desirable, an ambiguous representation that serves to reinforce and justify colonial domination (2001). David Rollo has also focused on Gerald's falsified depiction of a depraved Irish sexuality, arguing that Gerald uses this depiction as a justification for the rule of his own Cambro-Norman ancestors, who had been among the first to invade Ireland (1995). Catherine Karkov reads the figure of the werewolf in the *Topographia Hibernica* against the Irish text *Acallam na Senórach*, demonstrating how the werewolf functioned as a symbol of barbarity for the coloniser, but of heroism for the colonised (2003). A central object of examination in all of the readings is Gerald's descriptions of hybrid creatures, especially the werewolf. Whether this figure is seen as racialising and dehumanising or as more ambiguously sympathetic, it appears to figure as a response to the many 'contact zones' created by the Norman Conquest.

Guillaume de Palerne

The 'twelfth-century werewolf Renaissance', then, may be more directly linked to Norman expansion than has been previously observed and in ways that go beyond mere acknowledgment of the roots of the 'sympathetic werewolf' legend in Celtic folklore.[12] Perhaps the best-known of the werewolf tales, Marie de France's 'Bisclavret', begins with a multilingual emphasis that reflects the 'contact zone': '*Quant des lais faire m'entremet, / Ne voil ublier* Bisclavret; / *Bisclavret ad nun en bretan,* / Garwaf *l'apelent li Norman*' ['In my effort to compose lays I do not wish to omit *Bisclavret* – for such is its name in Breton, while the Normans call it *Garwaf*'].[13] Other examples of werewolf tales include an early thirteenth-century *lai*, 'Melion', which involves the daughter of the king of Ireland, and the Latin *Arthur and Gorgalon*, extant in a fourteenth-century manuscript, also involves a mixture of Arthurian and Celtic themes (Hopkins 2005; and Kittredge 1966). Let us now turn to another region of Norman conquest, Sicily, and the werewolf tale set there: *Guillaume de Palerne*.

The romance begins when Guillaume is four years old and a werewolf abducts him in order to save him from a plot against his life by his two nurses. Guillaume is first raised by a kindly cowherd and his wife and is then taken into the home of the emperor of Rome. Guillaume's natural nobility shines through all that he does and he rises to favour not only in the emperor's court, but in the eyes and heart of the emperor's daughter, Melior. The pair fall in love, but Melior is promised to the son of the Greek emperor. In order to remain together, she and Guillaume steal away disguised in the skins of white bears. The werewolf reappears to help the two fugitives as they head south through Apulia, a domain under the rule of Guillaume's father. Apulia and Palermo are under siege by the king of Spain, who wants Guillaume's sister to wed his son. Guillaume's now-widowed mother takes in Guillaume and Melior, who have changed their disguises from bears to deer, and Guillaume ends up liberating Palermo from the Spaniards, fighting under the sign of his protector, the werewolf.

As it turns out, the werewolf is the Spanish king's long-lost son, Alphonse. His stepmother, Queen Brande, had turned him into a werewolf to ensure the crown for her own son. Brande is summoned to Palermo and she transforms Alphonse back into human form. Guillaume and Melior marry and he assumes the crowns of Sicily and of Rome. *Guillaume* calls into question the nature of chivalric iden-tity, and, indeed, the nature of identity itself (Sconduto 2000: 121). Guillaume's noble nature clearly emerges as he lives in the Roman emperor's court, demonstrating the belief in inherited nobility so common in romance texts. Yet the poem also shows, especially through the figure of Alphonse the werewolf, that outward signs are not always reliable and that the possibility of radical transformation always exists

(Sconduto 2000: 125). Bynum has pointed to the relevant twelfth-century interest in the nature of change and transformation, noting that focus on the Eucharistic miracle becomes 'truly prominent' around 1200 and also arguing that writers from this period often use figures of hybrids and of doubles, 'and employ rhetorical strategies that force confrontation with paradox or contradiction' (2001: 104, 31). The characters of Guillaume and Alphonse seem to force such a confrontation for the reader. As boys, Guillaume and Alphonse are beloved sons who are also under threat, and, as men, they are noble knights whose nobility is hidden beneath misleading exteriors. Each literally appears as hybrid man and beast: Guillaume through willing, if necessary, disguise, and Alphonse through treacherous and involuntary magical transformation.

The romance underscores the importance of transformation through direct reference to that most central of Christian transformations, the Incarnation. As both Guillaume's mother and Alixandrine, Melior's wise and helpful friend, pray to God for assistance, their prayers ask for Christ's aid in a way that posits the Incarnation as a conditional:

> Hé, vrais dous peres Jhesu Cris,
> Rois sor tos rois poesteïs,
> Vraie paterne, omnipotent,
> Biau sire Diex, si vraiement
> Com ciel et terre et tous formas
> Et en la vierge t'aombras
> Et preïs incarnation,
> Sire, par sainte anoncion,
> Et forme d'ome et char humaine
> Et garesis en la balaine
> Jonas qu'ele avoit englouti,
> Si voir, sire, par ta merci
> Ces .II. enfans gart et deffent
> D'anui, de mal et de torment
> Et remet en prosperité. (Micha 1990: 131–2, ll. 3129–44)

> Oh, true gentle Father Jesus Christ,
> Most powerful of all kings,
> True Father of men, omnipotent,
> Good Lord God, if truly
> You formed heaven and earth and everything
> And in the Virgin You became incarnate
> And were made flesh,
> Lord, through Your holy annunciation,

And through the form of man and human flesh,
And if You protected in the whale
Jonah who had been swallowed,
If all this is true, Lord, then through Your mercy
Protect and defend these two children
From distress, from evil and from torment
And return them to prosperity. (Sconduto 2004: 92, ll. 3129–43)

Alixandrine's prayer is interestingly inflected by a note of doubt that connects the miraculous transformations of Christianity to those that she herself wishes to create in order to protect Guillaume and Melior. If God has truly become flesh through the Incarnation and taken the 'form of man and human flesh', then God should protect Guillaume and Melior, who have enveloped themselves in animal hides. Alixandrine's reference to Jonah reconfigures but also reinforces an unlikely but miraculous combination of animal exterior and human interior, asking for similar protection from the Almighty who has created all these elements in the first place. We have here a traditional emphasis on God's power and mercy combined with a marked emphasis on God's power of transformation.

Queen Felise echoes this emphasis on transformation in her later prayer, which parallels that of Alixandrine:

Diex, vrais peres, si voirement
Com vos par saint anoncement
Presistes incarnalité
En la virge d'umilité,
Qui en ses flans tant vos porta
Qu'a droit terme s'en delivra,
Et naquistes a loi d'enfant,
Si com nos trovosmes lisant,
De la sainte virge pucele
Qui fu et ta mere et t'ancele,
Et tu ses peres et ses fix,
Si voirement, biau sire Dix,
Garde m'onor, deffent mon cors
Contre mes anemis la fors. (Micha 1990: 172, ll. 4513–26)

God, true Father, if it is true
How you through holy annunciation
Became incarnate
In the Virgin with humility,
Who in her loins bore You so long
Until at the proper time she was delivered of You,

And You were born as a child,
Just as we find when we read
About the holy virgin maiden
Who was both Your mother and Your servant,
And You her Father and her Son,
If it is true, fair Lord God,
Then take care of my honor and protect me
Against the might of my enemies. (Sconduto 2004: 128, ll. 4513–26)

This prayer is uttered by Guillaume's mother, who will later encounter her own son in the guise of a deer. She is unaware of his true identity because the werewolf snatched him from her in order to save the boy's life. Her prayer also begins with reference to the Incarnation, but here keeps a sharper focus on the Virgin Mary, emphasising not only the power of a mother's love, but the paradoxes inherent in the Virgin's relationship to Christ. These paradoxes are echoed on a lesser scale in the relationship between Felise and her son, who will shed his animal disguise to reveal himself a man and who has, during their long separation, transformed from boy to man, from the abducted son of Palermo to its valiant saviour. These emotional prayers bring hybridity to the fore, both in theological and personal terms, making a connection between the God-man who is Christ and the individuals these prayers beseech him to protect. They confirm Christian beliefs while simultaneously stressing the power of transformation.

These representations of hybridity and transformation in *Guillaume* are not only part of explorations of chivalric identity or of identity and transformation more broadly, as Sconduto and Bynum have explored, but they also have a specific significance in relation to the romance's Sicilian setting. As Charles Dunn has shown, *Guillaume* has an unusual 'unwonted fullness of geographical detail' that stands in strong contrast to other romances set in the region. Comparing *Guillaume* to the famous and influential late-twelfth-century romances of Chrétien de Troyes, Dunn argues convincingly that the romance's Sicilian setting would certainly have been far 'more real to French crusading families than Chrétien's never-never land of Caerleon' (1960: 84–5, 139). What appears to have escaped the notice of critics of *Guillaume*, however, is how this very specific Sicilian setting intersects with the text's themes of hybridity and identity. It seems reasonable that a poet with such specific knowledge of and interest in the Kingdom of the Two Sicilies would also be aware of the existence of a wide variety of cultural and religious influences there, including those of Western and Eastern Christians, as well as Muslims and Jews. Sicily had been a Greek state, but fell to Muslim rule in the ninth century. When the Normans arrived, Muslim Sicily was in its cultural 'Golden Age'. The Normans took over and adapted to the bureaucratic practices of Sicily, using Latin, Greek and Arabic in governance, and employing and patronising Muslim artists, architects and poets (Mallette 2005a: 5).

Despite this cultural interchange, the stance of the Sicilian kings was demonstrably pro-Christian even as they tolerated Muslim practices. Metcalfe cautions us that one cannot simply read the art history of Sicily as providing a complete history of the region's culture or politics, which reveal strife as well as interconnection (2002: 303). Certainly the relationship between Christians and Muslims was also characterised by tensions and even violence, as evidenced by a massacre of Muslims in Palermo in 1161 and a later revolt by Muslims following the death of William II in 1189 (Metcalfe 2002: 314, 317). At the same time, as Metcalfe's own careful study reveals, while the formal stance of the Christian Sicilian kings reflected an unambiguous Christian triumphalism, actual practice was more complex, as in the case of the 'open secret' of 'palace Saracens', who continued to practise Islam even after official conversion to Christianity (2002: 304). There also seems to have been cultural intermixing among the lower classes. Metcalfe notes that the 'possibility that one could find Christians named Muhammed living besides Muslims with Greek names only compounds our inability to distinguish Sicilian Christians from Muslims' (2002: 313).

When a Muslim from al-Andalus, Ibn Jubayr, found himself shipwrecked in Sicily in 1184, he was amazed at the important role that Muslims and Muslim culture played there, sanctioned and fostered by a Christian ruler (Mallette 2005a: 1–4; Davis 1976: 72–4). The unique hybrid culture of Norman Sicily is preserved in monuments, such as the Capella Palatina or the church of the Martorana, and artifacts such as the coronation mantle made for Roger II in 1133–4, the border of which, like St Cuthbert's cloak, has an Arabic blessing for the king inscribed in Kufic script (Davis 1976: 74–5).

Ibn Jubayr also notes that Christian women in Palermo seem indistinguishable from Muslim women in appearance:

> The Christian women of this city follow the fashion of Muslim women, are fluent of speech, wrap their cloaks about them, and are veiled. They go forth on this Feast Day [Christmas] dressed in robes of gold-embroidered silk, wrapped in elegant cloaks, concealed by coloured veils, and shod with gilt slippers. Thus they parade to their churches, or (rather) their dens [a play on the words kana'is, 'churches', and kunus, 'dens'], bearing all the adornments of Muslim women, including jewelery, henna on the fingers, and perfumes. (Ibn Jubayr 1952: 349–50)

The complex nature of Norman-Sicilian culture is a rich field for further study, a task that its mix of cultures and languages makes particularly challenging. While additional research is necessary to understand further the balance between tolerance and friction between different groups, it is clear that Sicily in the period in which *Guillaume* is set is best understood as a 'contact zone' or as a hybrid culture, in which the Norman presence responded to very different conditions and in far different ways than those Normans who conquered England.

We can indeed see traces of Norman-Sicilian hybrid culture in the details of *Guillaume de Palerne*. At the double wedding of Guillaume and Melior and Brandin (Alphonse's younger half-brother) and Alixandrine, the presiding priest is referred to as 'patriarch Alexis', a name that evokes the Byzantine church. The ceremony, which involves a double crowning of bride and groom, appears to follow Eastern Christian tradition as well, as the poet relates: 'Then he unites them in marriage / According to the custom and the usage / That was practiced in that country' (Sconduto 2004: 238, ll. 8905–7; and Dunn 1960: 63). Of course, Queen Felise is the daughter of the emperor of Greece, an intercultural tie that would explain the wedding rituals. Furthermore, when Queen Felise has a dream that appears to give her power over both Rome and Spain, she calls for the counsel of a chaplain named Moysant, 'a good cleric and wise master, / Well indoctrinated in the arts, / Master of the arts and of canon law, / A very religious and virtuous man' (Sconduto 2004: 134–5, ll. 4781–7). Scholars have posited that this figure evokes the learned Muslims who served the king's court in Norman Sicily (Dunn 1960: 45). The name Moysant, or Moses, would imply, however, that this wise and learned counsellor is actually a converted Jew. This detail is in keeping with Metcalfe's assertion that members of the Jewish community in Sicily served as important transmitters of Arabic knowledge after the arrival of the Normans, because the Jews tended to preserve their polyglot skills and could readily act as translators and interpreters (2003: 68–70).

The portrayal of a converted Jewish rather than a converted Muslim advisor is an interesting one, however. Textual references to both culture and topography reveal the author's detailed knowledge of Norman Sicily, and a wealth of written and physical evidence points to the significance of Muslim culture there. Yet, *Guillaume* contains only one direct reference to Muslims: when Guillaume finally tearfully bids farewell to Alphonse, he pledges to protect him from any enemy, Saracen, pagan or Christian (Sconduto 2004: 245, ll. 9175–6). What can we make of the lack of direct reference to the Sicilian Muslim presence, especially in light of the actual Muslim presence in court life and the fact that Muslims 'formed the majority' of the population of Sicily for most of the Norman period (Metcalfe 2002: 289)?

Here, I would argue, we find the cultural hybridity of the contact zone expressed not directly, but instead through representations of hybridity: the werewolf and the disguises of Guillaume and Melior. Unlike Gerald of Wales's dismay and distaste for the Irish hybrids, however, we have in *Guillaume* a more ambiguous representation. The text has, of course, a Christian outlook, as evidenced by Alixandrine's and Felise's prayers and numerous other references. At the same time, however, just as we see an emphasis on transformation and hybridity even within words of prayer, we are presented with hybrid figures that encode the complex nature of Sicilian culture in ways that seem far closer to the subtle and ambiguous representations of Marie de France's *Lais*. The sympathetic nature of the hybrid figure is best seen in the werewolf, Alphonse, whose heroic nature is belied by his bestial exterior. He is, of course, an enchanted Christian prince, but the overall message of this figure appears to be that exterior trappings of identity are not the most important and that the innocent may be trapped and misjudged because of them.

Alphonse is made a werewolf by his stepmother. Scholars have remarked on the fact that wicked women often play a role in these werewolf tales, perhaps through derivation from Marie de France's 'Bisclavret', which features a treacherous wife, or through derivation from some other earlier source. The importance of gender in *Guillaume*, however, has not been further explored, despite the fact that the romance abounds in representations of female agency. Indeed, women's actions can be said to drive the plot. Guillaume must be saved from the two Greek women, Gloriande and Acelone, to whom he has been given for instruction and who are plotting to poison him and his father. Alphonse, the werewolf who saves him, has been transformed by his stepmother, Brande. And when Guillaume is finally in the Roman emperor's court, it is Melior who first falls in love with him and boldly maintains that she will marry only him, despite his unknown lineage. She and her lady, Alixandrine, are the ones who plan the lovers' disguise and escape. Finally, it is Felise, Guillaume's mother, who takes in the pair when they are in hiding in Palermo. Just as this text highlights hybridity, it also demonstrates a concern with the role of women, who are often able to pass more easily between different cultures and who can be given as brides as a means of cultural exchange. We can read in Ibn Jubayr's comments on the appearance of Christian women an instance of cultural 'passing', as these women are indistinguishable from Muslim women in their appearance.[14]

Do these highlighted roles for hybrid creatures and for women in some way account for the absence of Muslim figures in the text? Is the text highlighting both women as potential agents of cultural mixing and even of miscegenation? Are hybrids like the werewolf, who can be seen to figure this mixing, emblematising the hybrid world of the Kingdom of the Two Sicilies without either praising or condemning it? It has been noted that *Guillaume* depicts only mild punishment for those who do wrong. The nurses who plot against Guillaume and the stepmother who transforms Alphonse are not brutally punished for their deeds (Dunn 1960: 45, 130–1). This is in quite stark contrast to the ending of Marie de France's 'Bisclavret', in which the werewolf husband punishes his wife's betrayal by biting off her nose, a physical trait that then carries over to her female descendants. Indeed, all of the women in *Guillaume* are ultimately either justified in their actions or forgiven for them. I think, however, moments such as Melior's declarations that she will marry the man of her choice reveal an anxiety over female agency and the possible results of the sexual freedom this implies.

Set in a world in which Muslims, Christians and Jews co-existed, the tale suppresses references to non-Christian cultures, especially Muslim culture. These suppressed references are instead expressed through the hybrid figure of the werewolf and the disguised lovers, through whom we can see reference to cultural difference in the contact zone and perhaps discern an anxiety about cultural mixing that is reflected in various references in the text. Dunn points out that the name of Guillaume's father, Embron, is usually found in the *chanson de geste* genre as a name used for Saracen leaders (Dunn 1960: 42). Queen Brande, Alphonse's stepmother, stays in 'Carmans' when her husband is away, a town Dunn thinks must be linked to Carmona, a reference he has difficulty accepting, though, because Carmona was under Muslim control until 1247.

But what if Queen Brande has Muslim ties? Unlike Alphonse's biological mother, who comes from Gascogne, her origins are royal but unspecified. As Ana Grinberg suggests, Brande's power to transform Alphonse into a werewolf would then imply a magical power associated with Muslims, a not-unheard-of connection in the twelfth and thirteenth centuries, as we can note from Wolfram von Eschenbach's *Parzival*. Brande's ability to transform her stepson, the heir of the Spanish throne, into a wolf would then seem to express an anxiety about cultural contact between Christians and non-Christians. This intercultural contact is also relevant to Spain, portions of which were still under Muslim control, a situation that knights of Norman origin were eager to change, as evidenced in their participation in the Reconquista.[15] The character of Brande could also encode an anxiety about intermarriage and interfaith sexual contact in the wake of the Norman conquest of the area. Metcalfe notes that 'Christians targeted the conversion of the Muslim social elite' (2003: 53), a process that when successful would lead to mixing between the two religious groups. He has found eleventh-century evidence of possible intermarriage among the lower classes (2003: 75) and points out the complex nature of picking out 'ethnicity' in Norman Sicily:

> To add to the complexity of the situation, many 'Greeks' had intermarried with 'Lombards' and 'Normans' and even with Muslims and 'Berbers'. In all of the above cases, individual instances, usually in the form of mixed names, can be cited to show that the margins of these groups were often, and probably had been for some centuries, raggedly indistinct. (2003: 55)

Ibn Jubayr asserts that in King William of Palermo's court all the 'hand-maidens and concubines' were Muslim, which would likewise seem to indicate inter-religious mixing. He also tells the remarkable story of a young Christian nobleman who renounces Christianity so that he can marry a first cousin. Broadhurst, Ibn Jubayr's translator, notes that the actual story is more complex, but it involves a young nobleman named John who had renounced Christianity to marry the daughter of the Muslim Sultan of Iconium (1952: 388). Both versions of the story feature inter-faith unions, intimate intermingling between groups.

In *Guillaume de Palerne*, then, we can trace the impact of Norman conquest and the cultural intermingling that took place in its wake. Despite the text's great attention to local detail, explicit reference to Muslim culture and to Muslim figures have been suppressed, only to reappear through the motif of disguise and especially through the figure of the werewolf. The text is continually engaged with transformations ranging from the most holy, the Incarnation, to the black-magical metamorphosis of man to man-beast. These transformations seem to me to be metaphors for culture in the contact zone. The important role that women – from the Virgin, to Melior and Alixandrine, to Brande – each play registers the centrality of gender and sexuality to intercultural exchange. If, as suggested in our discussion of al-Andalus, we can begin to move medieval Iberia and Sicily from the periphery to the centre of postcolonial medieval studies, then perhaps even broader connections will be seen between the contact zones of these regions and those described by other authors whose works reacted to the Norman Conquest, such as Geoffrey of Monmouth and Gerald of Wales.

Reconsidering Hybridity

These connections and the similarities and differences that can be found both across cultures and times should lead not only to new readings of medieval texts, but to further refinements of concepts such as hybridity.[16] In her critique of postcolonial discourse, Ella Shohat (1992) pointed out that the terms 'syncretism' and 'hybridity' had for decades already been a part of Latin American modernisms, bringing us 'postcolonial hybrids *avant la lettre*'. While medieval texts do not employ these terms, these medieval literary werewolves provide examples of authors exploring the complexities of hybrid cultures and the dynamics of conquest and colonisation centuries prior to the height of European colonialism. If we read the twelfth-century 'werewolf Renaissance' as a production of the contact zones of Norman conquest, how does the medieval figure of the sympathetic human-beast inflect and inform the notion of the hybrid?

The term 'hybridity' has different meanings and functions in postcolonial studies. Best known perhaps is Homi Bhabha's idea of a mutually constructed discourse that poses a challenge to dominant colonial authority, and we can see the relevance of this definition to these werewolves and to the sly subversion exemplified by the *Lais* of Marie de France (Bhabha 2004). We have seen explored in these medieval texts 'contact zones' extant prior to what Pratt refers to as the 'shift in European planetary consciousness' in the mid-eighteenth century, before the 'emergence of natural history as a structure of knowledge', and before 'the turn toward interior, as opposed to maritime, exploration' that she sees as characterising this shift ([1992] 2008: 11). In works such as those of Gerald of Wales, which display an intense interest in the natural world and are focused on conquered lands within Europe, such as Ireland, we may find models that provide important predecessors for those dominant at the height of European colonialism and encounters beyond European borders.

Another definitional element of 'hybridity' to consider is that of power asymmetry. In their explorations of hybridity and the contact zone, Bhabha and Pratt, for example, address relationships in which the colonising power is far more powerful militarily than those being colonised. In the context of *Guillaume*, however, while the Christians have triumphed in Sicily, Islam and Christianity are overall far more equal in terms of power, and, indeed, if one considers the ultimate outcome of the Crusades, Islam has the upper hand. The elements of sympathy and ambiguity that one finds in medieval depictions of the werewolf could well be tied to the relatively more equal struggle between the 'conquerors' and the 'conquered', thus adding new dimensions to the way that we could consider representations emerging from these hybrid cultures and models of hybridity more generally.

There is also the troubling past of the term 'hybridity', which Robert J. C. Young reminds us was implicated in nineteenth-century racism. The linguistic roots of 'hybrid' go back to the Latin term for 'the offspring of a tame sow and a wild boar', and in the nineteenth century the term was used pejoratively to refer to racial miscegenation (Young 1995: 6). Young also notes that

> What has not been emphasized is that the debates about theories of race in the nineteenth century, by settling on the possibility or impossibility of hybridity, focused explicitly on the issue of sexuality and the issue of sexual unions between whites and blacks. Theories of race were thus also covert theories of desire. (Young 1995: 9)

Young traces the genealogy of the term 'hybrid' and the strange and disquieting ramifications of its complex, seemingly forgotten past, a past that has much deeper roots than the nineteenth century, as demonstrated by tales of desire like *Guillaume*. The literary half-human, half-wolf is evidence of a much longer history of narratives of hybridity expressed through the narratives of desire that constitute medieval romances. We will see issues of race manifesting themselves again in our discussion of *Parzival* and the *King of Tars*, texts in which the dynamics of interracial desire are presented through the representation of fantastic desire and monstrous progeny.

Hybridity in the Afterlife of the Norman Conquest: Ivanhoe

Before we turn to those romances, I want to consider one additional element: the enduring relevance of the Norman Conquest in later historical periods. In addition to the role that medieval ideologies may have played in the early ideologies of European conquest outside Europe, the history of the Normans also became an important part of the historiography within the British Isles and to ideologies of British Empire. It has proved just as powerful a source of legend as those myths and historiographies of the medieval Iberian experience were to Spanish imperial endeavours. As Michael Ragussis asserts:

> From the seventeenth century through the end of the Victorian period and beyond, the Conquest was the key event through which ideology regularly entered and shaped the writing of English history. The Norman Conquest became the most important event in English historiography because it was

the event by which the appeal to history was consistently used to establish English national identity. (Ragussis 1995: 106)

This quest to establish an English national identity not only had an impact on the metropole, but had implications for the British colonies as well, and images of the Norman Conquest became part of what Ananya Jahanara Kabir has termed 'imperial medievalism' (2006: 66).

A broad exploration of the imperial afterlife of the Conquest is beyond my scope here, but I would like briefly to look at an extremely well-known and influential treatment of it: Sir Walter Scott's hugely popular historical novel, *Ivanhoe* (1819), which was widely read in the British Isles, British colonial possessions and the United States. Scott (1771–1832) creates in *Ivanhoe* a vision of strife between the Saxons and their Norman conquerors:

> Four generations had not sufficed to blend the hostile blood of the Normans and Anglo-Saxons, or to unite, by common language and mutual interests, two hostile races, one of which still felt the elation of triumph, while the other groaned under all the consequences of defeat. (Scott [1819] 1998 16)[17]

This strife is eventually resolved through the rule of the legendary King Richard I, the Lionheart. The novel is set in 1194 when the historical Richard returned to England from Crusade and from imprisonment by Duke Leopold V; during Richard's absence, England was ruled by his brother John, who had aspirations of usurping Richard and who is portrayed in the novel as cruel and corrupt, in contrast to the valiant Richard.

Although Richard's virtues and his love of England seem greatly exaggerated in *Ivanhoe* when considered against medieval sources, Scott was clearly familiar with medieval history and literature. The novel is steeped in Chaucerian allusion and draws upon medieval romance, as evidenced in the encounter between Richard (disguised as the Black Knight) and an unknown hermit, a moment that reads in places like an episode straight out of a Grail romance. Scott also fabricates a manuscript source for his novel, the Wardour MS, a device that can be found in texts such as Geoffrey of Monmouth's *Historia* or Wolfram of Eschenbach's *Parzival*. And Scott compares his 'source' to the fourteenth-century Auchinleck MS, an actual compilation now housed in the National Library of Scotland in Edinburgh. Scott knew Auchinleck extremely well. He edited its *Sir Thopas* romance and was even allowed to take the manuscript home with him to consult. Many of the texts contained in the Auchinleck MS deal with 'Otherness', as the manuscript's 'Saracens' come to represent not only Muslims, but also

Scots and the French. It is through these representations of Saracens, Siobhain Bly Calkin has recently argued, that the manuscript presents a view of English identity through reference to these 'Others' (2005).

As Scott moved from his focus on Scotland in the Waverley novels to medieval England in *Ivanhoe*, the texts of the Auchinleck manuscript may not have been a direct inspiration, but English identity and the birth of England as a nation are undeniably central concerns. In keeping with this English focus, Scott even assumes the fictional identity of an Englishman, Laurence Templeton, in his 'Dedicatory Epistle' to the equally fictitious Rev. Dr Dryasdust, and he initials the numerous explanatory notes in the text as 'L.T.' Michael Ragussis has suggested that the figure of the Englishman Templeton is not only a device, like the fake manuscript source, but is itself a type of conversion from Scot to Englishman, a conversion that reflects other conversions or possibilities of conversion in the novel itself (Ragussis 1995: 99). These conversions or potential conversions, from Saxon to Norman, Scot to Englishman, or even, as we will see, Jew to Christian, are explorations of the effect on individuals of living in multiple worlds. For while this novel presents the Normans and Saxons as distinct 'races' (the term 'race' is used repeatedly in the novel), which is a way of looking at ethnicity later typified by Scott's fellow Edinburgh resident, Robert Knox (1791–1862), the novel is also about the contact zone and the possibilities of hybridity.

Scott (in his introduction through the voice of 'Templeton') even makes an argument for the historical novel itself as a new kind of temporally syncretic world in which the past can touch the present. In discussing how he as an author has tried to capture the manners and emotions of those living in the medieval period, he uses a striking analogy:

> What I have applied to language, is still more justly applicable to sentiments and manners. The passions, the sources from which these must spring in all their modifications, are generally the same in all ranks and conditions, all countries and ages; and it follows, as a matter of course that the opinions, habits of thinking, and actions, however influenced by the peculiar state of society, must still, upon the whole, bear a strong resemblance to each other. Our ancestors were not more distinct from us, surely, than Jews are from Christians; they had 'eyes, hands, organs, dimensions, senses, affections, passions;' were 'fed with the same food, hurt with the same weapons, subject to the same diseases, warmed and cooled by the same winter and summer,' as ourselves. The tenor, therefore, of their affections and feelings must have borne the same general proportion to our own. (10)

That Scott views the historical novel as a way to transcend difference is interesting considering the ways in which his narrative asserts essential differences between the 'races', between Saxons and Normans, Christians and Jews. His analogy makes reference to the famous lines in the *Merchant of Venice* (3.1), a Shakespearean passage that came to be seen in the early nineteenth century as an assertion of a common humanity. At the same time the Shakespearean lines bring to the fore the issue of differences between peoples and cultures in a way that serves to keep conflict in focus even as tolerance is preached.[18]

It is no surprise that Scott draws on *Merchant* in the passage, since the play is an important source for *Ivanhoe* and its Jewish characters Isaac of York and his daughter, Rebecca. The conflict between Jews and Christians, shaped through an Orientalist view of medieval English Jews, is an important part of the novel. While the conflict between Norman and Saxon, and the now-classic portrayal of the 'Norman Yoke' of servitude, is at the heart of the novel, it is in the novel's Orientalist vein that we see its most profound exploration of questions of hybridity. *Ivanhoe* appears focused on events transpiring on English soil, but it is in fact equally concerned with worlds beyond English borders and with the potential threat to pure English identities posed by outsiders from these worlds.

The Normans in *Ivanhoe* are represented as outsiders not only because they are French, but because they are steeped in a culture that has been greatly shaped by their experience on Crusade. When Brian de Bois-Guilbert, the Templar knight who comes to embody all that is negative about the Normans, first appears, he is linked unmistakably with crusading. He appears with two Saracen attendants, Hamet and Abdallah (29), who are 'natives of some distant Eastern country' (25), a description that means, as Scott explains in a note, that they are 'Negro slaves.' Scott (in the guise of Templeton) argues that this is not an anachronism, but instead proves a history of black slaves in England going back to the medieval period (513). Not only has Bois-Guilbert learned the culture of the Holy Land, speaking fluent Arabic (53), but he is also himself 'burnt almost into Negro blackness by constant exposure to the tropical sun' (24). Bois-Guilbert is represented as tainted by his exposure to the East. This exposure can be seen influencing Norman culture in general, as evidenced by the music of Eastern origin that plays at the fateful Ashby tournament and 'bids' both 'welcome' and 'defiance' to participating knights (79). The Norman knight seems to have been ruined by his time on Crusade, which has led him to an affiliation with the corrupt Templar order. The Templars are also strongly associated with their Eastern connections. The music they use to signal a charge in battle, for example, is characterised as having a 'wild Oriental character'

(394), one suited to the corrupt morality that has infected the knightly Christian order.

The fair-haired Saxon Ivanhoe has also been exposed to the East, but ultimately is not tainted by it. Ivanhoe can also speak Arabic and uses this knowledge to aid Rebecca and her father, Isaac of York, but unlike Bois-Guilbert, Ivanhoe is able to control his attraction to the beautiful Rebecca as soon as he realises that she is not a Christian. While he can adapt to Norman ways and prove a loyal retainer to Richard, a Norman king, Ivanhoe manages to maintain his ideals and his Saxon identity, ultimately marrying the Saxon princess, Rowena, and thereby continuing his Saxon line as well as avoiding any possible miscegenation. Ivanhoe represents an idealised hybrid, someone who can adapt without losing his cultural identity, figured by Scott as a racial one.

Miscegenation, the sexualised mixing of the races, is a forbidden form of hybridity in the novel and Rebecca, for all of her positive qualities, embodies its threat. To create her character Scott draws upon the figure of Jessica in Shakespeare's *Merchant of Venice*, a text whose language is equally as embedded in *Ivanhoe*, through both direct and indirect allusion, as that of the *Canterbury Tales*. In Rebecca and Isaac, Scott recreates the figures of the rich Jew and his desirable daughter. But here, instead of the disobedient Jessica who abandons her father for a Christian lover and takes with her money and valuables, we have a Jewess who is loving and obedient to her father. Rebecca is profoundly wise and highly educated, and she is also willing to die out of loyalty to the race of her ancestors, a race whose misery and lost glory she continually mourns. She is, finally, the most racially loyal character in the novel, choosing her people over her own desire for Ivanhoe.

This beautiful Jewess, like her Shakespearean model, represents an alluring and dangerous prize to Christian men, but unlike Shakespeare, Scott does not allow for the possibility of mixing Christian and Jewish blood. At the end of the novel Rebecca appears before Ivanhoe's bride, Rowena, and declares her intention to leave England for a life of service and celibacy in Muslim-controlled Spain. She is an idealised figure but one whose sexual attractiveness poses a danger to the racial purity of both Normans and Saxons. She must therefore be removed at the novel's end, sent off to an Orientalised realm where she can live in service, and she, notably, has vowed to produce no offspring herself.

Rebecca is not the only Jewish element that is excised from England in *Ivanhoe*. *Ivanhoe* is, of course, a historical novel, and it plays fast and loose with historical facts, as has already been noted in its portrayal of an idealised Richard the Lionheart. But Scott's treatment of Anglo-

Jewry is, nevertheless, striking in its omissions. The novel continually references the connection of Rebecca's father to York; he is, indeed, called Isaac of York, perhaps an allusion to one of the most famous Jews of medieval England, the wealthy Aaron of York, who served as the chief rabbi of the Jews in the early thirteenth century. But more important than an allusion to this individual figure is its connection to York's ill-fated twelfth-century Jewish community. On Friday 16 March 1190, York was the site of the infamous 'Shabbat ha-Gadol' massacre, during which the entire York Jewish community of 150 people, having sought royal protection, were trapped in Clifford's Tower by an angry mob. The castle's keep then caught fire through unknown means, threatening the Jews with immolation. In order to avoid forced baptism, most of the community, including women and children, committed suicide, with fathers killing family members and then submitting to death at the hand of the community's rabbi, who finally took his own life. Those who left the tower hoping to avoid death through conversion were slaughtered as they exited. Members of the mob then went to York Cathedral and burned documents pertaining to the Jews, notably records of debt owed to the Jews by Christians.[19]

The event was well documented by both Jewish and Christian medieval chroniclers, and while it has only recently become an acknowledged part of modern English histories of York, it should have been known to Scott through one of his acknowledged sources, Sharon Turner's *The History of England during the Middle Ages* ([1814] 1853: 325–6). The Castle of York, built for William the Conqueror, of which Clifford's Tower is a part, seems to have been significant to Scott, who locates the fictitious Rev. Dr Dryasdust as residing in 'Castle Gate, York'. If Dryasdust does signify the facts of history, those dry facts brought to life by a retelling like Scott's, then these facts could also be seen as residing in the area of York Castle.

The horrific facts of the castle, however, only haunt the edges of *Ivanhoe*, which does not reference the massacre. In *Ivanhoe*, set at the moment of Richard's return, Rebecca and Isaac are persecuted and threatened with death, but ultimately escape. The massacre, which occurred four years prior to the historical return of Richard that is a central part of the novel, is never mentioned. Just as *Guillaume* represses the hybrid history of Norman Sicily, so too, in *Ivanhoe*, Scott sublimates significant elements of the history of the contact zone for English Jews. Turner's discussion of the persecution of Anglo-Jewry during the period in which Scott's novel is set describes the massacre of Jews at London at Richard's coronation, an event which may have echoes in the scene in which Isaac of York is an unwelcome spectator at the great tournament at Ashby. Turner's account notes that the even more terrible York massacre occurred while Richard was away on Crusade, a time when King John, as described in *Ivanhoe*, exploited and mistreated the Jewish community. Turner's account of the massacre emphasises the treachery of the assailants, the helplessness of the Jewish community, their decision to die rather than convert, and, in his account, their choice to burn all valuables rather than surrender to the mob.

One can discern the most striking echoes of the details of the massacre in the second major episode in the novel, the imprisonment of Cedric, Rowena and other Saxons, as well as Isaac and Rebecca, in the Castle of Torquilstone by treacherous Norman captors who wish to ravish the women and extort treasure. In a famous scene, the Templar knight Brian de Bois-Guilbert wishes to make Rebecca his concubine, but she stands on the edge of the castle turret and makes clear that she would rather hurl herself to her death than accept him. Her fearlessness and willingness to commit suicide rather than submit to dishonour, which cause Bois-Guilbert to become even more obsessed with her, recall the infamous decision by the York Jews to die rather than be captured. In *Ivanhoe* the conflict between Christians and Jews is portrayed as religious and as financial, since Isaac is portrayed as unbelievably wealthy and stereotypically avaricious, but this tension is ultimately crystallised into the sexual desire of Bois-Guilbert for Rebecca.

Instead of the willing beautiful Jewess of Shakespeare, however, Scott gives us a woman who will not yield to oppression or to her own desires. She will ultimately embrace a life of celibacy, but we see her potential fate echoed in the fate of another woman whom she encounters in the castle, Ulrica, a bitter and half-crazed old woman. Ulrica was once a noble Saxon beauty who succumbed to the fate Rebecca defies, becoming the concubine of the Norman conqueror, Front de Boeuf, despite the fact that he had murdered her relatives and taken over their lands. She then later seduced his son. Ulrica, originally called Urfried, represents the darker side of hybridity. This willing victim ultimately betrays the Normans and sets fire to the castle, killing herself and the younger Front de Boeuf, but allowing Rebecca and the princess Rowena to escape. Ulrica's fate represents what could have become of Rebecca if she had given in to the desires of Brian de Bois-Guilbert, betraying her father and the values of her people; the flames of the castle recall the conflagration at York in which not Norman but Jewish bodies were consumed. And, indeed, the ultimate defeat and brutal deaths of these treacherous Normans might also be seen as a warning to those powerful men who succumb to the temptations of a foreign woman. Ulrica's fate also acts as a foil to the Saxon noblewoman Rowena. Rowena is in love with the Saxon knight Ivanhoe, although her guardian wishes her to marry the noble Saxon Athelstane, and she is held in Torquilstone because the Norman de Bracy desires her beauty and her riches. She too escapes the fate of Ulrica and ultimately marries Ivanhoe, keeping true both to her own desires and to her Saxon bloodline. Their union, the only success-ful one portrayed in the novel, celebrates the perpetuation of a pure bloodline; no hybrid unions actually occur.

If, as Robert J. C. Young argues, theories of race are also covert theo-ries of desire, then it makes sense that the racial politics of the novel, which sees Saxons, Normans and Jews as separate races, are enacted through narratives of desire. In the end the racially 'correct' union of Ivanhoe and Rowena triumphs, despite Scott's famous inquiry whether 'the recollection of Rebecca's beauty and magnanimity did not recur to his [Ivanhoe's] mind more frequently than' Rowena might have liked (401). Ivanhoe, the male hero of the novel, comes to represent a positive form of hybridity. He is able to serve his king well without losing his ties to Saxon roots, and he keeps his bloodline pure. The treacherous and unfortunate Ulrica dies without progeny, as does Rebecca, who will embrace a life of service and celibacy. Her alluring beauty is ultimately contained by strong moral values and a devotion to her own people.

Despite frequent references to the Crusades, no fully realised Saracen character is given a place in Scott's romance. While Scott may well have been familiar with tales of alluring Saracen beauties from medieval romance, his black Saracens are represented only as cruel brutes whose words remain unintelligible, never translated into English. When Front de Boeuf is prepared to torture Isaac for his money, it is these black Saracens who eagerly await his orders to perform the actual deeds. While Rebecca and her father represent Orientalised figures who must be banished (as all Jews ultimately were from England a century later in 1290), the Saracens are almost monstrous. They are lurking physical threats within England, threats that are presumably dealt with along with John and his supporters as Richard resumes the throne, thus paving the way for a hybrid union of Normans and Saxons to form an English people that is free of both Jewish and Muslim influence.

While *Ivanhoe* is only a single novel, it was hugely popular, selling 10,000 copies in its first two weeks, and its influence could be seen spread throughout the English-speaking world, with *Ivanhoe*-themed events taking place as far away as colonial India; *Ivanhoe*-inspired place names can still be found in former British colonies, such as Australia.

As was famously lamented by Mark Twain (1835–1910), *Ivanhoe* also had a great following in the ante-bellum American South, where white Southerners fancied themselves not Saxons, but chivalrous Normans. The novel arguably influenced authors such as Rudyard Kipling (1965–1936), whose poem 'Norman and Saxon A.D. 1100' appeared in *A School History of England* (1911). The poem is a Browning-esque monologue in which a Norman baron advises his son on how to treat the rough, but also honest and tough, Saxons. The poem could be profitably read against his better-known 'White Man's Burden' (1899) for a study of how ideas about this early conquest within England inflected views of imperialism once England had become a colonising power itself.

Race, Periodisation and Medieval Romance

On 18 March 2008, Senator Barack Obama gave a speech on race entitled 'We the People in Order to Form a More Perfect Union'. Many came to regard this address as a turning-point in his campaign for the Democratic nomination, which was then locked in a heated race against Senator Hilary Clinton.[20] The speech was occasioned by controversy over sermons given by Reverend Jeremiah Wright, Jr, formerly the pastor of Chicago's Trinity United Church of Christ, where Obama was a parishioner.[21] Video clips of Wright had circulated widely, showing him proclaiming, 'God damn America!' and, in reference to the attacks of 9/11, 'America's chickens have come home to roost', an allusion to Malcolm X's 1963 speech on the assassination of President John F. Kennedy. Obama was attacked for his connection with a minister whom some branded as anti-American. In response to the uproar over his relationship with Wright, Obama asserted, 'Race is an issue that I believe this nation cannot afford to ignore right now', and, through his speech, he attempted to open a national conversation on the subject. Delivering his address in Philadelphia, Pennsylvania, across the street from where the US Constitution had been debated and composed, Obama argued that the Constitution was an 'unfinished' document because it was 'tainted by the Original Sin of slavery'. He referenced his own heritage as the son of a black Kenyan father and a white mother from Kansas, and as the husband of an African-American woman 'who carries within her the blood of slaves and slave owners', thereby situating himself, as a person of mixed-race descent, within the American racial landscape.

Because Obama's speech referenced both black and white Americans' anger over issues of race, it was widely praised as an attempt to take on the issue of race from 'both sides'. Obama presented himself as an individual with an understanding of both black and white perspectives. The speech dealt with racial tension as it is most commonly approached in popular discourse in the US, as an issue of prejudice and discrimination based on colour and as an issue typified by tensions between whites and blacks. Obama's focus also makes sense given the context of the Wright controversy and the fact that Obama was campaigning vigorously in the closely contested 'battleground' states, including Pennsylvania, which would hold its primary election a month later. (In the end, Hilary Clinton took the state by a smaller-than-expected margin.)

Obama's speech also situated Wright's comments within the historical institution of the black church in the US. Even as he distanced himself from Wright's controversial words, Obama affirmed Wright's importance to him as the pastor who had helped him to deepen his faith, had consecrated his marriage, and had baptised his children. Obama was attempting to appeal to the 'two sides' of the US racial divide as he attempted to show that he was neither 'too black' nor was he not 'black enough'. As part of his appeal to a broad spectrum of voters, Obama also emphasised his Christian faith. Given that Wright was Obama's pastor, this Christian framing is understandable, but Obama's discussion also seemed designed to avoid a 'third rail' in his campaign: the controversy surrounding his purported 'Muslim roots'. Observing that not all religious worshippers agree with everything they hear uttered from the pulpit, Obama addressed the audience directly by referring to 'your pastors, priests, or rabbis'. His ecumenical inclusiveness did not, notably, extend to imams.[22] It was only at his inaugural address that Obama declared, 'We are a nation of Christians and Muslims, Jews and Hindus, and nonbelievers. We are shaped by every language and culture, drawn from every end of this Earth', and it was six months later on 4 June 2009 that he made a much publicised Cairo speech 'reaching out' to the Muslim world.[23]

The Obama campaign had very specific reasons for avoiding references to Islam. Just as the video clips of Wright's speeches circulated throughout the presidential campaign, so too did references to Obama's Kenyan-born father, his middle name Hussein, and a picture of him in a robe and turban taken during a visit to Africa. This costume, while traditionally Somali, was labelled 'Muslim'.[24] References to Obama's name and to the photograph were part of attacks against him; Obama's 'Muslim background', detractors charged, would make him unsuitable to lead the United States. Evidence of the sensitivity of the issue arose from within the Obama campaign itself three months after Obama delivered his speech on race. Two women wearing headscarves were removed from a place behind Obama's podium at a rally in Detroit so that they would not appear on camera with the candidate, a move that the campaign later officially condemned.

In terms of political tactics, it is obvious why Obama would not bring the issue of Muslims and Islam, another point of attack against him, into a speech designed to defuse controversy over his association with Wright. Indeed, many saw it as laudable that he chose to rise above the level of attack and rebuttal to address questions of race and racism head-on, thus elevating the level and the importance of the discourse on the 'Wright controversy' and on race and racism in relation to Obama's candidacy. Obama did not mention the racial-profiling of Muslims in his speech on race and his omission went unmentioned by critics, even though Obama was himself facing attacks as a 'secret Muslim'. Obama's only reference to Islam in the speech was to 'the perverse and hateful ideologies of radical Islam', and the racism inherent in attacking him as a Muslim remained unexamined.

The targeting of Muslims or those suspected of being Muslim is part of a variety of discriminatory practices ranging from airport screenings to arrests to 'extraordinary renditions'.[25] It was also being used in attacks on Obama not only out of prejudice towards Muslims, but as a way of attempting to disguise racism towards Obama himself as concern over the 'Muslim threat' to the United States, a tactic which assumes that these sorts of concerns are not themselves racist in motivation. The fact that the discourses of racism and religious bigotry were not often analysed together by the Obama campaign or by commentators on it is not only due to political calculation or to bias. Racism and discrimination based on religion or culture are often treated as separate issues, not only in popular discourse in the US, but also in academic discourse. The 'protean quality' of racism and its complex ideological make-up renders its history and multiple aspects extremely difficult to discuss.[26]

I want to stress here, though, the central importance of religious and cultural identities to racism. While some have heralded Obama's presidency as an important step toward a post-racial future, the distance still left to be travelled has to do not only with the issue of the colour-line, but with ever-increasing tensions along cultural lines. We can see this in the attacks against Obama's supposed Muslim identity, attacks which have to be seen not as distinct from racism against him as a person of colour, but as intimately tied to this racism. This moment when some are invoking the post-racial is actually a time for deeper study of the roots of racism. We need to re-examine the religious and cultural elements that dominate 'racism without race,' even as racism based on skin colour may seem to some to be fading.[27]

The concept of 'race' has been undergoing shifts in meaning in both academic and wider public contexts beyond the 2008 US election. In 1998, the American Anthropological Association (AAA) issued a 'Statement on Race', which concluded that 'present-day inequalities between so-called racial groups are not consequences of their biological inheritance but products of historical and contemporary social, economic, educational and political circumstances' (712–13). This statement draws upon recent scientific research that indicates that there is no genetic basis for categorising human beings into races. This research has also been reflected in editorial statements in medical literature. The noted journal *Nature Genetics* requires authors to 'explain why they make use of particular ethnic groups or populations, and how classification was achieved' (2000: 97–8).

In May 2001, the *New England Journal of Medicine*, citing the AAA statement, published an editorial by scientist Robert Schwartz that declared that 'Race is a social construct, not a scientific classification' (Schwartz 2001: 1392–3). The issue is, however, clearly not settled within the medical profession. The accuracy and efficacy of these perspectives was recently challenged from an epidemiological perspective by Neil Risch, who argues that 'Ignoring our differences, even if with the best of intentions, will ultimately lead to the disservice of those who are in the minority.'[28]

Both sides of this debate share a well-founded concern for the impact of racial categorisation on actual groups and individuals, and there is strong evidence for the impact of such debates outside the academic sphere (and in ways which the original researchers may never have intended), such as the controversial attempt for a 'Racial Privacy Initiative', which ultimately failed as a proposition on the California gubernatorial recall ballot of October 2003. Initiative advocates speak of what they call a 'colour-blind society', a goal based at least in part on the idea that 'race' is now a defunct category (Trounson and Vogel 2003; Bustillo 2002; and Erlanger 2001). While at the polar opposite of the political spectrum from positions such as Paul Gilroy's in *Against Race*, both approaches to the question of race demonstrate that 'race' as a concept is undergoing crucial shifts in meaning.

These shifts make the cultural – including theological – aspects of racism all the more important, but religion is often not factored into analyses of race and racism; instead it is often considered a distinct phenomena. One reason that religious and cultural discrimination are often discussed and analysed separately from racism is because of the same periodisation boundary that marks discussions of the nation and colonialism: racism is considered a modern phenomenon. Racist ideologies are associated with the pseudo-scientific theories and taxonomies that arose in the late seventeenth century. It was also during the seventeenth century, it is often argued, that the rise of secularism began from Enlightenment roots. Religion ends up painted out of discussions of racism with these two strokes: racism is modern and modernity is secular. While the 'Dark Ages' is often depicted as a time of superstition, prejudice and the brutal persecution of difference, most historical discussions avoid using the terms 'race' or 'racism' to describe these conditions. Some scholars are resistant to using the term 'race' in medieval contexts because 'race' and 'racism' were not used in the Middle Ages.[29] Others seem bent on preserving a clean demarcation between medieval prejudices and the atrocities of modern racism as exemplified by New World slavery and the Holocaust, thus creating a view of the Middle Ages that reverses the usual equation of 'medieval' with brutality and violence.

These attempts, however, either to inoculate terminology against anachronism or to quarantine the Middle Ages from the horrors of modern racism have ended up distorting a broader understanding of the multifaceted components of racism and of the concept of race. Although it is often taken for granted that racism is about prejudice based on colour or on the reprehensible hierarchies of human difference championed by such figures as Joseph Arthur Comte de Gobineau (1816–82) or Houston Stewart Chamberlain (1855–1927), racism and the concept of race have always had their foundations in elements of culture. These elements, including, importantly, religion, are unmistakable when we look back further than most studies of the history of race and racism tend to do.

I want first to turn to how the Middle Ages has figured (or not figured) in some prominent theoretical discussions of the history of the concept of race and then to consider how the limiting periodisations of typical histories of race have influenced other histories, specifically those related to colonial slavery. I will then turn to an important medieval genre, romance, to explore its context. I want to examine Wolfram von Eschenbach's early-thirteenth-century Middle High German romance, *Parzival*, in the context of medieval representations of somatic difference, including the lesser-known Middle English romance *The King of Tars*. These texts help to illuminate the tangled relationships between 'theological' and 'biological' notions of race in both the premodern and modern eras, connections that are often obscured by a frequent insistence on notions of biology (or more accurately, pseudo-biology) as the defining characteristics of 'race' and of 'racism'. These early writings demonstrate important connections between premodern and modern conceptions of race.

Race and Periodicity

How can we talk about race in the Middle Ages in an historically informed way? Medieval views of human difference were complex and even contradictory, although, as historian Robert Bartlett reminds us, no more than our own (2001: 42). Medieval authors considered not only genealogy, but also elements of 'environmental influence', ultimately placing the greatest importance upon 'the cultural and social components of ethnic identity' (2001: 45). For Bartlett, the idea of 'race' in the medieval period would appear to be much closer to what we today call 'ethnic group', a categorisation that emphasises linguistic, legal, political and cultural affinities over somatic features as markers of 'racial' difference. There are crucial distinctions between this type of notion of difference and those that animate, for example, the racist systems of apartheid or antisemitism under National Socialism. While Bartlett rightly notes such differences in his important book, *The Making of Europe*, he nevertheless uses the term 'race' in relation to the Middle Ages in his writings, demonstrating the relation of the concept of race to the more 'malleable' and, for the Middle Ages, more significant factors of religion, law, language and custom. These combined elements figured in the creation of 'Europe' as a construct in what Bartlett calls the 'Europeanization of Europe' in the Middle Ages (1993: 267–91). There is continuity, Bartlett argues, between this early Europe and early European notions of race and later attitudes: 'the mental habits and institutions of European racism and colonialism were born in the medieval world, the conquerors of Mexico knew the problem of the Mudejars; the planters of Virginia had already been planters in Ireland' (1993: 313).

While medievalists tend to be cautious about how the term 'race' is employed, outside the field their studies are largely ignored. In his book-length study *Race: The History of an Idea in the West*, Ivan Hannaford asserts that 'it is unhistorical to perceive the concept of race before the appearance of physical anthropology proper, because the human body, as portrayed up to the time of the Renaissance and the Reformation, could not be detached from the ideas of polis and ecclesia' (1996: 147). The idealised body of the Church that Hannaford references is not, however, simply abstracted but represented allegorically in medieval theological, philosophical, literary and visual works as the figure of

Ecclesia, often depicted in paired contrast with an allegorical figure for the Jewish people, Synagoga. While it would be inaccurate to equate either Synagoga or Ecclesia with the racialised figures of nineteenth- and twentieth-century discourses, the allegorical Synagoga is often depicted as a beautiful but fallen woman, who embodies a supersessionist view of the Old Law.[30]

Synagoga is part of a long line of representations of Jewish females that can be traced back to the biblical matriarchs and forward through Christopher Marlowe's Abigail in *The Jew of Malta* (c. 1592) and Shakespeare's Jessica in *The Merchant of Venice* (c. 1596) to the 'beautiful Jewess' of nineteenth- and twentieth-century literature, a figure that Sander Gilman has shown was very much part of racialised antisemitic discourses by the nineteenth century.[31] Using nineteenth- and twentieth-century biological models as the standard for whether one can make connections between ideological formations, as Hannaford would have it, hinders investigation into how medieval concepts, particularly theological ones, may have shaped later ones in ways about which we are still unaware. Hannaford's conception of the medieval seems very much governed by a misuse of the periodisation scheme of Jacob Burckhardt, who is often associated with a cultural privileging of the Renaissance over the medieval period; Hannaford repeatedly asserts the problematic notion that in the Middle Ages there was no notion of 'self'. Hannaford's discounting of medieval concepts is all the more troubling because of the influence his work has had. In *Against Race*, for example, Paul Gilroy relies strongly on Hannaford for his understanding of the history of racist ideologies prior to the seventeenth century, which may in part account for Gilroy's lack of serious consideration of theology or religion, components of which are, I would argue, still very much part of the racisms that he is examining as global discourses (2000).

I do not intend here to provide an exhaustive list of all the historical or theoretical examinations of race that have elided or distorted medieval contexts. More significant are the effects of such treatments. In *Racism: A Short History*, George M. Fredrickson has noted that investigations of antisemitism and studies of other forms of racism, such as 'white-supremacism', have remained separate and divergent bodies of scholarship (2002: 157). Fredrickson's project attempts to address that gap, and he is able to make important connections, in large part, I would suggest, because his study takes a longer view of the history of the concept of race, opening with a chapter charting 'the segue between the religious intolerance of the Middle Ages and the nascent racism of the Age of Discovery and the Renaissance' (2002: 12). Fredrickson may here appear to be reinforcing traditional periodisation boundaries, but his formulations actually serve to call familiar binaries into question even as he attempts to present clear and meaningful distinctions between terms.

For Fredrickson, racism 'exists when one ethnic group or historical collectivity dominates, excludes, or seeks to eliminate another on the basis of differences that it believes are hereditary and unalterable' (2002: 170). Whether or not one accepts this definition, Fredrickson's treatment is valuable not simply because his inclusion of medieval concepts allows for understandings of how those ideas about human difference sometimes do and sometimes do not appear to fit his definition. More importantly, his inclusion of the Middle Ages allows for sharper discussion of religious ideas in the concept of race and a deeper exploration of the very permeable boundaries between racism and 'culturalism'. 'Culturalism' is a reification of cultural difference that did not hold sway in the Middle Ages, but was merely 'nascent' (2002: 12). As Fredrickson shows, medieval contexts are notable for their lack of rigidity and their sometimes inclusive representations of cultural difference. These representations are expressed, as Fredrickson stresses, not in pseudo-scientific language, but in religious discourses that still have relevance to modern racisms (2002: 15–48).

In the early 1990s, Etienne Balibar noted the new prevalence of a type of racism based on notions of culture rather than of biology, arguing that Europe was experiencing 'a racism without race', directed primarily at Muslim immigrant populations (1991). His observation, as we will see, has proven remarkably astute. This 'neo-racism' does not rely on discourses of biology, but instead on notions of cultural difference. In contrast to the medieval instances discussed by Bartlett and Fredrickson, which posit cultural differences as changeable, in neo-racism, cultural difference is 'immutable'. As Balibar notes,

> Biological or genetic naturalism is not the only means of naturalizing human beings and social affinities . . . *culture can also function like a nature*, and it can in particular function as a way of locking individuals and groups a priori into a genealogy, into a determination that is immutable and intangible in origin. (1991: 22; italics in original)

For Balibar, antisemitism is the most supremely differentialist form of racism, based on perceptions of cultural difference in which the so-called Jewish 'essence is that of a cultural tradition, a ferment of moral disintegration' (1991: 24). This degraded essence is all the more threatening because it is not readily detected. Balibar argues that the whole of current differentialist racism may be considered, from the formal point of view, *as a generalized anti-Semitism*. This consideration is particularly important for the interpretation of contemporary Arabophobia, especially in France, since it carries with it an image of Islam as a 'conception of the world' which is incompatible with Europeanness and an enterprise of universal ideological domination, and therefore a systematic confusion of 'Arabness' and 'Islamicism.' (1991: 24)

Balibar focuses on the 'nationalist inflexion' given to antisemitism in early modern Spain, seeing the Spanish blood laws as the earliest 'crystallisation' point of modern antisemitism (1991: 23). Balibar connects modern-day attitudes to Muslims with premodern views of Jews, without addressing the historical connections between Islamophobia and antisemitism.

Medieval Christianity's encounter with Islam was not simply an echo or generalisation of Christian encounters with Jews, but rather it played a crucial role in shaping the history of antisemitism. Medieval Christian writers often grouped Muslims and Jews together. The infamous dress regulations of Lateran IV in 1215 decreed special sumptuary markers for both Jews and Saracens. But there were always also crucial differences in Christian attitudes towards Jews and Muslims, differences which R. W. Southern, in a now-classic formulation, argues were based on the fact that in contrast to Jewish populations within medieval Europe, who lived in small communities within larger Christian ones, the existence of Islam was the 'most-far reaching threat in Medieval Christendom. It was a problem at every level of experience' (1962: 3).

With the Crusades came increased Christian contact with Muslims. As Christian thinkers attempted to deal with Islam, they turned, as historian Jeremy Cohen has shown, to the figure of the Jew, who had been until that point 'the primary enemy in Christian religious polemic' (1996: 147). Christian polemic then shifted to incorporate both types of religious 'Other'. The Jew may have served as what Cohen calls 'a springboard for formulating a deliberate response' to Islam (1996: 146), but this response was not, as Balibar's model would have it, a generalisation. It was instead a complex interaction, which not only played a role in Christian thinking about Muslims, but altered Christian views about Jews as well. One important factor, as Cohen emphasises, is that the figure of the Jew lost its place of 'singularity' in Christian discourse (1996: 148). Cohen asserts that it was this grouping of Jews and Muslims together in Christian thought, along with the increased use of rational argumentation and a recent Christian awareness of Jewish post-biblical texts, that all contributed to the declining status of the Jews in medieval Christendom and the developing negative polemic against them (1996: 143).

It is essential to remember that Christianity has its origins in Judaism and to consider the special way that this relationship shaped medieval and modern Christian figurations of Jews and the Jewish. This originary relationship, however, does not justify the 'privileging' of antisemitism as a uniquely virulent prejudice or an understanding of antisemitism as historically isolated from other forms of discrimination. Such approaches blur crucial early history and blunt our critical tools for understanding the complex ways that different kinds of religious intolerance have developed and intersected with each other and with other forms of prejudice, including prejudice based on colour.

In Black and White: *Parzival* and *The King of Tars*

Recent work on Western European literary texts by medieval Christian authors has begun to reveal numerous examples of how somatic differences typically associated with ideas of race have been linked to representations of religious difference, particularly the difference of the Muslim or Saracen. These texts consistently link whiteness with goodness and purity. White skin is, in some medieval texts, not simply a conventional marker of beauty, as in the phrase 'Isolde of the white hands', but also, in Bruce Holsinger's provocative formulation, 'the color of salvation'. Holsinger's reading of whiteness in Bernard of Clairvaux shows how in their portrayal of blackness, some of Bernard's sermons reflect militant Crusading ideology and also seem to reflect more broadly representations of Saracens in vernacular writings (Holsinger 1998).

Although Wolfram von Eschenbach's *Parzival* provides a prime literary portrayal of a non-Christian character marked by blackness, general examinations of the history of the concept of race tend to give *Parzival* only passing mention, if they mention it at all. One of the jewels in the crown of the Middle High German canon, *Parzival* creates within its nearly 25,000 lines three different, overlapping realms: the world of Arthur, the world of the Grail, and the world of the Orient (Groos 1995). Like much of the romance tradition, *Parzival* builds on earlier texts, in this case the story of a naive young hero, Perceval, in Chrétien de Troyes's *Li Contes del Graal* (c. 1190). But one of Wolfram's additions to this source is the story of Parzival's father, Gahmuret, and his love affair with the beautiful, black queen of Zazamanc, Belacane, who is not a Christian, but a heathen, which in Wolfram's text denotes a conflation of pagan and Muslim attributes. Throughout this encounter, Belacane's blackness and that of her people are emphasised: they are 'as black as night' and Gahmuret feels 'ill-at-ease' among them, although he chooses to remain ['*liute vinster sô diu naht / wârn alle die von Zazamanc: / bî den dûht in diu wîle lanc. / doch hiez er herberge nemen*'] (17.24–25).[32] The blackness of Belacane and her people is mentioned repeatedly, and it is her nobility in spite of her colour that draws Gahmuret to her.[33] They fall in love and marry.

But, encouraged by a man from Seville, who, we are told, is not 'like a Moor in color', Gahmuret abandons Belacane. At the Spaniard's advice, Gahmuret conceals his actions 'from those whose skins are black in color' and, in an echo of the Aeneas and Dido story, steals away, leaving Belacane a letter explaining that if only she had been willing to convert to Christianity he would not have been forced to leave her.[34] Belacane bemoans that she would have been willing to convert, and indeed, in a familiar trope, the poet refers to her innocent tears as a type of baptism (28, 9–17). She is pregnant and later bears Gahmuret's son, Feirefiz, who is spotted black and white. Heartbroken at being abandoned, she is described as kissing again and again the sign of Gahmuret's paternity, her son's white markings (57, 19–20). Belacane eventually dies of grief, and Feirefiz virtually disappears from the narrative, only reappearing in the romance's penultimate book to challenge Parzival in combat. The two are half-brothers, since Gahmuret marries Parzival's mother after he deserts the black queen. Feirefiz appears without being named, a mysterious knight of great prowess and fabulous wealth. The brothers engage in a strenuous battle, during which Feirefiz displays his noble qualities. Indeed his actions during their encounter are arguably superior to Parzival's. Finally Feirefiz and Parzival recognise each other and embrace as brothers. Feirefiz accompanies Parzival to see King Arthur and then on to the Grail castle as Parzival completes his quest, finally asking the correct question of the Grail king and thereby ending the king's torment. Feirefiz falls in love at first sight with the Grail maiden, Repanse de Schoye, and converts to Christianity for love of her, ultimately conquering foreign lands in the name of Christianity and through their son, the legendary Prester John, eventually converting the land of India.

Despite the brevity of his appearances, Feirefiz is not an incidental character in the romance. Black and white and the contrast between them are at the centre of *Parzival* from its complicated images in its opening lines:

Ist zwîvel herzen nâchgebûr,
daz muoz der sêle werden sûr.

gesmaehet unde gezieret
ist, swâ sich parrieret
unverzaget mannes muot,
als agelstern varwe tuot.
Der mac dennoch wesen geil:
wande an im sint beidiu teil,
des himels und der helle.
der unstaete geselle
hât die swarzen varwe gar
und wirt och nâch der vinster var:
sô habet sich an die blanken
der mit staeten gedanken.

If inconstancy is the heart's neighbour, the soul will not fail to find it bitter. Blame and praise alike befall when a dauntless man's spirit is black-and-white mixed like the magpie's plumage. Yet he may see blessedness after all, for both colours have a share in him, the colour of heaven and the colour of hell. Inconstancy's companion is all black and takes on the hue of darkness, while he of steadfast thoughts clings to white. (ll. 1–14)

There are clearly biblical and, some have argued, mystical influences at play in this passage (Wilson 1960). In addition to its moral and spiritual meanings, the passage also has resonance with the romance's portrayal of its characters as either black or white, or in the case of Feirefiz, as a mixture of the two. Critics have treated the question of race in *Parzival* with responses ranging from assertions of Wolfram's 'relative tolerance' in both *Parzival* and his later text, *Willehalm*, to more negative assessments, exemplified by one critic who finds '*rassisches Ressentiment*' [racially motivated antipathy] in Gahmuret and Belacane's encounter (Ebenbauer 1984: 21).[35] Whether one views the character of Feirefiz as the subject of heroic praise or the object of prejudice, as the narrative progresses, Feirefiz becomes a shaping foil for Parzival, physically embodying the moral ambiguities and struggles that the narrator introduces in these opening lines (Blamires 1966: 438–41).

This exploration of the moral coding of black and white launches a poem of immense length and complexity that features black, white, heathen/Muslim and Christian characters. Erich Auerbach has asserted that the fundamental purpose of romance is a 'self-portrayal of feudal knighthood with its mores and ideals', and we can see this play out through the relationship between Parzival and Feirefiz (1968: 131). Feirefiz embodies the stained and imperfect nature of his half-brother, Parzival, who grows and develops to master his ignorance and his errors through a journey of blunder, growth and eventual triumph. In the text this ideal is figured as Christian and white, against a blackness that is linked with hell as well as with 'heathen' culture. The text's opening images figure that struggle as marked by colour, with black, the colour of hell, representing what must be overcome and with white representing 'the color of salvation' (Holsinger 1998: 156–86).

Parzival, then, can be seen as chronicling the growth of good, the whiteness of the soul, within one man, Parzival. Feirefiz, in contrast, becomes an emblem for the narrative retelling of that development. Just before the brothers recognise each other, Feirefiz asks Parzival to describe the brother he has never met and the latter replies that his brother is 'like a Parchment, written upon in black and white' *['als ein geschriben permint, / swarz und blanc her unde dâ']* (747.26–7). With this description Feirefiz becomes a symbol not only of the development of the knight, but of the romance text itself. Before he encounters the questing Parzival, Feirefiz has already achieved a high level of knightly renown through his vast riches, his successful relationships with noble women, and his exceptional fighting acumen. Yet it is Parzival, Feirefiz's white brother, who is ultimately the transformed and completed heroic character. Feirefiz's development as a lover, fighter and ruler seems complete by the time he meets Parzival. He is, however, still a heathen, and even though Feirefiz converts, his conversion is sudden and is driven by his desire for a beautiful woman.

While Feirefiz's conversion is recognised as such in the text, its portrayal is arguably comic (Blamires 1966: 452; and Christoph 1981: 222–7). The brevity of his conversion stands in stark contrast to the slow education in religion through which so many key characters guide Parzival. Even after Feirefiz's conversion and full and complete acceptance into the world of the Grail castle, he bears as a mark his blackness, the sign that he was born to the heathen queen, Belacane. The character of Feirefiz then is not simply an example of a heroic black character, or of proto-racial representation, but of complex negotiation of colour as a mark of difference against and through which the image of an idealised knight, the Christian and white Parzival, is developed.

In the early-fourteenth-century Middle English romance *The King of Tars*, colour as a mark of identity is represented even more dramatically than in *Parzival*. The romance tells the story of a young Christian princess who, for the sake of her people, marries a Saracen king, feigning conversion to his faith. Soon she bears a child who is greatly deformed, a mere lump of flesh, but upon baptism, the child is transformed into a beautiful, healthy baby. His father, the Sultan, then also converts and his black skin bleaches white. Here blackness is not indelible, but, instead, a convert can be 'washed white' with baptismal waters.[36] The romance, which appears in three manuscript versions, derives from a fascinating mix of historical accounts and folklore. The tale has a background in actual successful campaigns by Mongols, or Tartars, as they were referred to in the medieval period, in the late thirteenth century and an account of King Ghazzan's marriage to an Armenian princess. Within this context we find an analogue to the religious intermarriage in *The King of Tars*: various chronicles recount stories of such a union resulting in an offspring somehow monstrous, either as lump-like, freakishly hairy, piebald, or half-animal, a motif with roots in folklore.[37] Judith Perryman argues that *The King of Tars* takes these earlier accounts and creates from them characters that become generalised, losing their moorings to historical figures from the chronicle accounts and taking on symbolic roles. The historical Ghazzan was Muslim, but he was friendly to Christians. This is perhaps the reason that various European chronicles asserted for him a Christian identity. *The King of Tars* moves away from these historical complications to work on a symbolic level as an unequivocally Christian king is threatened by a Muslim sultan (Perryman 1980: 44–9). The text's focus on a clear-cut battle between Christianity and Islam is reinforced through its symbolic deployment of white and black to mark the two opposing faiths. We find here no sympathetic representation of a hybrid, as in *Guillaume de Palerne*'s werewolf, but a hybrid union of Muslim and Christian that is monstrous and unsustainable.

Siobhain Bly Calkin has stressed the romance's concern with interfaith union (2005). The narrator compares the Sultan's reluctance to marry outside of his religion to the reluctance a Christian man would feel about marrying a heathen:

> Wel loþe war a Cristen man
> To wedde an heþen woman
> Þat leued on fals lawe;
> Als loþ was þat soudan
> To wed a Cristen woman. (Perryman 1980: ll. 409–13)

> A Christian man would be very loath to wed a heathen woman who believed false law. Just as loath was that sultan to wed a Christian woman.

Such reluctance, the poem shows, is well founded, since the offspring of the Sultan and the Princess is so deformed that it is a 'rond of flesche' [round of flesh] (l. 580), with neither 'blod & bon' [blood and bone] nor 'nose no eye' [nose nor eye] (ll. 582; 584). The poem makes clear that although the Princess has officially converted, the marriage is still a mixed one, since her conversion is merely feigned for the sake of necessity. She dons Saracen dress and goes through the ritual motions of worshipping their gods, but remains steadfast to her faith.

As Bly points out, we learn abruptly of the Sultan's blackness just before he converts, 'þan cam þe soudan, þat was blac' [then came the sultan, who was black] (l. 799), and then, when he converts, his skin becomes white: 'His hide, þat blac & loþely was, / All white bicom, þurth Godes gras / & clere wiþouten blame' [Through God's face, his hide, which was black and loathly, became all white and clear without blemish] (ll. 928–30).[38] The Sultan's former blackness is clearly associated with his belief, and this reference then contrasts with the poem's opening description of the Christian princess, who is 'As white as feþer of swan' [As white as feather of swan] (l. 12). The Sultan's black appearance resonates with other descriptions of Saracens in the romance. The Princess, already described as swan-white in the poem's opening, has a dream in which she is attacked by black hounds (l. 448) and then comforted by Jesus, who appears to her 'in white cloþes, als a kni3t' [in white clothes, as a knight] (l. 451) to reassure her. When she wakes, she prays: 'on her bed sche sat al naked, / To Ihesu hir preier sche maked' [on her bed she sat all naked. To Jesus she made her prayer] (ll. 460–1). The Princess's naked body may be read as erotic, but it is also vulnerable and, because she is still a virgin, I would argue, innocent. Given the poem's opening description of her, she is also a vision of whiteness, likened visually to Jesus in his white robes and contrasting markedly to the hounds of her dream (and her Saracen husband).

As in the memorable opening lines of *Parzival*, black and white are the colours of evil and good respectively in this poem, and, as in *Parzival*, goodness is coloured white. Despite the text's assertion of the mutual distaste for interfaith marriage among both Christians and heathens, the fact that it is Christian baptism, rather than the worship of Saracen 'gods', that miraculously heals the child make it clear that Christianity is the superior faith.

Geraldine Heng's important analysis of *The King of Tars*, part of her study of race and the genealogy of the romance tradition, *Empire of Magic*, shows how *The King of Tars* raises numerous unresolved questions about the causes of the tale's monstrous birth. Whether it is the result of the Princess's union with the Sultan, his tainted Saracen identity or her false conversion, the malformed child provides a strong message about human difference in the midst of swirling doubts:

The inescapable, explicit lesson in this representational script of hideous birth is that religion, which we had assumed to belong purely to the realm of culture, can shape and instruct biology: a startling logic suggesting that secreted within the theory of religious difference in this tale is also a theory of biological essences seemingly indivisible from religion. (Heng 2003: 228)

The King of Tars provides us, Heng argues, with a 'twilight, interzonal space in which culture and biology overlap' (2003: 229). Heng's analysis reveals a deep entanglement of the discourses of nature and culture that reaches back into a period sometimes presumed to be free of racial discourse. What is most important about this insight is not, however, the revelation of an 'origin' for racism, but rather an understanding of the creation of normative whiteness. As Heng asserts, '*The King of Tars*, as a medieval artifact, supposes the normativity of whiteness, and of the white racial body, as the guarantor of normalcy, aesthetic and moral virtue, European Christian identity, and full membership in the human community, in complicity with the possession of a human essence conferred by religious discourse acting as biological determination' (2003: 232).

The stark linkage of spiritual and physical essences found in *The King of Tars* differs considerably from Wolfram's depiction of Feirefiz. These representations of blackness range from the exoticism of Wolfram's Belacane and Feirefiz to the 'loathsome' Sultan of *The King of Tars*. They share, however, a consistent linkage between Christian belief and a morally inflected whiteness. Although Feirefiz is not bleached white, we are told in the romance's opening lines that 'black is the colour of hell'. As Ania Loomba asserts, the character of Feirefiz 'does not tell us that differences in skin colour were not important at the time, but rather that religious and cultural differences were already colour-coded' (2002: 47–8). These models, however, do not, as neo-racism does, make 'culture' into a 'nature' (Balibar 1991: 22).[39] Unlike modern notions of racial essence, these texts seem to point to the possibility for change, although this change does require conversion and is based on a fixed belief in Christianity as the only true religion.

What are we to make of these differences? Representations such as those in *Parzival* and *The King of Tars* may be considered rare or exceptional in their representations of colour difference; and it does seem clear that they can neither provide us with definitive answers about race in the Middle Ages, nor locate for us medieval origins for the racisms that developed and held sway in the nineteenth and twentieth centuries. Nor are these examples definitive evidence of either a Dark Ages marked by ignorance, superstition, persecution, or a world 'before race' where markers of nobility and wealth trumped somatic and perhaps also religious difference. But it is precisely because of their ambiguities, their malleability and their emphasis on culture and especially religion that these examples are important.

Texts such as *Parzival* and *The King of Tars*, as well as 'The Man of Law's Tale' and the *Chanson de Roland*, which represents some Saracens as black, show us linkages between colour and cultural difference, specifically religious difference.[40] These examples, with their focus on whiteness as the normative marker of Christian identity, can perhaps help us face more squarely contemporary occurrences of what Balibar calls 'neoracism' and George Fredrickson calls 'culturalism', encouraging us to understand racism as a phenomenon that is not merely about somatics or biology, but which also can incorporate notions of cultural, specifically religious, difference as well. Such work might also lead us to consider connections between the glamorised and commodified images of black bodies of twentieth- and twenty-first-century popular culture analysed by Paul Gilroy in his book *Against Race* (2000) and the differently but equally glamorised and exoticised bodies of Belacane and Feirefiz, who are also likewise imagined by a culture noted for its focus on the visual. In order to see these possible discursive links, the Middle Ages must be taken into account not as a period frozen or static in time, as I believe this period is still often depicted, but as a period that continues to inform imagination and ideology in ways that are more than simply nostalgic.

Longer Histories of Race

The nostalgia often referred to *vis à vis* the Middle Ages is the evocation of a monolithic white Christendom, portrayed as the pure medieval origin of modern European nation-states. Such a vision is the premise of the 2001 film comedy *Black Knight*, which features Martin Lawrence as Jamal, an African-American from South Central Los Angeles whose presence in fourteenth-century England is seen as so incongruous that it is the central joke of the film.

There are, of course, many other forms of nostalgia for the medieval past. A very interesting example comes in a widely read work by Amitav Ghosh, *In an Antique Land*, a text that combines the genres of memoir, history and novel to relate the parallel stories of Amitav, the narrator (modelled on the author), a young anthropologist from India doing fieldwork in Egypt, and an Indian slave owned by a Jewish merchant in the twelfth century whom Amitav is researching. Amitav's search for a record of the slave is inspired by a brief mention of him in a manuscript from the Cairo Geniza, a centuries-old Jewish repository of documents, the contents of which are now scattered across the globe, along with so many other antiquities from nations colonised by Europeans. *In an Antique Land* intertwines the narrative of Amitav's experience in two Egyptian villages and his reconstruction of the stories of the slave, whom he believes was called Bomma, and the master, Ben Yiju, a Jew who resided in India for much of his life. The two main threads of the narrative, framing the stories of individual fates, are woven into the tapestry of larger events, with the history of trade, exchange, wars and colonialism, both connecting past and present and juxtaposing them.

The narrator's search to uncover the identity and story of the slave transforms into nostalgia for a lost cosmopolitanism, presenting us with a medieval world often eclipsed by a more typical focus on European Christendom. While Ghosh does not completely idealise the Middle Ages, he does depict it as a time of freer trade and exchange across continents and between groups of different faiths, an openness contrasted, in one scene from Amitav's youth, to sectarian violence between Hindus and Muslims.

As several critics have noted, it is in Ghosh's treatment of the medieval institution of slavery that his depiction of medieval cosmopolitanism becomes most problematic. Ghosh situates the master/slave relationship between Ben Yiju and Bomma within the religious traditions of the Sufi mystics and the Vachanakara saints of southern India, who 'drew some of their most powerful images from the institution of slavery' (Ghosh 1993: 262). Drawing upon the work of historian S. D. Gotein, Ghosh argues that the medieval institution of slavery lived by Bomma was entirely different from the slavery of the modern plantation system; medieval slavery, as Ghosh depicts it, often created ties that mirrored kinship or that could be seen as a means of career employment (1993: 260). Indeed, slave status such as Bomma's could even have positive aspects, as the narrator speculates that:

> The elements of slavery in the ties that bound an apprentice to a master craftsman, an accountant to a merchant, would have appeared, perhaps, not as demeaning bonds, but rather as links that were in some small way ennobling – human connections, pledges of commitment, in relationships that could just as well have been a matter of a mere exchange of coinage. (1993: 263)

Critics have pointed out the problematic nature of this characterisation of medieval slavery. Kathleen Biddick goes back to the work of Gotein, who, she argues, wanted to emphasise a world of ties between Jews and Muslims, a desire to show 'affinities' that stemmed from his own subject position as a German Jew who had emigrated to Palestine in 1923. Biddick sees Gotein's views as part of a 'strange silence and uneasiness about slavery in the medieval world by historians of medieval economics and trade such as Janet Abu-Lughod and Phillip Curtin' (Biddick 2003: 98). This medieval human trafficking was foundational to medieval economic exchange and was marked by brutality, including castration and rape (Biddick 2003: 99; and Desai 2004: 139–40). Ghosh's treatment of slavery creates a 'periodization of a medieval Golden Age superseded by modern colonialism' (Biddick 2003: 101). This periodisation notably also occludes issues of race. While the novel critiques the violence of imperialism, there is no place within it to show that the medieval interlinked networks of trade and exchange valorised in the novel were also part of the same global systems that produced not only modern imperialism but the modern forms of slavery that Ghosh represents as so distinct from the world of Ben Yiju and Bomma.

Ghosh's periodisation of the history of slavery conforms to dominant historiography. Indeed, it is not only that medieval and modern slavery are seen as distinct, but that the 'later colonial slavery systems' are sometimes even seen as part of the 'advent of modernity', as a marker of the distinction between medieval and modern (Blackburn 1997: 3). There are, of course, important shifts, for example in terms of scale, that make New World slavery distinct; but this periodisation often obscures its roots in much longer, interconnected histories, including those of trade and capitalism as well as nationalism and the role of theology and religious institutions in all of these.

Expanding upon the ideas of the influential historian Fernand Braudel, Giovanni Arrighi writes that the history of capitalism extends back into the Middle Ages to the city-states of northern Italy, chiefly Genoa and Venice. The economic dominance of these city-states can be seen as the first in a series of cycles of capitalist expansion that then went on to Dutch, British and finally US dominance. Europe's role as 'a monstrous shaper of world history' was not something that simply occurred all of a sudden in the sixteenth century; rather, it should be understood as the result of 'a series of stages and transitions, the earliest dating from well before what is usually known as "the" Renaissance of the late fifteenth century' (Braudel 1984: 92, quoted in Arrighi 1994: 11). Cycles of trade existed for centuries and stretched across Eurasia. People living in the West sought Eastern goods (Arrighi 1994: 38). The medieval Italian city-states developed and maintained a monopoly over strategic routes that linked Europe to India and China through the Middle East (Arrighi 1994: 40). Iberian expansion had the goal of gaining access to routes to the East. The Iberian imperial expansion which spread colonialism and the slave trade was financed through Genoese capital as this trading power shifted toward dominance in high finance, an industry it developed (Arrighi 1994: 125–6). As David Wallace notes, '[m]any features of later European colonialism – as the slaving Mediterranean prepares to enter the black Atlantic – are clearly forming throughout this earlier period. To say this is not to suggest seamless continuity with later, full-blown plantation slaving in the Americas; differentiation of human experience will stem, above all, from questions of scale' (2004: 189).

One significant strain of continuity is a connection to the theologies of Crusade. Portuguese and later Castilian expansions into Africa were motivated by a desire for territory and profit, but their goals were often expressed through the ideologies of the Crusades and Reconquista, as conquest over the infidel. Scholars debate whether this ideology was simply a screen to mask a profit motive considered inappropriate for nobles and monarchs, or a genuine expression of belief, or a mixture of the two. In any case, Christian ideology and the Church were clearly enmeshed in these ventures. Infante Henrique of Portugal (1394–1460), for example, linked his exploits in Guinea in West Africa to the conquest of the North African Muslim city of Ceuta (1415), highlighting the link between these battles and the Crusades (Bennett 2005: 23).

The Church claimed responsibility for and jurisdiction over the souls of both infidels, such as Jews and Muslims, and pagans, such as the inhabitants of Guinea. The Church's involvement did allow for some recognition of the humanity of non-Christians in regions such as Africa, but papal bulls also gave Christian rulers the right to subdue and enslave them. The *Romanus Pontifex* (1455) bestowed on Portugal rights to territory and conquest on the African coast. The document begins by describing Pope Nicholas V in his role as Father, contemplating all of the world's nations in all of its climes, asserting that the Pontiff desires to convert non-believers and save their souls. The bull then goes on to laud the exploits of Infante Henrique and King Alfonso of Portugal, 'athletes and intrepid champions' *[athletas et intrepidos pugiles]* of the Christian faith, for their efforts against the Saracens in Ceuta and elsewhere in Africa (Davenport 1967: 13, 21). They have been exploring the lands in an attempt to make contact with Indian Christians, presumably subjects of the fabled kingdom of Prester John, in order to join forces against the infidel. In recognition of these efforts and the establishment of Christian institutions in the lands conquered by the Portuguese, the Pope not only grants the Portuguese crown territories, trading and fishing rights south of the cape of Bojador, but also, crucially, the right to attack and subdue non-Christians (Davenport 1967: 13–26).

> *Nos, premissa omnia et singula debita meditatione pensantes, ac attendentes quod cum olim prefato Alfonso Regi quoscunque Sarracenos et paganos aliosque Christi inimicos ubicunque constitutos, ac regna, ducatus, principatus, dominia, possessiones, et mobilia ac immobilia bona quecunque per eos detenta ac possessa invadendi, conquirendi, expugnandi, debellandi, et subjugandi, illorumque personas in perpetuam servitutem redigendi, ac regna, ducatus, comitatus, principatus, dominia, possessiones, et bona sibi et successoribus suis applicandi, appropriandi, ac in suos successorumque suorum usus et utilitatem convertendi* (Davenport 1967: 16, qtd in Blackmore 2009: 48)

> We . . . weighing all and singular the premises with due meditation, and noting that since we had formerly by other letters of ours granted among other things free and ample faculty to the aforesaid King Alfonso [Alfonso V] – to invade, search out, capture, vanquish, and subdue all Saracens and pagans whatsoever, and other enemies of Christ wheresoever placed, and the kingdoms, dukedoms, principalities, dominions, possessions, and all movable and immovable goods whatsoever held and possessed by them and to reduce their persons to perpetual slavery, and to apply and appropriate to himself and his successors the kingdoms, dukedoms, counties, principalities, dominions, possessions, and goods, and to convert them to his and their use and profit. (Davenport 23, qtd in Blackmore 2009: 49)

As Josiah Blackmore notes in his important *Moorings: Portuguese Expansion and the Writing of Africa*, this chilling passage does not distinguish between 'Moors' and 'blacks', a distinction often found in contemporary Portuguese writings about Africa. Instead the terms are primarily addressed toward Saracens, a decidedly negative term for Muslims in Latin or Portuguese, or pagans (2009: 49). There is no room for neutrality here, and the bull acts as an authorisation for the slave trade (Blackmore 2009: 49).

While presented as part of a desire to spread Christianity, the bulk of the bull seems concerned with establishing a specific relationship between the papacy and the Portuguese crown in Africa. The undifferentiated and vilified Saracens, 'enemies of the Christian name' capable of 'savage excesses' (Davenport 1967: 21), are primarily discussed as the objects of conquest and of trade, activities that, it is believed, will eventually win more souls to Christ. And, indeed, the bull does describe the conversion of some captured Guineans and other '*nigri*' [blacks] who were sold and eventually converted to Christianity. While blackness was not yet an immediate marker of slave status, it was slowly becoming one as black Africans became slaves in increasing numbers. What we can see in a document like *Romanus Pontifex* or in texts such as the *Crónica da Tomada de Ceuta* (Chronicle of the Capture of Ceuta) by Gomes Eanes de Zurara (1410?–74?), also brilliantly analysed by Blackmore, is how the discourse of theology merges with those of sovereignty and commerce, among others, to create a vision of Africans that allows and justifies their enslavement. The divide between theological and secular, so much a part of our contemporary definitions of racism, falls apart here.

Romanus Pontifex is viewed as a landmark document in the history of slavery, a papal sanction that began the widening of the scope of the slave trade and heralded even further competition among European powers for territory and profit. At the time of its writing, blackness was seen as a mark of difference, but not yet as an absolute mark of servitude. The justification for violence is not based on somatic difference, but on religious difference, as inhabitants of the African coast are viewed in terms that recall the view of the Saracen infidel at the time of the Crusades. While the succeeding conditions of slavery in the Americas and the Caribbean lost that original theological element, a re-examination of the opposition to the Saracen reveals a significant strand in the longer history of race. While colour came to be the mark of 'Otherness' in the racist ideologies that justified slavery, it was enmeshed with the earlier hostility to non-Christians that the Pope used to justify Christian conquest in the first place. These elements have remained part of racism, to some extent lying dormant, and now re-emerging in new forms in a post- 9/11 world as new wars of religion have been declared.

It seems clear in the wake of recent 'racial profiling' against Arabs and Muslims that while somatic markers are still crucial to contemporary racisms, neo- or otherwise, racism is not merely concerned with biology, nor was it ever. As Ania Loomba and Jonathan Burton put it, 'Even the most "scientific" assertion of race as biology was in fact "cultural" – which is the whole point of calling it *quasi*-biological' (2007: 23). What we are seeing, as these quasi-scientific notions have had all of their credibility stripped away, is that the cultural components of racism are once again among the most prominent and important. Because, however, our definitions of racism and our discourses about it are so focused on notions of science and on the issue of colour, we are left without a sufficiently powerful vocabulary to deal with current permutations of racism. In the case of the racial profiling of Muslims, the concept of race is returning to what Appiah describes as a 'premodern' notion of race, in which somatic difference is a marker or sign of unbelief, not its cause. Current discussions over the still-urgent problem of the colour-line, like Obama's campaign speech, need to be expanded and complicated to include the cultural components of racism, especially the religious/theological components of racial ideologies that can transform 'culture' into 'nature'.

A Global Vision: *The Travels of Sir John Mandeville*

When scholars of postcolonial studies addressing more recent historical periods examine 'historical roots', they tend not to dig deeper than those moments that are typically seen as the beginning of colonial contact: when the 'Old World' encountered the 'New', with Columbus's 1492 voyage acting as a standard periodisation marker. Columbus's journey and similar voyages and encounters are obviously of great importance; but as they have often been used as almost absolute markers of periodisation, they have also had an ossifying effect, obscuring what came before and limiting how subsequent events are seen. European attitudes towards the rest of the world and its inhabitants did not spring into being fully formed in 1492, nor at any other discrete historical moment: they developed over time. In this case study, I want to use a widely popular narrative, *The Travels of Sir John Mandeville*, also known as the *Book of John Mandeville*, as a focal point through which to introduce medieval narratives of travel, trade and cross-cultural contact prior to the 'Renaissance Age of Exploration'. The *Travels* is a true precursor to the more commonly acknowledged markers of colonialism's beginnings. Andrés Bernáldes recounts that Columbus examined the *Travels* prior to his voyage and that it also shaped his expectations during it (Bernáldes 1992: 62–3, 138–41 *inter alia*); Frobisher carried a copy with him to Baffin Bay (Mandeville 1983: 9).

The *Travels* was originally composed in French, or possibly in Anglo-Norman, and appeared around 1360. The narrative enjoyed immense popularity and is now extant in over 250 manuscripts. As one might imagine with a text translated into English, Dutch, German, Latin and a host of other languages, its manuscript history is complex.[41] The *Travels* is dominated by the engaging persona of Sir John Mandeville, its purported author, who claims to be reporting his first-hand experiences of the world. Sir John's exact experience and even his existence, however, are the subject of debate, and it is now widely agreed that he did not make all of the journeys he describes; he perhaps never ventured further than a library. Because of the questions surrounding the authorship of the *Travels* and the text's complex manuscript tradition, I will refer to the '*Mandeville*-author' rather than to the persona of 'Sir John' or 'Mandeville' as the author of the text.[42] Although the *Mandeville*-author's overall use of sources is extremely fluid and really quite masterful, his borrowings are readily apparent to anyone familiar with his sources, even though he quite frequently embellishes and changes their details. An important probable primary source was a compendium, Jean de Lonc's *Livre de Merveilles*, into which the *Travels* was eventually included (Moseley 1974: 7). The *Mandeville*-author also drew from a range of travel narratives from missions to Asia, as well as legendary material such as the story of Prester John, supposedly a Christian ruler, who shows up in various texts as existing in numerous far-flung lands, such as India and Ethiopia. Prester John's legend circulated orally and in texts such as a forged letter of c. 1160 that addressed the leaders of Western Christendom, boasting of Prester John's enormous wealth and representing a hope for wider Christian dominion in lands beyond Western Europe (Friedman and Figg 2000: 504–5; Uebel 2005).

I will first survey the background to the *Travels*, including both narrative and cartographic sources, and then turn to the *Travels* itself, discussing its structure and orientation, and attempting finally to unravel a textual knot: the strikingly odd connection the *Mandeville*-author makes between the apocalyptically destructive Jews, allegedly trapped in the Caspian mountains by Alexander the Great, and the legendary Amazons who keep guard over them. What we find in the *Travels*, I will argue, is another example of the ways in which representations of women and Jews, figures that are both original and 'Other' to medieval Christians, are seen as interconnected threats to Christian identity.

Background to the *Travels*: The Global Outlook from Medieval Europe

Although most medieval people did not journey further than very short distances from their homes, the Crusades seem to have inspired new curiosity about travel (Dalché 1995: 55, quoted in Edson 2007: 46–7). The *Mandeville*-author doubtless drew upon this increased interest in the wider world as well as from the narratives of actual explorers, including narratives of thirteenth-century missions to Asia to interact with the Mongols, a group whose conquests drew the attention of leaders across Europe. The Mongols, also called the Tartars in medieval texts, were a nomadic Asian people whose military prowess helped them to create the largest land-based empire ever known between 1206 and 1368. They launched devastating attacks in Poland, Moravia and Hungary in 1241 and continued to be regarded as a grave threat by European leaders even as the Mongol leadership structure fractured. While feared, the Mongols were at the same time regarded as potential allies against Muslims and as potential converts to Christianity.

The earliest narrative of a Western Christian mission to Asia is the *Ystoria Mongalorum* (1247), written by John of Plano Carpini (c. 1180–1250), a Franciscan sent as an emissary to the Mongols by Pope Innocent IV in 1245.[43] The Pope chose John because of his religious devotion and his maturity rather than his linguistic or cultural training. John made the arduous and dangerous journey eastward with a small group of companions when he was sixty-five, presenting to the Mongol emperor, Great Khan Guyuk (1206–48), letters that exhorted the Mongols to give up their 'barbarian' ways. The missives failed to impress the emperor, who sent replies that expected the Pope's subservience to Mongol rule.

In 1253 Franciscan William of Rubruck (c. 1215? –c. 1270?) was sent by the French king, Louis IX, on an evangelical mission to the Mongols. His record of the journey, his *Itinerarium* (1255), is considered to be the fullest record by a European of the Mongol empire and includes the first European account of Buddhism. Another Franciscan, Odoric of Pordenone (c. 1265–1331), was sent east in 1320 on a journey that was explicitly missionary in nature (Odoric 1929; 2002). Although his narrative report does not record any conversions, it was widely read and included in Le Lonc's *Merveilles*. It was also used as a source by the *Mandeville*-author. Despite the religious objective of his journey, Odoric also remarked upon commercial possibilities in the East. There are some notable similarities between Odoric's narrative and the now more-famous account of Eastern travels by Marco Polo (1254–1324), the *Divisament dou monde*, written in 1298 from a Genovese prison with the help of 'ghostwriter' Rustichello of Pisa, a writer of romance. This chronicle of Polo's many years in the East with his brothers was a rich source for many, including the *Mandeville*-author (Polo 1975; 1992).

For those interested in medieval travel writing beyond the sources used by the *Mandeville*-author, we have numerous other records from medieval travellers. Benjamin of Tudela (d. 1173?) travelled throughout the Mediterranean basin between 1159 and 1168, and his *Itinerary* remains an important source about Jewish and non-Jewish communities of the time (Benjamin 1995). Ibn Jubayr (1140s–1217) was a Muslim from Valencia. A record of his travels survives, including his experiences of Norman Sicily, where he was shipwrecked in 1184. Ibn Battutah (1304–68), trained as a lawyer, left his home in Tangier in 1325 on the *hajj* and then continued to journey throughout the Muslim world and into the Indian subcontinent, finally returning home in 1349. *Al-Rihla*, or *The Journey*, is an account of his travels created from his notes and oral recollections by Ibn Juzayy, and is still considered an important source for the study of Muslim communities in the fourteenth century.[44]

There are some close connections between medieval travel narratives such as these and medieval cartography, as the two forms influenced each another (Edson 2007). There were various types of maps in Christian medieval Europe, including *mappaemundi* (maps of the world) and marine charts. The oldest extant marine chart is the 'Pisa Chart', made in Genoa between 1275 and 1300. The exact ways that these charts were produced and used remain in dispute, as does their origin. We are not sure the extent to which Christian medieval navigators in Western Europe had access to magnetic compasses, for example, or could consult the cartography of Muslim map makers such as al-Idrisi (d. 1154), who worked in the court of Roger II of Palermo.

The *mappaemundi* are not maps in the modern sense; that is, they are not tools used primarily to convey geographic information. The medieval map, especially the *mappamundi*, 'was a vehicle for conveying every kind of information – zoological, anthropological, moral, theological, historical' (Harvey 1991: 19). *Mappaemundi* exemplify the moral and theological functions of medieval cartography, 'present[ing] the entire history and philosophy of the human race organised within a geographical framework' (Edson 2007: 15). These maps take the history of Christian salvation and depict it spatially on a diagram of the world, often based on the T-O form, the most basic models of which figured the great Ocean in an 'O' that encircled the land masses of the earth, divided by the three central waterways that divide the lands (see Figure 1).

The *mappaemundi* often figure Jerusalem as the centre of the world, a feature which derives from the biblical verse Ezekiel 5: 5, 'I have placed Jerusalem in the midst of the nations and with all the lands around it', and also from Isidore of Seville, who called Jerusalem *'umbilicus regionis totius'*, 'the navel of the whole region of Judea', an expression later expanded by Rhabanus Maurus to make Jerusalem the 'navel' of the whole world. This emphasis on Jerusalem as centre of the world, a location that is featured and emphasised in the *Travels*, may have also been influenced by the importance of the Crusades. According to Ingrid Baumgärtner, it became common to figure the world's centre in Jerusalem after it was lost to Crusaders in 1244 (2001: 309–10). The

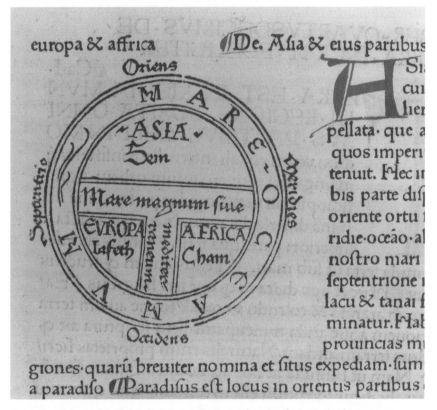

Figure 1 Example of a T-O map, which is also the first printed map in Europe. From Isidore of Seville (1472), *Etymologiarum sive Originum libri XX* (Augsburg: Günther Zainer), London: British Library IB. 5441. By permission of the British Library

mappaemundi noted places in the Holy Land as well as the three known regions, Asia, Europe, and Africa. They also pictured the so-called monstrous races, which included not only humans with the heads of dogs, the Cynocephali, people born with only one leg who shaded themselves with their large feet, the Monculi, and the headless Blemyae, but also giants and wild men.

The two largest *mappaemundi* we have today (or have record of) are the Hereford Map (c. 1290), housed in Hereford Cathedral, and the Ebstorf Map (c. 1240) from lower Saxony. The latter was destroyed in the bombing of Hanover in 1943, but has been reconstructed in a detailed copy (Friedman 2000: 45) (see Figures 2 and 3). The two maps share some key characteristics, including their explicit focus on

Figure 2 Hereford world map, c. 1290. With permission of the Dean and Chapter of Hereford and the Hereford Mappa Mundi Trust

Christ, who appears near Paradise on the eastern edge of the Hereford map, with a circle containing Jerusalem and a crucifixion scene figured beneath him. This 'circular world' can itself be seen as a metaphor for the body of Christ (Kline 2001: 53). The Ebstorf Map literally integrates the body of Christ into the map as the world is superimposed over his body with his head emerging from the east, his hands, marked with stigmata, from the north and south, and his feet from the west. These are

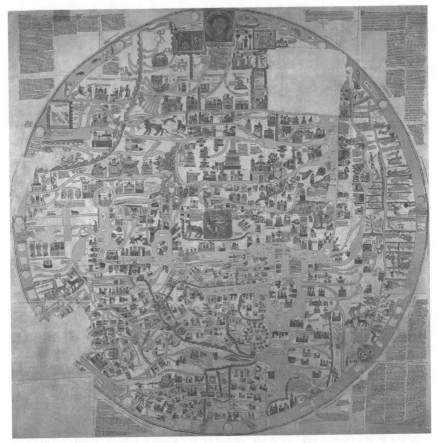

Figure 3 Ebstorf world map, c. 1235. (Reconstruction of original, which was destroyed in World War II.) By permission of Dr Martin Warnke

not maps that anyone could literally use to navigate the world, but are instead guides to the world's moral and spiritual order.[45]

The *Travels*

Just as gazing at complex depictions of the world like the Hereford and Ebstorf maps can evoke a sense of wonder and plenitude, reading the *Travels* can produce a similar experience (Greenblatt 1991). While the *Travels* may seem almost overwhelming, in terms of the variety and scope of what is depicted, it is as carefully ordered as a *mappamundi*. This structure, the text's art of 'selection and arrangement', is key to the narrative's success and appeal (Howard 1980: 65). The *Travels* begins with Jerusalem, centring on it as the *mappaemundi* do. If the text is a travel-romance as Bennett (1954) has characterised it, it is reminiscent in its opening focus on Christ of the thirteenth-century Old French Grail romances, which frequently begin with references to the Passion (Lampert-Weissig 2007). In the *Travels* the emphasis is on Jerusalem as the site of Christ's suffering, chosen by the Saviour himself:

> Since it is so that the land beyond the sea, that is to say the Land of Promise which men call the Holy Land, among all other lands is the most worthy land and mistress over all others, and is blessed and hallowed and consecrated by the precious blood of Our Lord Jesus Christ, in which land it pleased Him to take life and blood by Our Lady Saint Mary and to travel round that land with His blessed feet. (Mandeville 1983: 43)[46]

The Holy Land is consecrated through Christ's choice to be born and to die there and through contact with his body: his blood and feet. Christ seems manifest in Jerusalem, which can itself be seen as a Christian relic (Heng 2003: 264; Howard 1980: 71).

The *Mandeville*-author's focus on the Holy Land is coupled with a desire to reclaim it; the text is clearly haunted by the Crusaders' loss of Jerusalem in 1244. The narrator speaks of Christ's manifest presence in Jerusalem and exhorts his readers:

> This is the land that is promised to us as heritage; and in that land He willed to die, and to be seised of it, to leave it to His children. Each good Christian man who is able, and has the means, should set himself to conquer our inheritance, this land, and chase out therefrom those who are misbelievers. For we are called Christian men from Christ our Father; and if we be true children of Christ, we ought to lay claim to the heritage that our Father left to us, and win it out of strange men's hands. (44)

The narrator goes on to claim that it is the 'pride, envy and covetousness' of Christian lords that has led to the loss of Jerusalem, but he believes that if they can join together and journey again to the Holy Land, the Christian heritage can be regained. This sense of heritage and entitlement to Jerusalem, this centre-point of the world, infuses the entire text through the narrator's continual assertions of Christian superiority, even at those moments when he seems at his most tolerant and respectful in the face of cultural and religious difference.

The first fifteen chapters of the *Travels* describe the journey to the Holy Land and the region itself, complete with a detailed description of Jerusalem. The book's second half covers the rest of the world, reaching to China and to the realms of the 'monstrous races'. The text is held together through the persona of Sir John, who often inserts himself into the narrative, creating a sustained sense of a character with whom the reader can connect. He claims to have been at most of the locations he describes, including personal details such as his possession of a thorn from the Crown of Thorns (48) or the healthful effects of his draughts from the Fountain of Youth (123). Only in a few instances does he acknowledge a lack of direct experience. For example, he has been unable to visit Paradise himself and can only describe it secondhand (184).

We do not have space to cover the entire text of the *Travels* here, and there are, fortunately, already many excellent analyses available, as noted above. One thread common across these discussions is the recognition, often admiring, of the seeming openness and tolerance of the narrator, Sir John, toward other cultures. He appears to view the world through the cultures he describes, and unlike many contemporary narratives by Western European Christians, his observations about difference, including Muslim difference, seem relatively tolerant. His descriptions of Muslim customs and of Islam are less inaccurate than many other contemporary accounts, although they are always tempered by a view of Christian superiority and with an eye to Muslim conversion to Christianity.

Reading the *Travels* side by side with the Hereford Map, David Lawton has shown the influence of Orosius (died c. 420) on both. Orosius's *Historiarum adversum paganos libri VII* (The Seven Books of History against the Pagans) interprets world geography within an explicitly Christian frame, viewing the diversity of people in the world as a challenge to Christians. Lawton writes that for Orosius, 'Cultural diversity is read . . . as both a cause for limitless celebration, an index of Christian superiority, and as somewhere between an insult and a rebuke, an active chastisement' (2001: 22). We can see the desire for conversion and for the global spread of Christianity in Sir John's remarks about the Khan, who seems an ideal ruler, except that he is not a Christian (144).

The *Travels*, the Jews and the Amazons

If we read the *Travels* in the light of such a worldview, with its longing for a universal and global Christianity as well as its anxieties in the face of difference, we may begin to better interpret the *Mandeville*-author's very notable exception to his tolerance: his treatment of the Jews. As numerous critics have noted, the Jews stand out as the villains of this text, and its frequent explicit references to their Christ-killing, well-poisoning conspiracies are accompanied by implicit ones such as the citation above, where Christ is referenced through his suffering; this suffering, we are told, comes at the hands of the Jews. Benjamin Braude has pointed out that just as the *Mandeville*-author uses his sources to shape relatively tolerant portraits of a wide variety of peoples, so too does he seem to go out of his way in his use of sources to portray the Jews in a negative light (1996: 138). Braude argues that these portrayals are not simply stock antisemitism, but that they are tied to the *Mandeville*-author's belief that Jerusalem and the Holy Land rightfully belong to Christians. Although Muslim forces had recently regained the Holy Land, the *Mandeville*-author sees the struggle for Jerusalem in larger, apocalyptic terms, with the Jews acting as the ultimate and, indeed, true threats to Christian claims to the world's sacred centre and, through it, to worldwide salvation and dominion (Braude: 1996).

There are many accusations of Jewish perfidy in the text. Beyond the references to the Jews as torturers and murderers of Christ, Sir John reports that a Jew directly confessed to him that the Jews would 'have poisoned all Christendom' with a deadly preparation from a poison-bearing tree, had they not somehow failed to carry out their plot (132). The reference upon which I wish to focus describes a group of Jews, called Gog/Magog, locked up by King Alexander in the Caspian Mountains. It is a long passage that needs to be quoted at some length:

> The Jews of the Ten Lost Tribes are shut up in these hills; they are called Gog and Magog, and they can get out on no side. King Alexander drove them there, for he intended to shut them up with the work of his men. When he saw he could not, he prayed to God that He would finish what he himself had begun. And although he was a heathen, God of His special grace heard his prayer and closed the hills together, and they are so big and high that they cannot be passed. And on the other side is the Caspian Sea; but no one can escape on that side because the sea comes up out of the earth under these hills, and runs on one side of the country through a great desert, reaching as far as the land of Persia. Even if it is called a sea, it is not one in fact, but a lake, the biggest in the world. So if the folk that are enclosed there desired and attempted to cross that sea by ship, they would not know where they would arrive and would not understand [any language except their own. And so they cannot get out]. And know that now the Jews have no land of their own to live in in all the world except among those hills. Even so they pay tribute to the Queen of the Amazons, and she has those hills guarded very well so that they do not cross them into [her] country, which borders those hills. Nevertheless it sometimes happens that one of them climbs over those hills and gets out, but no great number of them could climb out together because of the great height and the difficulty of the climb. And there is no other way out except by a little [path] made by men's diligence. That track is about four miles long, and then there is a

great desert where no water or shelter is to be found for men because there are dragons and snakes and other poisonous animals; so except in winter no man can travel that way. This narrow path they call Clyrem; and as I said the Queen of the Amazons has it guarded very carefully. (165–6)

Here the *Mandeville*-author's noted paratactic style seems to convey a kind of nervousness as he shifts back and forth between a portrayal of a prison that cannot be breached and numerous reassurances that many safeguards are in place if the impossible does occur and there is a Jewish jailbreak. The passage continues in an apocalyptic vein:

If it should happen that any of them get out, they can speak no language except Hebrew and so cannot speak with other men when they come among them. Folk in the country nearby say that in the time of the Antichrist those Jews will sally out and do much harm to Christian men. And so all the Jews in the different parts of the world learn to speak Hebrew, for they believe that the Jews who are enclosed among those hills will know that they are Jews (as they are) by their speech when they arrive. And then they will lead them into Christendom to destroy Christian men. For those Jews say they know by their prophecies that the Jews enclosed among the hills will issue out and the Christians will be under their sway, just as they have been under Christian domination. (166)

Finally, we are told, in the time of the Antichrist, the Jews will indeed break out of their prison, led by a digging fox that they will follow until they reach the stone gates erected by Alexander. When the Jews breach these gates they will wreck havoc on Christians.[47]

Ian Higgins has analysed the location of this episode within the narrative, arguing that by placing this description of the enclosed, menacing Jews so near to the description of the Khan, the *Mandeville*-author seeks to 'neutralize the formerly threatening Tartars by setting up a once and future enemy in their place' (1997: 183). Higgins points to the numerous ways in which descriptions of the Jews invert the descriptions of other peoples described in the text, including Christians. There is an ironic contrast between the Jews' landless state and their desire for world domination, as well as one between the fact that Christians hold a great deal of land but lack the one piece of real estate they most desire: Jerusalem. Further, in ironic contrast to the cross-cultural relations that the *Mandeville*-author describes between his Christian narrator and a vast range of cultures, the Jews' international connections are not bridges between peoples, but conspiratorial and potentially deadly threats (Higgins 1997: 184). There is also one final parodic inversion that Higgins captures:

the inversion of Christian History in the Jews' destructive escape. Whereas Adam and Eve in the beginning were expelled by God from the Paradise to which their Christian descendents now desire to return, the Jews in antiquity were locked up with God's help and their descendents want to escape from their anti-Paradise – an escape that, ironically, will herald the triumphant Christian return to their origins. (1997: 185)

Portrayed through these parodic inversions, the Jews become a kind of anti-people in the *Travels*, inverting (and perhaps also perverting) the history of humanity from Paradise to the Apocalypse. This view includes an adversarial place for the Jews in the long reach of salvational history, a role that leads finally to Jewish destruction and Christian triumph. Just as this view of the Jews locates them at the beginning of Christian history (as Christianity's precursor) and at its end (as essential to the prophecies of the Book of Revelation), so too are these Jews relegated to a mountainous prison on the edges of the known world, contained until the proper time for their appearance.

This role for the Jews in the Christian salvational scheme is not at all unique to the *Travels*, although it is expressed here in a very clearly spatialised way: the Jews are mapped not only in time, but in space. Another notable feature of this depiction of Gog/Magog is the way that it links these destructive Jews with the legendary Amazons. Other than an occasional passing remark, little has been said about this connection (Higgins 1997: 182; Braude 1996: 147). One exception is a study by Vincent DiMarco that attempts to trace the shifting roles of the Amazons through a dense thicket of sources and to understand them in relation to the equally complex source history of the legend of the Jews enclosed by Alexander (1991). DiMarco concludes his recounting of the sources with the tantalising suggestion that we consider what he calls 'the underside of an image of the Amazons' and see in stories about them, including the *Mandeville*-author's, an expression of 'the hopes and anxieties latent in Christianity's struggle for hegemony' (1991: 81). I agree with this suggestion and think it is best addressed through an understanding of the interrelated roles of the figure of Jew and Woman in medieval Christian thought, roles which I see as foundational to models of Othering in medieval contexts and beyond.

We first encounter the Amazons in the *Travels* on an island next to Chaldea, known as 'Maiden Land or the Land of Women'. The Amazons, we are told, came to adopt their warlike way of life when the king of Scythia killed all of their men. Since that time the Amazons have not allowed any men among them for more than seven days, nor have they raised any male children: these are either sent to their fathers or killed. According to the *Mandeville*-author, the Amazons join with men only occasionally for purposes of procreation or pleasure. They are said to cut and cauterise one breast from each girl to improve her fighting ability, and they are always ruled by a queen (116–17). In the *Travels* and beyond, the Amazons represent a 'mythic form of female masculinity' (Lochrie 2005: 104). They are chaste, limiting their sexuality to certain times but not abandoning it altogether. The Amazon myth may have originated from actual encounters with female fighters, but representations of them also had a moral dimension that went far beyond any real contact (Pohl 2004: 25). Amazons were often depicted in a distant and barbaric past, either that of another people or of an author's own, or in a distant locale. Their exact geographic location in legend has varied over time (as it varies even between episodes in the *Travels*), something that could be attributed to the way in which the Amazon kingdom inverts normative gender hierarchy (Pohl 2004: 26–8; Lochrie 2005: 103–4).

Because they were fighters and ruled their own female-only society, the Amazons 'violated European norms' in a dramatic fashion. They were thereby pictured as spatially opposed to the geographic centre, depicted as living in frontier regions on *mappaemundi* to illustrate graphically their inversion of social order (Baumgärtner 2006: 320). The Amazons are contradictory figures, often praised for their control over their sexual desires but also generating anxiety because of their transgression of normative gender roles. Orosius blames the Amazons, whom he associates with the Goths, for the Fall of Rome, associating them with the shame of pagan society and beliefs. They are women who violate Christian order because pagans cannot manage to contain them (1964: 36–7; Pohl 2004: 28).

Amazons have also long been linked to the concept of nation, figuring in myths of national origin, such as Paul the Deacon's history of the Lombards, the *Historia Langobardorum* (c. 796) (Pohl 2004: 26).[48] Their story is part of the national origin myths in late antiquity and the early Middle Ages that involve differentiating between in-group and out-group (Pohl 2004: 30). Lochrie analyses the role of the Amazons in relation to the formation of the nation. Reading the representation of the Amazons as balancing their potentially destabilising and threatening characteristics against their originary roles, she draws upon Julia Kristeva's concept of abjection as adapted by Anne McClintock in *Imperial Leather: Race, Gender and Sexuality in the Colonial Context* (1996). Kristeva has argued that the abject haunts the borders of the Self, acting as an Other that is an uncanny 'me' and 'not-me'. McClintock extends the concept of abjection, that process of acknowledging and rejecting the 'Other', arguing that it is part of the formation of the nation in the nineteenth and twentieth centuries through the creation of 'abject zones' and the stigmatisation of those who inhabit them, peoples who are to be rejected but who still have a connection to the nation itself. Lochrie argues that in medieval contexts:

> The Amazon provided just such an abject zone and race/gender for a variety of European cartographers, Spanish, English, and German, as part of their larger project of representing a sacred cosmology. Within the biblically charted world of the *mappaemundi*, the abjected races form part of another project of representing the political and social identities of the Western cartographers. (2005: 111)

Lochrie extends her understanding of medieval 'abject zones' to her discussion of the *Travels* and to Chaucerian texts, creating a compelling reading of the Amazon within medieval English texts. The curious connection between Amazons and Jews made by the *Mandeville*-author, however, remains unexamined.

I would argue that it is significant that the queen of the Amazons guards the enclosed Jews, because both women and Jews, in distinct but parallel ways, represent threats to the hegemony of Western Christian societies. This connection is intrinsic to the Kristevan concept of abjection. The second half of *Powers of Horror* (1982), the text in which Kristeva introduces the concept of abjection, is devoted to analysis of the notoriously antisemitic writings of Louis Ferdinand Céline (1894–1961); the figure of the Jew is essential to the concept, both as Kristeva presents it and, I would argue, in the way that abjection has functioned historically in Western European ideologies.

In *Gender and Jewish Difference from Paul to Shakespeare*, I argued that the figures of Jew and Woman held particular places in Western European Christian thought (Lampert 2004). Both the Jew and the Woman are figures of origin: women, through their reproductive capacities, are the source of all human life, and Judaism is the source of Christianity. While both Jew and Woman are marginalised in patristic and medieval thought, they cannot be fully rejected or eradicated. Put simply, women are necessary at the very least for their reproductive roles, and the Jews are not simply Christian precursors, but according to Christian prophecy, they are essential for Christ's return. Jews are needed to constitute the Remnant, the 144,000 Jews who Revelation 7 prophesies will convert to Christianity. Drawing from such ideas of the necessity of some kind of 'preservation' of Jews in order to prepare for the Endtime, Augustine developed what is now often referred to as his 'doctrine of relative toleration', forbidding Christians from slaying Jews because of the prophesied role of the Jews in Christian salvational history. The Jews are to be preserved as relics of the Old Testament, living in a state of domination until they can fulfill their preordained roles.

The figures of Jew and Woman came to represent ways of reading and understanding both Scripture and the world that were associated with a fallen state, with the literal and the carnal. The Jewish and the feminine are seen as categories to be overcome, to be superseded by a new masculine, Christian hermeneutics that reads, in keeping with 2 Corinthians 3: 6, not through the letter, but through the spirit. Women and Jews were figured as unable to understand the word of God, at least until they could transcend their state – women through a masculinisation that required abandoning their sexuality and Jews through conversion to Christianity (Lampert 2004: 21–57).

The Amazons could be seen as part of this transcendent masculinisation (Baumgärtner 2006: 321); but in the *Mandeville*-author's account, while they are able to moderate their sexuality, they do not aspire to the Christian ideal of virginity, nor do they limit their sexuality entirely to procreation. And, as independent warriors, they have spurned the male offspring who could have replaced their lost men. The Amazons, then, come to represent a rejection of male-domination that threatens social order. The Amazons must also be understood in relation to other examples of female sexuality depicted in the *Travels*. Women in the *Travels* are not exclusively sexualised. There are frequent references to the Virgin and to some female saints, and the Amazons and the wives of the Tartars are noted for their fighting ability (158). But we also encounter many women who are part of exotic polygamous relationships and others whose sexuality is often figured as dangerous.

In the story of Hippocrate's daughter, found on the Isle of Lango, we have a beautiful, young woman who is transformed into a dragon by the goddess Diana. The girl must remain in this state until a 'knight comes who is so bold as to dare and go to her and kiss her on the mouth', which will return her to her former state, although she will then die a short time later (53). One young man arrives on the island and glimpses the girl during a rare moment when she is not in her dragon form. Mistakenly believing that she is a prostitute, he requests to be her lover. She instructs him to leave and be knighted and to then return, telling him that no matter how she appears upon his return, she will do him no harm. The young man returns, but upon seeing her dragon form he flees to his ship, to her great sorrow. The knight dies soon thereafter, and from that time any knight who sees the maiden will die, unless he dares to kiss her, in which case he will become lord of her and her island (53–4). Beyond her desirable youth and beauty, this young woman also somehow signals sexual availability to the young man who discovers her, however mistaken his assumption. The situation is one of isolated, alluring and ultimately deadly beauty, all tied to the fate of a woman who has been cursed by a goddess associated with chastity, perhaps indicating some prior transgression.

This sense of transgressive sexuality and its dangers are echoed in the story that follows. This episode is set in Cyprus, where a country is lost through 'the folly of a young man' (55). He loves a beautiful damsel who dies suddenly and, overcome with desire, he opens her grave and lies with her. Nine months later he is called by a voice instructing him to reopen her grave. He does so and a gruesome head escapes from the grave, flying around the city and causing it to sink into the ground, leaving a treacherous void. Once again, sexual allure leads to death and destruction. The nine-month interval figures a perverted reproduction, inspired by lust for the body of a beautiful woman.

Other tales reveal similar dangers in the lure of female sexuality, such as the tale of the lady with the sparrowhawk. Desire for her leaves the king of Armenia cursed to perpetual war (115). There is also the account of the people who have young men called 'gadlibiriens', or 'fools of despair', who are employed to deflower new brides, since the taking of maidenheads risks death (175). Their custom comes from an ancient legend that maidens at one time had snakes within their bodies that stung the penises of their husbands, killing them. This story is followed by a tale of another island land whose women have precious stones in their eyes, which enables them to kill men through an angry glance (175). The Amazons and other threatening females appear to challenge Christian patriarchal hegemony. The goal of universal Christian domin-ion that the *Mandeville*-author shares with Orosius entails the triumph of Christianity over all other religions, including (and perhaps especially) its source religion, Judaism. Just as Jews threaten Christians throughout the globe through violence, poison and conspiracy, these women pose a threat through their sexuality. Women and Jews are figures of abjection, posing a threat from without that also comes from within, given the inextricable originary status of both figures.

In the *Travels* we find a new type of spatial representation in which the figures of sexually dangerous women and violently threatening Jews are both placed on the edges of the known world.[49] Their temporality is also often shifted toward the past or the future so that threats from women appear to exist in an ancient past, their frequent association with serpents or serpent-like creatures hearkening back to Eve. The Jews are also embedded in the past, as the founders of that ancient navel of the world, Jerusalem, and are needed, if also feared, as part of an apocalyptic future. In the present, Sir John seems keen on stressing the physical distance of both types of threatening figures, telling us repeatedly (and repetitiously) of all the safeguards in place to restrain Gog and Magog in their remote mountain prison in the case of the Jews. In the case of women, Sir John tells us that he has declined the offer of an exotic foreign bride from the sultan of Babylon. He was offered 'a rich marriage' with 'a great prince's daughter', at the price of his salvation, since the match would require his conversion to Islam (59). The potential threat posed by the figures of women and Jews seems held at bay, but it is a threat always lurking nearby.

As I puzzled out the connection between the Amazons and Gog and Magog in the *Travels* and read some of the excellent scholarship dealing with either women or Jews in the text, I found myself facing another mystery. Why had theoretical analysis of the two figures, Woman and Jew, remained separate when there are clear connections both in the text and through the concept of abjection? There are many possible reasons, of course, including scholarly interest, limitations of theme and space, and so on, but it seems to me that contemporary political disputes may also play a role in shaping the ways that certain concerns come together (or fail to come together), especially in relation to the treatment of the figure of the Jew in postcolonial studies.

The disputes, centred on the Israeli-Palestinian conflict, are bitter, brutal and urgent in their day-to-day actual manifestations, but, although they are, in this case, subtly expressed, they also seem to shadow current scholarship, even when that scholarship is not explicitly dealing with contemporary issues. For example, I found the outstanding scholarship in Braude's work on the Jew in the *Travels* to be marred by his unnecessarily derisive and dismissive attitude toward what he calls 'trendy Saidism' (1996: 133–5). His negative tone is so noticeable that I questioned whether it could simply be attributed to his methodological conservatism or whether other factors were in play. The disdain for Said, emphasised by the fact that Said's name replaces the usual reference to the theory of Orientalism, seemed to me to extend beyond *Orientalism* to Said's engagement with the Palestinian cause and the bitter debates about the relationship between anti-Zionism and antisemitism that are now later manifestations of the history that Braude traces in its medieval forms.

I found a parallel situation, although from the opposite perspective, when I re-examined McClintock's 'abject zones' in relation to Lochrie's reading. I noted McClintock's repeated use of Palestinians and the Occupied Territories to illustrate her conceptualisations. Her examples make good sense, but I wondered if the way they were shaped did not end up de-emphasising the importance of antisemitism to the original formulation of the Kristevan concept, and if this shaping also had to do with contemporary debates concerning Zionism and antisemitism (1995: 71–4).

The historical connections between antisemitism and Islamophobia have been closely intertwined since the medieval period. It is only through examination of the longer history of these associations that we can even attempt to understand clearly how these prejudices manifest themselves.[50] Thus, while Braude argues that Said could have not written *Orientalism* if he had read the *Travels*, I would argue that, of course, Said could have, but that a more nuanced view of medieval texts and contexts would have then reshaped his theories (Braude 1996: 135). Suzanne Akbari has recently revealed the historical grounds, rooted in medieval culture, for Said's statement that 'The transference of a popular anti-Semitic animus from a Jewish to an Arab target was made smoothly, since the figure was essentially the same' (Said [1978] 1994: 286). In doing so, Akbari opens new paths for the study of Orientalism, antisemitism and Islamophobia. Akbari has noted that because of the contemporary 'polarization of Arab and Jewish identity', it has been difficult to create a climate in which the relationship between antisemitism and anti-Muslim sentiment can be understood (2005: 32).

Such longer histories would help us to continue in the vein of recent work such as Aamir Mufti's *Enlightenment in the Colony: The Jewish Question and the Crisis of Postcolonial Culture*, in which he attempts to 'make the cultural and critical legacies of the Jewish Question speak to debates and dilemmas that are distinctly postcolonial' (2007: 4). Mufti's focus on the Enlightenment is a crucial one for understanding the development of colonial and postcolonial ideologies. Enlightenment ideals of universalism, citizenship and subjecthood did not spring into history fully grown, any more than the Age of Discovery inaugurated colonialist ideologies out of nothing. Enlightenment ideas built on notions of reason and universality that were constructed in explicit opposition to representations of Jews and Judaism and associations of them with irrational backwardness that are rooted in the patristic and medieval periods (Lampert 2004: 8–9; Sutcliffe 2003). While a fuller understanding of a longer history will likely not be the key to solving current crises and injustices, it can go some way towards untangling the sources of contemporary stereotypes and helping us to question them.

It can also assist in giving new perspectives on a wide range of connected concepts. Karma Lochrie continues her engagement with the *Travels* by exploring it through the lens of cosmopolitan utopianism, arguing that we can find in the *Travels* 'a nonmodern utopianism' that offers 'new possibility for . . . revitalization' of utopianism itself (2009: 598). One potential problem for such a positive reading of the *Travels* is the text's portrayal of Jews and, according to Lochrie, '[t]he question becomes whether Mandeville's blind spot utterly compromises his cosmopolitanism, utopian vision in the rest of the book' (597–8). I would argue, though, that this 'blind spot' – the text's treatment of Jews – is not one particular to Mandeville. It is intimately connected to his Christian vision. A better question might be: how does seeing this view of Jews not as incidental, but as integral, change our understanding of cosmopolitanism? Understanding this may be a key to understanding some very negative uses of 'cosmopolitanism', used in the twentieth century as a form of antisemitic excoriation by National Socialists and Stalinists.

As Walter Mignolo, drawing upon world systems theory for his analysis of cosmopolitanism, notes '[t]he first global design of the modern world was Christianity, a cause and a consequence of the incorporation of the Americas into the global vision of an orbis christianus' (2000: 721) and then provides a brilliant mapping of cosmopolitanism that takes into account the ways in which the Christian project has been a source of both imperialist and emancipatory impulses (2000: 723), impulses that date back to the end of the fifteenth century in his scheme and, I would argue, through a text such as the *Travels*, much earlier than this. The figure of the Jew and questions of gender are not the focus of Mignolo's essay, but they are, I would argue, nevertheless integral to the ways in which concepts such as cosmopolitanism are constructed and have been constructed up from their medieval Christian roots. If we can see Christianity as the original cosmopolitan project, then the special and vexed relationship of Judaism to Christianity and the vexed role of 'woman' in Christian thought need to be taken into account in our understandings of cosmopolitanism, even in its most utopian permutations. Considered in this way it is clear that animosity toward the Jews and anxieties about gender are not just blind spots for the *Mandeville*-author. They are structural components of his Christian world vision, a vision that has permeated Western thought. We must try to understand antisemitism as part of the very structure of the concepts we use in order to begin any process of revitalisation.

Notes

1. I have chosen the convention of transliterating Arabic words and terms without diacriticals. I follow the lead of Karla Mallette, who notes that 'those who read Arabic will recognize the words without these aids, while those who do not would only be distracted by them' (2003: 695).
2. For this background I am drawing on Menocal (2002: 5–49) and Lasater (1974: 15–34).
3. On language in al-Andalus, see López-Morillas (2000).
4 For a discussion of the medieval Hajj, see Lindsay 2005 and Vanchez 2001.
5. On the history of *kharja* studies, see Armistead (1987), Menocal (1987), Rosen (2000), and Mallette (2003).
6. My discussion here draws upon Aidi (2006), Tofiño-Quesada (2003), Blackmore and Hutcheson (1999), and Glick (1992). On the search for origins and *tradicionalismo*, see Espósito (2000: 466–7).
7. There is a large literature on the *Cid*. I have found useful Aizenberg (1980), Burshatin (1984; 1985), Hart (2006), Mirrer (1994), and Navarrete (1972).
8. For background on the Normans, I have drawn upon Bartlett (1993), Brown (2003), Davis (1976), Gillingham (2000), Le Patourel (1976), Mallette (2000; 2003; 2005a), Metcalfe (2002; 2003), and Norwich (1992).
9. See Michael Faletra (2000; 2007); and Laurie Finke and Martin Shichtman (2004).
10. See Otter (2006) and Warren (2000).
11. The literary scholarship summarised here draws extensively on the important work of historians Robert Bartlett, R. R. Davies and John Gillingham.
12. On the 'sympathetic werewolf' and other classifications of werewolf types, see Smith (1894).
13. Marie de France, trans. Rychner, 1966: 61, ll. 1–4, quoted in Kinoshita 2006a: 106; English translation: Marie de France, trans. Burgess and Busby, 1999: 68.
14. On 'passing' and the 'perils' of miscegenation in a premodern context, see Lampert (2004: 138–67).
15. My student Ana Grinberg first suggested the importance of the Spanish link in a graduate seminar and is now at work on the role of Spain in *Guillaume* as part of a larger project on representations of Muslims and monstrosity in medieval Europe. I am grateful to her for bibliographic background on the Middle English version of *Guillaume* and for drawing my attention to the Sicilian setting of the tale in our class discussions.
16. An important and useful discussion of the concept can be found in Loomba 1998.
17. Subsequent references to this edition will appear in the text. In addition to the important readings by Valman (2007) and Ragussis (1995) cited below, my treatment of *Ivanhoe* draws upon Abramczyk (1903), Alexander (2007), Barczewski (2000), Chandler (1970), Davidson (2006), Lincoln (2007), MacDougall (1982), Mitchell (1987), Simmons (2006), Sutherland (1995), Watson (2008), Scott (2005), and Young (2008).
18. For more on Scott's views on Jews, which were not always so accepting, see Valman (2007: 23–24). A sympathetic Shylock appeared on the English stage with Edmund Kean's famous performance in 1814. For a history of *The Merchant of Venice* on stage, see Gross (1992).

19. My account of the massacre draws on Dobson [1974] 1996.
20. A transcript of the speech is online at http://www.nytimes.com/inter active/2008/03/18/us/politics/20080318_OBAMA_GRAPHIC.html, accessed 3 August 2009.
21. http://www.pbs.org/moyers/journal/04252008/transcript1.html, accessed 4 October 2008.
22. http://www.usatoday.com/news/politics/election2008/2008–06–18-detroit-event _N.htm, accessed 4 October 2008.
23. http://www.nytimes.com/2009/01/20/us/politics/20text-obama. html?pagewanted=2, accessed 3 August 2009.
24. http://www.msnbc.msn.com/id/23337141/, accessed 3 August 2009.
25. See the Committee on International Human Rights of the Association of the Bar of the City of New York and The Center for Human Rights and Global Justice, 'Torture by Proxy: International and Domestic Law Applicable to "Extraordinary Renditions"', New York University School of Law, June 2006, http://www.chrgj.org/press/press_releases.html, accessed 3 August 2009.
26. On the 'protean quality' of racisms and for an excellent discussion of the history of the concept of race with emphasis on the early modern period, see Loomba and Burton (2007: 1–36).
27. The phrase is from Balibar (1991). See below.
28. Risch et. al. 2002; 2007. See Wade (2002) and Foster and Sharp (2002: 844–50).
29. See Appiah (2002: 11) and Nirenberg (2007: 73–4).
30. Schlauch (1939: 448–64) and Seiferth (1970).
31. Gilman (1993) and Lampert (1998).
32. Middle High German excerpts from *Parzival* are found in *Wolfram von Eschenbach*, ed. Karl Lachmann (Berlin: W. de Gruyter, [1926] 1961). References are to stanza and line. The English translations are all from Wolfram von Eschenbach, *Parzival*, trans. Helen M. Mustard and Charles E. Passage (New York: Vintage, 1961).
33. For example, 24.6–10: 'If there was anything brighter than daylight – the queen in no way resembled it. A woman's manner she did have, and was on other counts worthy of a knight, but she was unlike a dewy rose: her complexion was black of hue' ['*ist iht liehters denne der tac, / dem glîchet niht diu künegin. / si hete wîplîchen sin, / und was abr anders rîterlîch, / der touwegen rôsen ungelîch,/ nâch swarzer varwe was ir schîn*] (24.6–11).
34. 'In the city of Seville was born the man whom, some time later, he asked to take him away. He had already guided him many a mile; he had brought him here; he was not like a Moor in color. And this ship captain replied, "You must quietly conceal this from those whose skins are black; my boats are so swift that they can never overtake us, and we shall get away."' ['*Von Sibilje ûzer stat / was geborn den er dâ bat / dan kêrens zeiner wîle. / der het in manege mîle / dâ vor gefuort: er brâhte in dar. / er was niht als ein Môr gevar. / der marnaere wîse / sprach "ir sultz helen lîse / vor den die tragent daz swarze vel. / mîne kocken sint sô snel, / sine mugen uns niht genâhen / wir sullen von hinnen gâhen*"'] (54. 27–30–55.1–8).
35. See also Frakes (1997).
36. On this trope in the early Christian tradition, see Snowden (1970: 196–207).
37. See Bly (2002: 150–7); Metlitzki (1977: 136–41). See also the introduction to the modern edition, Perryman (1980: 42–50). Subsequent references to this edition will appear in the body of the text.
38. Bly (2002: 183). Other related recent discussions are Heng (2000), Kruger (1997), J. J. Cohen (2001), Hahn (2001), Robertson (2001), and Dinshaw (2001).

39. See also Loomba (2002: 38).
40. See Kinoshita (2001).
41. For an important study of *Travels*, especially in relation to its manuscript history and the author's sources, see Higgins (1997). Additional studies I recommend beyond those cited in this section are Biddick (1998b), Campbell (1988), Grady (2005), Kupfer (2008), and Lomperis (2001).
42. See Higgins (1997: 9–10) for a discussion of the text's authorship.
43. A translation of Carpini's narrative is in William of Rubruck (1955: 3–72); the original text is in John of Plano Carpini (1929).
44. This survey of medieval travellers is of necessity very brief. See 'Further Reading' for additional references. For this discussion, I have relied especially on Verdon (2003), Jackson (2005), Friedman and Figg (2000), Dunn (2005), and Edson (2007).
45. For this section on cartography I have consulted, among others, Edson (2007), Lavezzo (2006), Moseley (1983), Friedman and Figg (2000), Friedman (2000), and Kline (2001: 149–50).
46. Subsequent references to this edition will appear in the text. Because the *Travels* exists in so many versions, I have decided, following Lawton (2001), to rely on the Moseley translation for Penguin, which provides a composite of different manuscript versions. It also has the advantages of wide accessibility and linguistic ease for non-specialists.
47. On the sources for the legend of the enclosed Jews, sometimes called the Red Jews, and Mandeville's probable use of sources, see Anderson (1932), Braude (1996), DiMarco (1991), Gow (1995), Higgins (1997), and Westrem (1998).
48. See also Lochrie (2005) and Geary (2006).
49. For a compelling reading of the Jew as insider/outsider in the *Travels*, see Akbari (2005: 48–9).
50. See also, for example, Jeremy Cohen (1996).

Chapter 3

The Dark Continent of Europe

Es waren schöne glänzende Zeiten, wo Europa ein christliches Land war, wo *Eine* Christenheit diesen menschlich gestalteten Welttheil bewohnte; *Ein* großes gemeinschaftliches Interesse verband die entlegensten Provinzen dieses weiten geistlichen Reichs. (Novalis [1799] 1978: 732)

There were once beautiful, splendid times when Europe was a Christian land, when *one* Christendom dwelt in this continent, shaped by human hand; *one* great common interest bound together the most distant provinces of this broad religious empire. (Novalis 1997: 137)

Modern history was born in the nineteenth century, conceived and developed as an instrument of European nationalism. As a tool of nationalist ideology, the history of Europe's nations was a great success, but it has turned our understanding of the past into a toxic waste dump, filled with the poison of ethnic nationalism, and the poison has seeped deep into popular consciousness. Cleaning up this waste is the most daunting challenge facing historians today. (Geary 2002: 15)

Recently commentators and journalists have begun to point to the great increase in Muslim immigration to Europe over the past decades, predicting, given the low birthrates among other groups in Europe, that the Muslim population will quickly grow into a European majority.[1] Many of these forecasts, however, go far beyond simple discussions of demographics. Predicting a 'takeover' of Europe by Muslims, they are part of a broader and contentious discourse about 'Islam in Europe'. Dutch politician Geert Wilders has, for example, publically proclaimed that Moroccan immigrants are 'colonising' the Netherlands (*De Telegraaf*, 17 September 2008). Bat Ye'or's (Gisèle Littman) *Eurabia* (2005) warns that Muslims could take over Europe and reduce all non-believers to the subservient status of 'dhimmitude', a kind of second-class citizenship. Melanie Phillip's *Londonistan* (2006) contends that policies in Great Britain have turned it into a haven for Muslim terrorists and extremists, and Necla Kelek concludes her 2005 *Die fremde Braut* (The Foreign Bride) with a declaration that assimilation of the Turkish population in Germany has been a failure with dangerous consequences.[2] Along similar lines, Oriana Fallaci (2002; 2006), Bruce Bawer (2006), Mark Steyn (2006) and Walter Laqueur (2007) each write of what they see as negative and even dangerous changes in Europe resulting from Muslim influence. Their polemics and numerous others toll the death knell of European civilisation and, by extension, of the West.[3]

The 'Islam in Europe' debate is not, of course, merely a matter of fiery rhetoric and spilled ink; it has concrete implications for European residents. Recent years have seen debates and legislation concerning the wearing of the veil in France; protests over cartoon depictions of Mohammed in Denmark in 2005–6; controversy and violence concerning the films *Submission* (2004) and *Fitna* (2008) in the Netherlands; and debates regarding the construction of mosques in countries such as England, Germany and Switzerland.[4] These and additional examples can be found all across Europe. Each case is shaped by the particular histories and cultures of the specific communities involved, as well as by questions of economics and immigration, but they are also each part of a larger set of conflicts concerning European identity and the nature of the European secular state. These debates over the nature of Europe, the identities of its inhabitants, and the fate of 'European civilisation' often draw upon representations of the Middle Ages, frequently as filtered through nineteenth-century medievalisms. Very important among the dominant representations is the idea of Europe as Christendom, which, as political scientist Christine Perkins argues

> continues to be reflected in every aspect of European life and thought: in, for example, the continuing historical, social and political significance of canon law within European constitutions, in the 'high' culture of art, music and literature which reflects not only the Christian world-view but also the powerful status of the Church and its relations with the State, in the architecture which still provides the day-to-day context of European city life, and at every level of education. (2004: 4)

This image of medieval Europe as Christendom permeates cultural and political discourses, and shapes policy and institutions in fundamental ways.

We can, for example, see the importance of the idea of Christendom and Europe's Christian heritage in the vigorous debates over the wording of the European Union's Constitution, as representatives of member states argued about whether Europe's 'Christian roots' should be mentioned. The Vatican and states such as Poland and Italy played a strong role in advocating mention of Christianity in the document, although reference to any specific religion was eventually omitted. The current draft instead recognises Europe as (in the rather foggy wording of the English-language version) a 'continent that has brought forth civilisation'.[5] While an assertion that European civilisation is 'Civilisation' itself is not made explicit, the document also does not explicitly frame European civilisation as one among many in world history; it could readily be seen as enforcing Eurocentrism by implying that Europe has indeed been the region to develop 'Civilisation with a capital "C"'.[6]

While Europe's 'Christian roots' are not mentioned in the Constitution, controversy over the role of Christian identity in determining what Europe is, and what it will be, has not, however, been resolved by any means. Current economics and immigration are important factors in determining which nations will be allowed to join the EU, but the debate over Turkey is haunted by the past; the spectre of Ottoman Muslims at Christian gates is raised for some when Turkey's admission to the EU is considered (Kösebalaban 2007). Even though the religious aspect of the admission controversy is not always referenced as explicitly as it is in the constitutional debate, the view that European civilisation is Christian clearly plays a role in decisions about Turkish inclusion. This prevalent, popular notion of Europe, which has at its core a view of the European Middle Ages as a pure European Christendom (which then gave rise to a humanist Renaissance and finally a secular Enlightenment) has not only imaginative, but concrete political ramifications.

In this final chapter I want to explore additional examples of how the medieval past is invoked in the 'Islam in Europe' debate. The range of controversies, polemics, incidents and locations I will consider are indicative of a pan-European phenomenon with global implications. These examples of contemporary medievalisms, which often make potent historical claims, 'disrupt the assertion that medievalists do not work for or in "the land of the living"' (Ingham 2003: 53). Indeed, as I want to argue below, 'the land of the living' and the question of to whom it belongs are precisely what is at stake in the medievalisms of the 'Islam in Europe' debate.[7]

It is my goal in this chapter to draw attention to the role of medievalisms in the Islam in Europe controversy. The subject of 'Islam in Europe' is itself very broad and complex with issues such as religious freedom, gender rights, racism, economics, migration and, of course, the legacy of European colonialism all playing roles – roles that vary significantly depending on the specific geographic context. I will focus on the importance of memory and of place in public discourse in order to suggest how postcolonial medieval studies can provide new perspectives on these discussions. For example, in the specific set of controversies surrounding mosque and minaret construction that we will survey, it is taken for granted that the European landscape is one naturally dominated by Christian architecture, an architecture that is also synonymous with medieval Europe and, more specifically, with medieval European Christendom. In the Cologne mosque controversy, for example, the famous Cologne Cathedral is used by opponents of immigration and 'Islamisation' as a symbol of European Christian values, a physical sign of historic continuity and homogeneity, even though the structure itself is the product of construction not over years, but over centuries.

By challenging Christianity's normative position, reconsidering Europe's boundaries and peeling back the layers of the palimpsest that is the landscape of Europe, postcolonial medieval studies offers important perspectives on the 'Islam in Europe' controversy. The scholarly perspectives afforded by bringing medieval and postcolonial studies together allow us to see very clearly that medievalisms themselves are layered. By attempting to understand the various lenses that have been used to filter the past we can, perhaps, work to challenge the destruction of cultural memory that novelist Juan Goytisolo has dubbed 'memoricide'. (2000: 25). As Sharon Kinoshita has noted, artists appear to be ahead of the curve in terms of exploring challenges to old and ossified paradigms (2007: 75). I will conclude by looking at how the treatment of memory and place appear in recent fiction dealing with Islam and the West and questions of memory and place by Goytisolo, Salman Rushdie, Tariq Ali and Amitav Ghosh.

Mapping the Future of the Past

In our discussion of medieval maps in the last chapter, I noted that *mappaemundi* such as the Hereford and Ebstorf maps are not literal navigational tools, but are meant to chart moral, spiritual and political worlds; ideological shaping of this sort is, of course, not limited to *mappaemundi*, but informs all types of cartography.[8] Perhaps the most influential contemporary example is Samuel P. Huntington's 1993 essay 'Clash of Civilizations?' which presents his vision of post-Cold War global politics.[9] Huntington divides the world into seven or eight 'civilisations': 'Western, Confucian, Japanese, Islamic, Hindu, Slavic-Orthodox, Latin-American and possibly African', asserting that 'the most important conflicts of the future will occur along the cultural fault lines separating these civilizations from one another' (1993: 25). But while Huntington's essay sets out to deal with potential clashes between multiple civilisations, its central preoccupation is the '1300 years' of conflict on the 'fault line' between Islam and the West.

The main battleground for the clash between Islam and the West is Europe, whose future is of prime concern:

> The Cold War began when the Iron Curtain divided Europe politically and ideologically. The Cold War ended with the end of the Iron Curtain. As the ideological division of Europe has disappeared, the cultural division of Europe between Western Christianity, on the one hand, and Orthodox Christianity and Islam, on the other, has reemerged. (Huntington 1993: 29–30)

For Huntington, the new dividing line of the 'Velvet Curtain of culture' has replaced the 'Iron Curtain of Ideology'. This line is the same line as that of 'the eastern boundary of Western Christianity in the year 1500', as Huntington literally divides a map of Europe with a year: 1500 (1993:30) (see Figure 4). This date is, of course, part of the common periodisation of the great epochal shift figured between the Middle Ages and the Renaissance, and, more importantly, also references the fall of Constantinople to the Ottomans in 1453. This watershed in the history of the 'cultural division' between 'Islam and the West' has often been seen as marking the end of the Middle Ages.[10]

Through Huntington's narrative of a clash between Islam and the West, the past is brought into the present and, on the map of the 'Eastern Boundary of Western Civilization', the temporal becomes spatial. This shift to the spatial obscures historical specificity as Islam and the West become separated by time and space in ways that seem better associated with iron than with velvet. The map appears in his book-length expansion of his article in a section called 'Bounding the West', an exercise meant, it seems, to provide Westerners with answers in the face of an uncertain future:

> The civilizational paradigm thus provides a clear-cut and compelling answer to the question confronting Western Europeans: Where does Europe end? Europe ends where Western Christianity ends and Islam and Orthodoxy begin. This is the answer which West Europeans want to hear, which they overwhelmingly support sotto voce, and which various intellectuals and political leaders have explicitly endorsed. (1996: 158)

Huntington's paradigm of global politics offers skittish world leaders a readily recognisable vision of boundaries and clashes. His divvying-up of the world is reminiscent of a medieval T-O map in its schematic

Figure 4 Europe c. 1500, map by Ib Ohlsson, in Huntington (1993),
'The Clash of Civilizations?' 30. Reprinted by permission of *Foreign
Affairs* (72.3, Summer 1993). Copyright 1993 by the Council on Foreign
Relations, Inc.

simplicity, but the worldview it provides is binary rather than tripartite, translating the Cold War antagonism between democratic West and communist East into a conflict between a Christian West and a Muslim East. Huntington does not clarify the distinction he makes between ideology and culture, but his re-mapping of the post-Cold War world creates a new (yet retro) periodisation. With the end of the Cold War, then, we have moved, in Huntington's view, from global conflicts motivated by secular concerns to those fired by the flames of holy war. And, indeed, while the *mappaemundi* set out to show a world united through a single spiritual order, Huntington portrays a world where religion divides rather than unites.

Huntington's 'Clash' thesis draws upon a 1990 article by the prolific Orientalist Bernard Lewis, who therein coined the phrase 'clash of civilisations'. Of the conflict between 'Islam and the West', Lewis wrote:

> We are facing a mood and a movement far transcending the level of issues and policies and the governments that pursue them. This is no less than a clash of civilizations – the perhaps irrational but surely historical reaction of an ancient rival against our Judeo-Christian heritage, our secular present, and the worldwide expansion of both. It is important that we on our side should not be provoked into an equally historic but also equally irrational reaction against that rival. (1990: 60)

Lewis's formulation of a clash between 'us' and 'them' relies upon additional binary oppositions: those between medieval and modern and between a religious, even fanatical, past and a secular present. It also is based on a relatively recent conflation of a centuries-old binarism: that between Judaism and Christianity. 'Judeo-Christian' civilisation is a post-Holocaust combination of two religious traditions held as inimical in centuries of Jewish, Christian and 'Western' thought and belief (Qureshi and Sells 2003: 4–8). The idea of a Judeo-Christian European civilisation elides European Jewry's long history of persecutions, expulsions and genocide, and creates a new identity for European civilisation that is compatible with secularism and at odds with 'Islam'.

Edward Said observed that there is no denying that 'the writing of history is the royal road to the definition of a country, that the identity of a society is in large part a function of historical interpretation, which is fraught with contested claims and counterclaims' (2004). Conceptions of 'Europe' and of 'European civilisation' also depend upon historical narratives with specific inclusions and exclusions, not only of persons, but also of regions and of times. Arguing that the narrative of European civilisation is one based on ideas of 'improvement and accumulation', Talal Asad concludes that:

> It follows from this view of Europe that real Europeans acquire their individual identities from the character of their civilization. Without that civilizational essence, individuals living within Europe are unstable and ambiguous. That is why not all inhabitants of the European continent are 'really' or 'fully' European. Russians are clearly marginal. Until just after World War II, European Jews were marginal too, but since that break the emerging discourse of a 'Judeo-Christian' tradition has signaled a new integration of their status into Europe. Completely external to 'European history' is medieval Spain. Although Spain is now defined geographically as part of Europe, Arab Spain from the seventh to the fourteenth centuries is seen as being outside 'Europe,' in spite of the numerous intimate connections and exchanges in the Iberian Peninsula during that period between Muslims, Christians, and Jews. (2003: 168)

The view of medieval Europe that Asad describes has developed through several centuries of historiographical shaping that developed alongside the rise of European colonialism, and which is still very influential.[11] (See Menocal [1987] (2004) and Dainotto 2007.)

As we have seen, Spain and Sicily (each pictured as safely to the west of Huntington's dividing line) have histories of hybrid cultures that defy easy definitions and boundary-drawing. And, at least in part because of their 'mixed' pasts, Spain and Sicily, while still considered part of the West, have frequently been relegated to a kind of second-class status in Europe. Often excluded from Europe altogether are the Balkans, recently the site of so much violence. Because Huntington's divisions are religious ones, his boundary for the Western world must cut jaggedly across national borders in the Balkans, as if attempting to navigate the mix of religious groups in this region. The status of the Balkans as part of Europe is continually debated, not simply because of the difficulty of establishing the artificial boundaries of the 'continent' of Europe, but also precisely because of the cultural boundaries that Huntington invokes. Referred to as 'Turkey in Europe' in the eighteenth and nineteenth centuries, the Balkans are deemed as separate from 'Europe' because of their Ottoman history, which, much like the history of al-Andalus, does not align with a definition of Europe as Christendom.[12] By challenging traditional periodisations and geographic paradigms, we alter our view not only of the past, but of the present and future as well. If the Balkans and the Iberian Peninsula are included as integral parts of Europe, then fault-lines such as those traced by Huntington become very blurry indeed.

Whose Long Memories?

In countries such as the US, Germany and Australia journalists have spoken of the 'long memory' of the Arab world, specifically noting mentions of the Crusades as in Osama bin Laden's 1998 'Declaration of the World Islamic Front for Jihad against the Jews and the Crusaders', and in the rhetoric of groups such as Hezbollah and Hamas. Journalists and commentators reference calls to reclaim Muslim control of the Iberian Peninsula and restore the glory of al-Andalus as evidence of the Muslim world's fixation on the past, and also frequently remind readers of the Crusades' lasting impact.[13] In the conclusion to *The Crusades: Islamic Perspectives*, Carole Hillenbrand argues that the Crusades left 'profound and lasting psychological scars' on those in the Muslim world and urges readers to bear in mind that 'many Muslims today still remember with pain – centuries later though it may be – what was done in the name of the Cross. As so often in the Islamic world, the events of the distant past have a sharp contemporary relevance' (2000: 614). In addition to scholarly accounts such as Hillenbrand's, we find much more schematic descriptions of 'historical memory in the Middle East' as 'long and deep' (Macintyre 2001) and headlines such as the one in the *Sydney Herald* proclaiming, 'Long Memories of the Crusades Overshadow the Future' (12 April 2003).

As Thomas Madden argues, however, this 'Muslim collective memory' may not actually be as long as is typically supposed:

> It is commonly said that memories in the Middle East are long, that although the crusades may have been forgotten in the West, they were still vividly remembered where they happened. This is false. The simple fact is that the crusades were virtually unknown in the Muslim world even a century ago. The term for the crusades, *harb al-salib*, was only introduced into the Arab language in the mid-nineteenth century. The first Arabic history of the crusades was not written until 1899. (Madden 2005: 217)

There were, of course, medieval accounts of the Crusades in Arabic, but 'the memory of the medieval Crusades' is not a static entity that has existed intact in any language since medieval times. The tradition in the Middle East, Madden contends, is instead the product of the expansion of European colonialism, which brought to this elements such as a European version of the legend of Saladin.[14] Such nineteenth-century European visions are nowhere better captured than in Kaiser Wilhelm II's visit (costumed in full Crusader garb) to Damascus in 1899. Upon finding the tomb of Saladin neglected, Wilhelm ordered a new mausoleum built and had laid upon it a bronze wreath inscribed, 'From one great emperor to another' (Madden 2005: 219). Leaders such as Syria's Hafez Asad and Iraq's Saddam Hussein later took up this romanticised vision of Saladin as a symbolic rallying point. Such visions of the Crusades are not ancient memories carefully preserved, but medieval histories 'stripped' of their historical context and 'dressed up . . . instead in the tattered rags of nineteenth-century imperialism' (Madden 2005: 222).

Kaiser Wilhelm's visit to Damascus indicates quite clearly that Middle Easterners are not alone in having 'long memories'. Often though, it seems that discussions of the 'long memory' of those in the Middle East are tinged with the sense that there is something backward about those who hold on to such memories: that they are, at best, desperately in need of being pulled into the modern world and, at worst, atavistically barbaric.[15] This perspective is in keeping with the commonly expressed notion that many Muslim-dominated countries are hopelessly trapped in a medieval, barbaric past, a common theme in recent debates on 'Islam and the West' or 'Islam in Europe'.[16] But this is not the only use of the 'medieval' in these debates. Examination of contemporary discourse in the media and in political forums reveals frequent recourse to medieval themes on both the national and European-wide levels. These frequently and openly deployed examples of 'long memories' are also based on visions of the Middle Ages created centuries later.

¿No hay moros en la costa? : Political Medievalisms in Contemporary Europe[17]

A striking example of the use of a medieval-inspired myth in contemporary Europe is a 2007 campaign advertisement for Jean Marie Le Pen, leader of the right-wing *Front National* (FN), a party that began on the fringes of French politics in the 1970s, but has gained in popularity more recently.[18] The ad focuses on the figure of Joan of Arc (c. 1412–31), a favourite symbol of the FN. It uses clips from Luc Besson's 1999 film, *Jeanne d'Arc*, interspersed with text calling for true 'Français' to 'Lève-toi!' (Stand up!) and, by voting for Le Pen, to take a stand for France.[19] Joan of Arc is one of 'three main national symbols of the party, also including 'the people' and 'the land'. Each 1 May, FN leaders honour the saint; this date marks a change from her traditional feast day (8 May), a shift that appears designed to supplant annual celebrations on the Left of the *Fête du Travail* or May Day (Davies 2001: 106; Margolis 2003: 104).

One segment of the Le Pen campaign ad intersperses scenes of Joan horribly wounded in battle with images from the war in Iraq and the torture and abuse of prisoners by US soldiers in Abu Ghraib prison, and calls to resist globalisation. In the ad, Joan *is* France, a France now being wounded by US-inspired globalisation and imperialism (figured with a maniacal Uncle Sam with glowing eyes) just as Joan was once wounded in battle. The advertisement links Joan to France and to Le Pen, who, like Joan, the ad implies, is willing to sacrifice for France, a theme popular in FN politics (Davies 2001:19). Joan is not the only medieval symbol adopted by the FN; the party also celebrated Clovis, the 'Christian Father of France', on the 1500-year anniversary of his baptism in 1996, although Clovis's violent history eventually made Joan the favoured choice as primary FN symbol (Geary 2002: 157; Gopnik 1996). For the FN, both Clovis and Joan represent a national-ist history tied to French Catholicism. This image of a Christian France is held up in contrast to those who are not 'truly French', and is also buoyed by images of Charlemagne as another French Christian leader, one who specifically battled Islamic threats to Europe (Davies 1999: 105).

As Nadia Margolis has shown, Joan has been used as a symbol for those holding both right- and left-wing political sentiments in France since the nineteenth century, when her image and history were revisited. Although Joan's role as symbol has long been debated, those on the right have more prominently and consistently adopted her image (2003: 59). Undeniably, though, we have here an example of a 'long memory'. This memory has not existed in unchanging form for centuries, but has been shaped by writers, such as the influential historian of France Jules Michelet (1798–1874), and by events such as the Franco-Prussian war and the two World Wars in which Joan was figured as the essence of the true France (Margolis: 2003: 59–64). The FN now deploys Joan of Arc as a symbol for specific political purposes, including the promotion of an image of France as a nation that is ultimately incompatible with immigration, specifically the immigration of Muslims. This anti-Muslim immigration stance is also asserted with appeals to 'history'. As Le Pen remarked in a 1987 speech:

A deux mille ans de distance, ce sont pratiquement les mêmes peuples qui nous font courir les mêmes dangers. N'est-il pas vrai que les moudjahidins iraniens sont les descendants de ces Perses qui furent vaincus à Marathon, que le monde islamique, qui vient battre les frontières de l'Europe et la pénètre lentement, est composé des fils de ces Turcs qui vinrent jusqu'à Vienne et de ces Arabes que Martel vainquit à Poitiers?[20]

For two thousand years, essentially the same people have posed the same dangers to us. Aren't the Iranian *mujahidin* the descendants of the Persians who were defeated at Marathon; isn't the Islamic World, now striking at Europe's frontiers and slowly penetrating her, composed of the sons of the Ottoman Turks who reached Vienna, and the Arabs whom Charles Martel routed at Poitiers?

Le Pen here refers to a conflict between East and West that has lasted over 2,000 years, with the battles of Marathon, Poitiers and Vienna conflated into one long and continuous clash. His formulation also figures the West as a sexualised victim, slowly penetrated by the sons of the Turks and Arabs who threatened her in the past.

Such rhetoric is not merely rhetoric. Serbian nationalists (with whom Le Pen has been shown to have ties) employed such 'clash of civilisations' symbolism to urge followers on to murderous and devastating ends in the Balkans.[21] They used the story of Prince Lazar, who died in the Battle of Kosovo in 1389, as propaganda in the campaign leading up to genocide in Bosnia. This retelling of the Lazar story employs the ideology of what Sells calls Christoslavism, which purports that all true Slavs are Christians. Sells argues that by using a nineteenth-century Christoslavic version of the Lazar story, the dramatic epic *The Mountain Wreath* (*Gorski vijenac*) (1847) by Petar Njegoš, Serbian nationalists were able to turn the story of Lazar into a new Passion, replacing the traditionally vilified Jews with Muslims, or 'Turks' (Sells 1996: 41–6).[22]

The use of this re-imagining of a medieval battle is exemplified by then-Serbian president Slobodan Milošević's address to a huge crowd at *Kosovo Polje*, or Blackbird's Field, on 28 June 1989, the 600th anniversary of Lazar's death. In this speech Milošević conflated past battles against a Muslim enemy with battles to come, and he hailed Serbia as a once and future bastion of European civilisation (Sells 1996: 68–9.) While paying lip service to interfaith co-existence in Kosovo, Milošević's speech was an appeal to Serbian unity, arguing that it was a lack of unity that had led to Serbian defeat six centuries earlier. The speech was also, crucially, an appeal 'to the values of Europe, meaning to Christianity, to modernity, to Civilisation with a capital "C"', and it drew on 'Orientalist stereotypes' about Bosnian Muslims to paint a picture of inter-religious conflict that Arne Johan Vetlesen compares to Huntington's 'clash of civilisations' thesis (2005: 153).

Michael Sells argues that this vision of an eternal clash was part of why Western European countries and the US were so slow to intervene in Bosnia: the situation was painted as the result of 'age-old antagonisms' and 'a coded set of stereotypes about Muslims had helped make the killings of Bosnian Muslims appear natural and helped naturalize the refusal to stop it' (1996: 11). Widely read books such as Robert Kaplan's *Balkan Ghosts* (1992) figured the Balkans as 'too close to the Orient (read Islam) to be a true part of Europe', and as mired in age-old Christian-Muslim antagonisms that made violence inevitable (Sells 1996: 124). This view of a world locked in a timeless struggle paralysed intervention, a situation exemplified by a 1994 remark by US president Bill Clinton: 'Until these folks get tired of killing each other,' Clinton said, 'bad things will continue to happen' (Sells 1996: 127). Such stereotypes of irrational peoples trapped in the past and unable to 'catch up' with modernity, another version of attribution of 'long memories', accounts in part for the lack of early outside intervention against the genocide.

When we are in fact dealing with mythic 'memories' such as those deployed by al-Qaeda, Milošević, and groups such as the FN, we find ourselves wading neck deep in the 'toxic waste dumps' of memory that Patrick Geary describes in one of the epigraphs to this chapter. In each case images and symbols of the Middle Ages are filtered through modern medievalisms that are then used to promote particular ideologies. The cases I have referenced are all extreme examples linked to campaigns of xenophobia, violence and mass murder, and the Serbian nationalists have been roundly condemned. The success of Jean Le Pen in the 2002 French presidential elections, however, arguably makes a case for the FN as more mainstream than fringe. Le Pen garnered the second largest number of votes in the presidential election, just behind Jacques Chirac, and beating the Socialist candidate Lionel Jospin.

While the FN's status as a fringe group may be up for debate, other prominent figures with undeniably international influence have used medievalisms in the contemporary 'Islam in Europe' debates. On 12 September 2006 Pope Benedict XVI gave an address entitled '*Glaube, Vernunft und Universität*' (Faith, Reason and the University) at the University of Regensburg, in which he cited a 1391 treatise purporting to relate a dialogue between the Byzantine emperor Manuel II Paleologus and a learned Muslim interlocutor. Benedict cited the emperor as asking the Muslim, 'Show me just what Mohammed brought that was new, and there you will find things only evil and inhuman, such as his command to spread by the sword the faith he preached.'[23] Pope Benedict uses the example of this supposed dialogue to begin an argument against the elevation of science, which, Benedict claims, is responsible for the association of religion with irrationality. As a result, he argues, secularists insist that the ideal of reason is incompatible with matters of faith. This particular thesis is in keeping with some recurring themes in Benedict's writings, which often lament secularisation as a cultural trend that has come to degrade humanity through the devaluation of spirituality and of human life itself.

Pope Benedict, a former professor of theology specialising in patristics, presented a complex argument geared toward an academic audience. There are scholarly grounds on which to critique his presentation, such as the imbalance between his careful parsing of Christian terminology in Greek, specifically the concept of *Logos*, and his relatively thin treatment of passages and concepts from the Muslim tradition, such as *Jihad*. One could also note his failure to acknowledge the often one-sided nature of medieval 'interfaith' dialogues.[24] More important than these philological and historical points, however, is the Pope's overall rhetorical strategy. After controversy over the address erupted, the pope's defenders stated that he had not intended to offend; however, his opening example – the treatise, with its denigration of Islam and its connections between Islam, violence and irrationality – is confrontational and remains a shadowy presence throughout his address. The Pope's overarching theme was the clash between the religious and the secular, but he ended up offending Muslims, whose reactions ranged from op-ed pieces demanding an apology to public protests and violence, including, it is suspected, the murder of an Italian nun working in Somalia, Sister Leonella Sgorbati.[25]

The Pope's choice of a fourteenth-century text, written as Byzantium was on the verge of falling to the Ottoman empire, and the subsequent outcry over his remarks provide yet another example of the important role that the Middle Ages plays in current culture wars. These examples seem to compound one another. Some days after the controversy erupted, on 23 September 2006, the former Spanish prime minister José María Aznar gave a talk at the Hudson Institute in Washington DC, in which he wondered why, in light of the calls for the pontiff to apologise, there were no calls for apologies by Muslims for conquering Spain in 711 and occupying it for eight centuries. For Aznar, the Pope's medieval citation was more than simply a scholarly reference; it was part of a history of conflict between Islam and the West that is still regnant, as evidenced by the crosses of St James of Compostela (the Moor-killer) emblazoned on the uniforms of Spanish soldiers who were deployed as part of the Iraq occupying force in 2003 (Tremlett: 2003).

Praising the spirit of the Reconquista, Aznar then went on to dismiss as 'estupidez' the Alliance of Civilisations, a UN organisation founded in 2005 by Aznar's successor as prime minister of Spain, José Luis Rodríguez Zapatero, and the prime minister of Turkey, Tayyip Erdogan

(*El Mundo* 2006). The Alliance is pledged to furthering dialogue and understanding between groups, and attempts to challenge the notion of a 'clash of civilisations' between Islam and the West.[26] Supporters of the Alliance, such as Juan Luis Cebrían, former editor at the Spanish daily, *El País*, also draw on medieval history to counter views such as Huntington's and Aznar's. In an opinion piece in *El País*, Cebrían refers to José Ortega y Gasset's well-known introduction to a Spanish translation of Ibn Hazm's *Tawq al-Hamama* (*Neckring of the Dove*), in which Ortega y Gasset reminds the reader that medieval Europe and its culture are inseparable from the culture of al-Andalus. Focusing specifically on the idea of civilisation, Cebrían argues that civilisations cannot and should not be limited by a focus on religion, and he condemns the Reconquista as 'insidious' (Cebrían, cited in Hamilton 2007a). Other well-known figures in Spain, such as the novelist Juan Goytisolo, also responded to Aznar's references to medieval history by offering an opposing view of the Spanish medieval past, one that views the Muslim presence in Spain as a key part of Spanish history and culture, not as a black mark upon it (Goytisolo 2006).

Debates on the past and present importance of al-Andalus and of the Reconquista clearly infuse political discourse on the national level in Spain. They are also important in local and regional settings, not only politically and culturally, but also economically, as highlighting Spain's Moorish past has become significant in advertising Spain as a tourist destination. Two annual festivals that involve community re-enactment of medieval events are now the focus of tension and debate as well as celebration: '*Moros y Cristianos*' (The Festival of Moors and Christians), observed in Spanish coastal regions in the south and east, and the '*Día de la Toma*' (Day of the Taking) in Granada, which commemorates the end of the Reconquista on 2 January 1492, when the Moors were expelled from Granada. These festivals are post-medieval in origin and are now community events and tourist attractions (Rogozen-Soltar 2007; Flesler and Melgosa 2003). The *Moros y Cristianos* festival had, until 2006, featured a 'giant turban-clad puppet known as *Mahoma* (Mohammed)', the head of which was stuffed with gun-powder and exploded when set alight with a cigar. This custom has been only recently halted out of fear of violent reprisals, after the publication of depictions of Mohammed in Denmark sparked death threats and international protest. Now instead

of the usual head-explosion or effigy burning, after the costumed reenactments of battles between the Christians and the Moors, participants simply dragged the puppet *Mahoma* through the streets. Afterward, a Spaniard dressed up as a Moorish leader performed a theatrical conversion to Christianity and was publicly baptized. (Rogozen-Soltar 2007: 863)

The festivals, their meaning, forms and continued existence have been much debated in the wake of recent international conflict. The Archbishop of Granada has defended the *Día de la Toma* and stated its importance in Christian terms by connecting it directly to the events of 9/11 (*El País*, 3 January 2002). An Arabic-language poster advertising the *Moros y Cristianos* festival in Alcoy, the largest of such celebrations, was found to translate the title of the event as 'árabes y sionistas' (Arabs and Zionists), linking this commemoration of a medieval event with the current conflict in Israel and the Palestinian territories (*El País*, 8 April 2004).

This translation highlights the ways in which these festivals reflect international tensions as well as what anthropologist Mikaela Rogozen-Soltar sees as a struggle by Andalusians 'to format their society as secular, western, modern and European' (2007: 864). Also figuring importantly here are tensions over immigration in Spain and particularly in the regions where these festivals occur, as Spain experienced a large increase in the migration of Muslims in the 1990s (Corkill 2000: 49). The region of Valencia has one of the highest percentages of Muslim immigrants, who have settled into both geographical areas and occupations that were similar to those of the Moriscos prior to their expulsion (Flesner and Melgosa 2003: 161). The festivals, which rarely include Muslim community members as participants, 'can be understood as a mechanism deployed to clarify, year after year, that the Christian side is the true "owner" of the territory of the Peninsula, the "natives" opposing the "invading" Moors' (Flesner and Melgosa 2003: 155).

The tensions within Spain, that is, the struggles surrounding 'long memories' of al-Andalus, take place in prominent newspapers, international forums, and annually in local events. And, of course, these tensions over Iberia are most violently evident in the 3/11 bombings of 2004, which resulted in 191 deaths and 1,755 wounded. These bombings too were linked to calls from such groups as al-Qaeda to reclaim al-Andalus, a perversion of the longing found in a tradition of Arabic poetry and fiction for a lost medieval region and culture (Granara 2005). The tensions that exist in the Spanish case did not begin in the modern era. They developed out of medieval conflicts, the memories of which have been shaped and filtered by modern historiography and modern medievalisms. Attempting to disentangle these layers of history, one of the projects of postcolonial medieval studies, is precisely the type of analysis that can aid in providing context and balance to public discourse.

The Hand of the Dead in the Land of the Living

To a visitor to Europe, gazing at the passing countryside of France or Germany from the window of a moving train, the church steeples punctuating the rural landscape mark it as unmistakably Christian. The loud tolling of church bells early on Sunday mornings also announces (as it perhaps jolts the visitor out of slumber) the Christian history of many European locales, despite Europe's now much-touted secularism. The Christian symbolism of Europe's landscape is obviously a large part of what is at stake in debates over mosque construction in Europe. Just as portraying a territory as 'virgin', or as an empty space waiting to be settled and civilised, is a way of justifying a right to that land, so too is portraying a land as already full, as already having a cultural landscape so old, so established, that it seems inevitable, natural and eternal. Place is not, however, unchanging and eternal. As Bill Ashcroft observes,

> Place is never simply location, nor is it static, a cultural memory which colonization buries. For, like culture itself, place is in a continual and dynamic state of formation, a process intimately bound up with the culture and the identity of its inhabitants. Above all place is a *result* of habitation, a consequence of the ways in which people inhabit space, particularly the conception of space as universal and uncontestable that is constructed for them by imperial discourse. (2001: 156, cited in Howe 2005: 35)

Ashcroft's observations are not only relevant to places typically considered to be colonised, but also can be applied to the former colonial centres of Europe. It is useful, I will suggest here, to consider place as a 'palimpsest, a kind of parchment on which successive generations have inscribed and reinscribed the process of history' (Ashcroft, Griffiths and Tiffin 1995: 392).

Recent work in medieval studies has explored the layered nature of medieval space, demonstrating that the very past that is so often represented as intact and eternal is itself created through processes of historical change. Nicholas Howe has examined the impact of Roman ruins in Anglo-Saxon England, which he sees as a

> postcolonial society in the most literal sense of the term: as one that existed after the Roman Empire ceased to function as a political, military, and economic entity in Britain and before *Englalond* emerged late in the Anglo-Saxon period as an incipient nation within the larger sphere of Christendom. (Howe 2005: 25)

Howe argues that '[t]he stones that litter the texts of Gildas, Bede, and the Old English poets can be read as the visible traces of a colonial past' (2005: 34). Seth Lerer also makes this layered past come alive in his reading of the traces of Roman architecture found in a description of a Roman floor in *Beowulf*, demonstrating the impact of cultural layering in the contact zone and the historical legacy it leaves (2005). Jeffrey Jerome Cohen has shown the architectural impact of Norman conquest in medieval Norwich and how the subsequent 'architectural wounding of a city affects the subjectivities of those who inhabit its altered geographies' including the conquering Normans, those 'native' to Norwich, and the town's Jewish community, which was subject to the first incidence of ritual murder accusation in Europe in 1144 (2006: 112). Neither 'Medieval England' nor its landscape is or ever was a monolithic entity, and the continual process of change in England's landscape and architecture is still discernible through centuries of layers.

Such questions of architectural symbolism, or even architectural 'wounding', not only apply to medieval Europe, but are also still very much in play in Europe today. We find the current situation presciently satirised in Spanish author Juan Goytisolo's 1982 novel *Paisajes después de la batalla* (Landscapes after the Battle), which opens with the transformation of Le Sentier, a Parisian garment district. Le Sentier's locals have noticed the appearance of indecipherable chalk graffiti throughout their neighbourhood. They take it to be the work of children, until one night

> Más tarde, alguno, en una pausa de insomnio, se había asomado a tomar el fresco a la ventana a altas horas de la madrugada y había divisado una silueta inclinada sobre la parte baja de la pared del inmueble contiguo: un sujeto de pelo rizado y negro, del que no consiguió ver la cara pero que, de eso estaba seguro y podía jurarlo, no era en ningún caso de los nuestros. (Goytisolo 1982: 10–11)

> Later on someone suffering from insomnia had leaned out of his window in the wee hours of the morning to get a breath of fresh air and had spied a silhouette bending over the bottom stretch of wall of the building next door: a person with kinky black hair, whose face he didn't manage to get a glimpse of, but in any case, of this he was certain and would swear to it: he definitely was not one of us. (Goytisolo 1987: 2–3)

Goytisolo describes how all of the signs in the district are, over a short period of time, transformed into Arabic. He employs metaphors of water to describe a slow beginning, the trickle of change, as the increasingly dismayed locals of Le Sentier find that their local bars, dance clubs and even their McDonald's now bear signs exclusively in Arabic. They perceive the influx of foreigners as an invasion: '¡Eso sí que era el colmo, colonizados por aquella gentuza!' (Goytisolo 1982: 14) ['This was the last straw: colonized by those barbarians!' (Goytisolo 1987: 5)].

Without focusing on any one character, Goytisolo takes us into a kind of general consciousness of the Le Sentier locals. While the narrative voice maintains an ironic distance from them, we nevertheless see things through their eyes and with their limitations. Goytisolo neither translates nor transliterates the Arabic words and phrases that appear, and he never refers to these mysterious markings as Arabic. Those readers who cannot read Arabic experience the signs as the Le Sentier locals do: as indecipherable signs in a foreign language and a foreign alphabet. For those who can read them, the signs are actually completely mundane place markings, a combination of Arabic words and transcriptions of French words into Arabic lettering, such as the name of a bar, a transcription of the word 'sandwich', and sign postings to the famous Parisian sites, the Place de l'Opéra and the Place de la Concorde. What seems to be foreign and threatening is actually simply a translation of what might otherwise be seen as mundanely French. The crowning irony of the description is in one man's dismay that his trusted party newspaper, the communist daily *L'Humanité* has also had its sign replaced. He remains ignorant that the sign has only replaced the signifier, not the signified. Fear and ignorance have obscured the meaning of 'humanity' itself.

Goytisolo's satire, which appeared in 1982, focuses on a Parisian neighbourhood, but it anticipates the current swell of controversy across Europe over the construction of mosques and minarets. The signs in Goytisolo's Parisian neighbourhood first appear in chalk in a transient fashion that could be mistaken for the work of a child, but slowly foreign signs become new markers of the landscape, even indicating the way to traditional Parisian landmarks. But what happens if foreign signs give way to the creation of new landmarks, public structures such as mosques? In Switzerland new construction has provoked political action. In 2008, the *Schweizerische Volkspartei* (SVP; Swiss People's Party) successfully gathered 115,000 signatures to add a constitutional amendment banning the construction of minarets in the country; the referendum was approved in November 2009.[27] Currently only two mosques, one in Geneva and one in Zurich, have minarets. The SVP has a strong anti-immigrant platform, and SVP advertisements from 2007 figure three white sheep on a background of the Swiss flag who are literally kicking a 'black sheep' off the flag under the heading *'Sicherheit schaffen'* ('Achieve security').[28]

Despite the gently cartoonish appearance of the sheep, the depictions of black and white sheep also clearly figure race, and have been widely criticised as racist and xenophobic. The SVP, however, argues that Switzerland itself is the target of aggression by Muslim immigrants and that the minarets are 'symbols of political-religious imperialism' having little or nothing to do with religion.[29] By arguing that minarets have no religious significance, supporters of the minaret ban are attempting to undermine any comparison between minarets and church bell towers. A graphic exemplifying literature for the committee behind the initiative figures the minaret as a weapon, as one pierces a map of Switzerland as though launched through it, visually tearing the fabric of the country. This sort of imagery stands in opposition to the idea of the palimpsest, in which meaning is layered. In the palimpsest, while earlier forms may be harder to see, they are not destroyed.

The arguments deployed by supporters of the Swiss anti-minaret initiative have much in common with Geert Wilders's contention, cited above, that Muslim immigrants are 'colonising' the Netherlands. In his anti-Islamisation film, *Fitna* (2008), Wilders begins with inflammatory citations from the Koran and then moves to images of the presence of immigrant culture in the Netherlands. These images are presented in a way that suggests not peaceful co-existence, but rather the impending doom of autochthonous Dutch culture. Footage of women in burkas pushing baby carriages is overlaid with a graphic charting an ever-increasing Muslim population in the Netherlands. Other intercut images are of satellite dishes being installed, representing the immigrant communities' connection to outside rather than Dutch communications; uniformed Dutch policemen are shown taking off their shoes when entering a mosque, symbolising the state's capitulation to Muslim custom. Also shown are women in headscarves walking behind a heterosexual couple demonstrating their affection publically on a park bench, again figured not as a sign of tolerant co-existence, but as an illustration of the incompatibility of Dutch sexual openness with the custom of the hijab. Finally, a segment entitled 'The Netherlands under the Spell of Islam' features multiple shots of Dutch mosques and minarets. It concludes with an image of a 'postcard' with the message '*Groeten uit Nederland*' (Greetings from the Netherlands). The postcard has images of these mosques superimposed over it. Intended to represent a takeover of Holland by Muslims (www.themoviefitna.com; accessed 8 October 2008), the image operates through a central assumption that there existed a 'natural' Dutch landscape, but that that landscape, and by extension the culture, is being altered and even destroyed.

Similar arguments and imagery are in play in Cologne in the controversy over construction of a 'mega-mosque', which when completed
will be Germany's largest. Although there has been much successful
fundraising for the mosque, including by prominent Christian groups,
the proposed construction has generated controversy in the press, as
well as protests, spearheaded by the group Pro-Köln (Pro-Cologne).[30]
The group uses Cologne Cathedral as its symbol, and its literature often
visually contrasts the cathedral to the image of a mosque.

The cathedral's Christian symbolism is recognised well beyond
the Cologne community; it is a UNESCO World Heritage Site, and
UNESCO's official description of it refers directly to its symbolic value:
'Apart from its exceptional intrinsic value and the artistic masterpieces
it contains, Cologne Cathedral testifies to the enduring strength of
European Christianity.'[31] Pro-Köln posters figure the two places of
worship superimposed on each other, as the construction of the mosque
is seen as the imposition of Islam on a Christian city in which Islam, and
Muslims, really have no place.

Others have stressed that the mosque is a political rather than a
religious symbol. In a debate on the construction, the noted German
writer Ralph Giordano protested against the idea of a central mosque,
which he feels gives a 'false signal' that Muslims are integrated into
German society while, he believes, in fact integration has failed.
Noting that Cologne has fifty to sixty mosques for its large Muslim
population, he rejects the symbol of integration and equality that a
large, central mosque would assume, and he focuses on the structure's
political, rather than religious meaning. That other structures, such
as the cathedral, are also political in nature is not part of Giordano's
and similar commentaries, an omission that underscores the way in
which a normative Christian identity for Europe is so often taken for
granted.

Such interpretations of the mosque controversy are supported by
the commentary on the controversy by author Dieter Wellershoff.
In an article entitled *'Wofür steht die Kölner Moschee?'* (What does
the Cologne Mosque stand for?), Wellershoff argues that while the
proposed mosque is not as large as Cologne Cathedral, the mosque is
problematic for some because it symbolises a bringing-together of the
religious and the political: *'religiöse Gleichberechtigung'* (religious equal
rights) (*Frankfurter Allgemeine Zeitung*, 14 June 2007). Wellershoff
observes that some Cologne inhabitants seem to view the proposed
mosque as though it were a ship from outer space suddenly landing in
their neighbourhood ('wie ein dort plötzlich gelandetes Objekt aus einer

anderen Welt erchienen'), a description that calls to mind the first confused reactions of Goytisolo's fictional Parisians.

Literature distributed by supporters of the mosque's construction attempts to quell fears of an alien invasion. The Diyanet İşleri Türk İslam Birliği (DITIB; Turkish-Islamic Union for Religious Affairs), an organisation established in Cologne in 1984 that has ties to the Turkish government, is raising funds for the now-approved construction.[32] They have produced a pamphlet that carefully explains that the mosque is being built because of the structural unsuitability of current facilities. The pamphlet also emphasises that this is not a 'Zentralmosque' (Central Mosque), as some detractors have deemed it, but a mosque in Cologne's centre. The DITIB's pamphlet also provides a scale-drawing demonstrating how the mosque and its minarets will be many metres shorter than noted Cologne landmarks, including the cathedral. The most notable image on the pamphlet, however, is a colour photograph of two fair-skinned young children, a little girl and a little boy, standing on stools facing a large, old wall of brick, presumably the side of a building. They appear to be drawing, in chalk, the outline of a house, although the house is so tall that it seems impossible that they have created the picture entirely by themselves. The caption superimposed over the photo reads 'Aufeinander zugehen, Miteinander leben', a phrase that implies the building of mutual understanding and translates into something like 'Approach each other, coexist'; 'Aufeinander zugehen' serves as a modern call for convivencia.[33] The simplicity and impermanency of children's chalk drawings in the photo bring to mind elements in Goytisolo's satire, where the first signs of a foreign 'invasion' appear scribbled in chalk graffiti. The children's drawing could also be said to have elements of layering, as the chalk outline of a house in no way obscures the brick wall of the structure it is drawn upon, depicting a very fragile and even impermanent image of a palimpsest that seems intended to convey the mosque construction as both non-threatening and innocuous.

Of course it can be very difficult to discern that a palimpsest is layered – to see it for what it is. While groups like Pro-Köln may attempt to represent Cologne Cathedral as the cityscape's static anchor, both the famous cathedral and the cityscape are, in fact, palimpsests. The cathedral was begun in the thirteenth century, but it was continually worked upon through the nineteenth century and rebuilt after it was damaged by bombings in World War II. The cathedral's official website refers to it, in fact, as an 'ewige Baustelle', (perpetual construction site) and expresses the hope that it will long remain that way, as the continual work upon it is a sign of how highly it is valued.[34] Each layer of the cathedral's growth builds upon a medieval foundation, but adds new layers of significance on both the religious and secular levels as well as to local, regional and global meaning. If the cathedral has an 'eternal essence', that essence is change itself; this beautiful and imposing structure has been built through centuries of growth and through both peaceful and violent change.

The notion of place as palimpsest allows us to acknowledge the hand of the dead in the land of the living. An acknowledgement of such layering can also, however, lead to controversy over precedence, as places of worship literally have been layered on to one another. In Spain, a famous example of a culturally layered architectural site proves just how contentious these disputes can be. Muslims in Córdoba have been prohibited to pray in the Mezquita de Córdoba, a cathedral converted from a mosque in 1236, when Córdoba fell to Christian forces; the mosque itself was originally a church in Visigothic Spain (construction began around 600 CE). The site's multilayered history is still evident in its architecture,[35] which can be seen as physically embodying the controversy over the nature and inheritance of Iberia that is argued out in the speeches of Aznar and the pages of El País.

One insight that postcolonial medievalism affords is a clear view of Europe and its many landmarks as palimpsests in themselves. Novalis's idealised vision of a unified Christendom, referenced to in one the epigraphs to this chapter, never really existed. Alternatively, as recent historiography of al-Andalus has shown, even if one accepts the idea of convivencia, cultural conflict between groups, negotiation and even violence were also part of how people functioned together. The supplanting of one religious community by another, as in the history of the Mezquita de Córdoba, is itself layered, as are histories of co-existence. Landmarks that remain from medieval times can be understood as examples of 'architectural wounding' or as physical artifacts of historical development and change, depending on perspective. Clean lines and simple divisions, such as Huntington's, cannot convey the complexity of Europe's landscapes (or, I would assert, of any other landscapes). Where, for example, can we place Jews and Judaism in Huntington's seven-civilisation scheme?

The landscape of Europe's 'Jewish Question' is indeed complex, and some of those layers, specifically physical traces of European Jewry, have been destroyed or scattered to the winds – or they lie hidden in the ground. The major symbols of the Cologne mosque controversy are a cathedral and a mosque. Images of the Cologne synagogues destroyed in *Kristallnacht* ('Night of Broken Glass'), 9 November 1938, a pogrom that many historians regard as the beginning of the Shoah, do not figure prominently in its discourse but this act of memoricide still shapes the debate. The Holocaust is arguably the controversy's crucial subtext and, indeed, the crucial subtext for all debates about race, racism and cultural prejudice in Germany. A 2009 film by Pro-Köln compared the party to the persecuted German-Jewish population under National Socialism in a way that is, at the very best, characterised as brazen and ludicrous.[36] Ralph Giordano, a noted German-Jewish author, has, nevertheless, dismissed the group as Cologne's 'local variety of contemporary National Socialism', and the group's leaders have been accused of having Neo-Nazi ties.[37] Giordano has himself voiced strenuous opposition to the mosque, and his objections have received notable press coverage, arguably not only because of his intellectual stature but also because of his status as a Holocaust survivor. Cologne has been said to be the home of the oldest Jewish community in Germany, with roots dating back to the fourth century, and so its landscape holds many memories and bears many scars, including those of the 1424 Jewish expulsion from the city and the ravages of the Shoah.[38]

Such scars of memoricide exist throughout Europe. An instructive example takes us back to York, discussed in relation to *Ivanhoe* in Chapter 2. I noted how the novel obscures the history of the 1190 massacre of Jews at Clifford Tower even as details of the event seem to emerge like repressed memories through Scott's choice of narrative detail. In twentieth-century York, life imitated art, and a hidden Jewish presence also returned to light. A site thought to contain medieval Jewish remains was about to be paved over to create a car park for a Sainsbury's supermarket. The York Archaeological Trust intervened, and the site was shown to be a twelfth-century Jewish cemetery. A small plaque at the entrance to the supermarket car park now commemorates the burial site, a prosaic challenge to the death of memory.[39]

The longer history of the Jewish presence in Europe is related to the 'Islam in Europe' question on numerous levels. As Matti Bunzl has asserted in an important essay on the relationship between Islamophobia and antisemitism in Europe, Islamophobia is based on the presumption that Islam is fundamentally incompatible with European civilisation (2007). He has argued that one path to countering the intensification of Islamophobia is a more careful examination of the perceived nature of European civilisation and the historical narratives upon which it is based. I agree with Bunzl's overall argument, but his focus on the contemporary and modern periods obscures, I think, some important connections in the longer histories of antisemitism and Islamophobia. This longer view points to how Islamophobia is at once a problem across Europe and, at the same time, is often focused on notions of place and community that demonstrate again and again that Europe is not yet post-national or even on the verge of it. Specific local histories, many dating back at least into the medieval period, are still very much alive in popular imagination. And while Europeans may be seen now as predominantly secular, European civilisation is still perceived (despite the creation of 'Judeo-Christianity' as a concept) as fundamentally Christian. This is a Europe that grew out of the Christian institutions that still influence its legal and political systems, just as churches and cathedrals still mark its landscape. It is in these debates over the sites of Christian and Muslim places of worship that we have a vantage point to see the longer history of these conflicts.

I want to turn finally to some attempts to examine these issues through prose fiction. At the same time as Huntington and other theorists of international relations have been producing schematised maps of Europe's past and future landscapes for pundits and politicians, literary artists have been trying to capture and convey the complexities of the longer and often hidden histories of East and West.

Resisting Memoricide: Medievalisms of East and West in Contemporary Fiction

El sitio de los sitios

Juan Goytisolo coins the term 'memoricide' ('el memoricidio') in an essay with that title about his visit to war-ravaged Sarajevo (1993). The piece is part of a collection of essays previously published in the Spanish daily El País as Cuaderno de Sarajevo: anotaciones de un viaje a la barbarie (Sarajevo Notebook: Notes on a Journey into Barbarism).[40] The essays are accompanied by photographs of Sarajevo by Gervasio Sánchez and 'annotated' with marginal facsimiles of notes in the author's own handwriting. Through these material details the book emphasises its role as an artifact against memoricide.

Goytisolo recounts the sites of memory that he viewed as he walked through Sarajevo's bombed-out streets, such as the efforts to rebuild the sixteenth-century mosque of Gazi Husref Bey, which had survived, though severely damaged, eighty-six mortar blasts (1993: 55; 2000: 25). He then describes 'the most desolate spectacle' in Sarajevo, its famous library, which was destroyed completely in 1992:

Como señala la Oficina de Información del Gobierno de Bosnia-Herzegovina, dicho acto 'constituye el atentado más bárbaro cometido contra la cultura europea desde la Segunda Guerra Mundial.' En verdad – y tal era el propósito de la gavilla de mediocres novelistas, poetas e historiadores con vocación de pirómanos, cuyo *Informe* a la Academia de Belgrado fue el germen de la ascensión de Milosevic al poder y del subsiguiente desmembramiento de Yugoslavia – dicho crimen no puede ser definido cabalmente sino como *memoricidio*. Puesto que toda huella islámica debe ser extirpada del territorio de la Gran Serbia, la biblioteca, memoria colectiva del pueblo musulmán bosnio, estaba condenada *a priori* a desaparecer en las llamas de la vengadora *purificación*. (1993: 55–6)

As the press office of the government of Bosnia-Herzegovina points out, this act 'constitutes the most barbarous attack on European culture since the Second World War.' The fact is that a band of mediocre novelists, poets, and historians with a vocation as arsonists, whose report to the Belgrade Academy was the seed of Milošević's rise to power and the subsequent breakup of Yugoslavia – the crime cannot be properly described except as *memoricide*. Since every trace of Islam must be removed from the territory of Greater Serbia, the Library, the collective memory of the Bosnian Muslim people, was condemned a priori to disappear in the avenging, purifying flames. (2000: 25)

The destructive and avenging flames seem to be an attempt at revenge against the Ottoman Empire, a purification of a 'Christian territory' that recalls the Reconquista.[41] Two photographs of the ruins of the library appear in the book's collection of photographs, captioned by very similar descriptions. One photograph shows a broad band of light streaming into the library, reminiscent of medieval images of the Annunciation. Here, however, the streaming light serves to sanctify the image of the ruins of *'la memoria colectiva de los musulmanes bosnios'* (the collective memory of Bosnian Muslims), using Christian iconography to critique the 'clash' between Muslims and Christians that has led to this destruction.

Goytisolo goes on to describe the treasures destroyed in the bombing and also to relate a conversation with a leader of the Jewish community, who describes the deportation and murder of Sarajevo Jews by the Nazis and then this more recent transformation of Sarajevo from a 'Little Jerusalem', a model of co-existence, into a ghetto where there is not even a place to bury the dead properly. Sarajevo has been transformed from a place where cultures could live together to one where not even the dead can co-exist.

Goytisolo returns to the themes from the 'Sarajevo Notebook' essays in his 1995 novel, *El sitio de los sitios*, which appeared in English in 2002 as *State of Siege*. *Sitio* in Spanish can mean both 'place' and 'siege', so the title could be translated in multiple ways, as befits its complex structure. The story begins when a Spaniard named JG arrives in Sarajevo and then is presumably killed by a mortar shell when his hotel room overlooking Sniper's Alley is hit, although the body cannot be found. A UN military official who is attempting to investigate JG's death is joined in the second half of the novel by a scholar. Goytisolo introduces him along with his description of the destruction of the Sarajevo library, where not only priceless manuscripts but also all of his research on the medieval saint Ben Sidi Abu Al-Makârim have been lost. The structure of the novel evokes a medieval figure, a twelfth-century Sufi mystic and philosopher, Ibn Arabi, from whom Goytisolo draws the strong connection between real and dream worlds in his text (Black 2004: 241).

As the novel unfolds, shifting between real and dream worlds, it turns out that the mysterious JG was not a Spaniard after all; he was actually a Moroccan with the same name as the saint whom the scholar is researching. His poems, discovered posthumously, turn out to reproduce verbatim those composed by the scholar. The scholar attempts to unravel the mystery, feeling (like the reader) as though he is 'a fly trapped in a very finely woven textual spiderweb' (2002: 109). ['Me sentía como una mosca atrapada en la urdimbre de una finísima telaraña textual' (1995: 146)]. Goytisolo creates a labyrinth of identities, a perplexing and disturbing mixture of connections and alienations across time and cultures. The poems, collected in an appendix as if in a scholarly tome, act as their own new fragments against memoricide, the destruction of the memory of Muslim presence in Sarajevo.[42]

More accessible in the novel than the twists and turns of the murdered poet's identity is its satire, which critiques the European indifference to Sarajevo's plight that Goytisolo referenced in the essay 'Memoricide'. In the novel, the unfolding fate of a down-at-the-heels Paris *arrondissement* begins much like the 'takeover' of Le Sentier in Goytisolo's earlier novel: graffiti scrawled in foreign tongues intimates troubles to come. In this case, those troubles are enormous. Just like Sarajevo, this Parisian district falls under a full-scale siege. Metro stations are closed, barbed wire fences are erected, and bullets whizz through the air. District residents are cut off from the rest of the city and then begin a process of singling out immigrants that a resident 'pensioner of Jewish origin' links directly back to the Nazi occupation of Paris during World War II (2002: 55; 1995: 75).

The Parisian siege is portrayed as a frightening yet ironic parallel

to that of Sarajevo. Just as Sarajevo has lost its mosques and libraries, events rendered in horrifying detail in other sections of the novel,
Parisian district landmarks are violently destroyed:

> Un obús se había estrellado en el gran cine de la esquina contiguo al inmue-
> ble – clausurado desde el inicio del cerco – provocando el derrumbe de su
> emblemática y refulgente torre, orgullo del distrito. Aquel ataque, sin obje-
> tivo militar alguno, les apabulló. El cine se hallaba en el mismísimo bulevar,
> en la primera línea del frente: no podía atribuirse por tanto a un error de
> tiro. Habían apuntado a ciencia y conciencia, para despojar el barrio de
> lo que fue su símbolo: un auténtico memoricidio! Minutos después, los
> morteros y lanzagranadas completaron la labor destructiva: las luminarias
> y viejos carteles descoloridos de filmes de Walt Disney y Vanesa Paradise se
> desplomaron. (1995: 77)

> A shell had exploded in the gigantic movie theater – closed since the
> beginning of the siege – on the corner adjacent to the building, causing
> its glowing emblematic tower, the pride of the district, to collapse. That
> attack, with no military objective whatsoever, stupefied them. The movie
> theater was located right on the boulevard, on the front line: therefore its
> destruction could not be attributed to erroneous targeting. It had been
> aimed, consciously and deliberately, in order to deprive the district of what
> had been its symbol: a real act of memoricide! Minutes later, mortars and
> grenade launchers finished the work of demolition: the neon signs and
> faded old posters advertising Walt Disney and Vanessa Paradis came tum-
> bling down. (2002: 56–7)

Virtually ignoring the siege, the global media that the theatre embod-
ied does not mourn the loss of the district as the residents mourn their
multiplex. By the end of this section of the novel, the siege has already
endured for 1,001 days, and one can barely find it mentioned on radio
or television – 'Tragedies that go on for too long are boring' (2002:
50) ['Las tragedias que duran demasiado abburen' (1995: 68)]. As in
Paisajes después de la batalla (Landscapes after the Battle), a detached
narrative voice presents the views of narrow-minded or racist residents
under siege through the filter of its nameless narrator, a former *flâneur,*
especially through his discussions with his neighbour.

The section concludes with the narrator reading a Paris 'Entertainment
Guide', which lists movies, concerts, museums, Seine boat tours, and so
on, and he finds that his district does not receive an asterisk rating like
the others, but instead is 'marked with a little square indicating that a
visit to it was not worthwhile, contrasted with the others by virtue of
its brevity. It read: DISTRICT UNDER SIEGE' (2002: 59). ['La cor-
respondiente al suyo, marcada con el cuadrito indicativo de que se

desaconsejaba la visita, contrastaba con las restantes por su laconismo: DISTRITO SITIADO' (1995: 80).] No longer of interest to tourists and consumers, this district fades into oblivion, suffering a fate as cruel as that of Cambodia or Rwanda or Bosnia, but suffering it ironically in the 'homeland of human rights' (2002: 47) ['la patria de los derechos humanos' (1995: 64)]. Goytisolo takes the 'clash of civilisations' to the heart of Europe through his fictional 'district under siege', demonstrating that a common humanity should not know ethnic and religious borderlines. By turning European indifference on its head in the quintessential European city, he explodes the hypocrisy of Europe's lack of reaction to Sarajevo's fate.

The medievalisms of his novel, its allusions to Muslim mysticism and philosophy, attest to the long-standing Muslim presence in Europe, a presence as intricately interwoven as the spiderweb structure of his postmodern novel. As structurally fragmented as his narrative is, it becomes an artifact meant to counter acts of memoricide, like the destruction of the library, a fragile but still powerful challenge to find links across times, locations and cultures.

The Moor's Last Sigh

> Ah, the dead, the unended, endlessly ending dead: how long, how rich is their story. We, the living, must find what space we can alongside them; the giant dead whom we cannot tie down, though we grasp at their hair, though we rope them while they sleep.
>
> Must we also die before our souls, so long suppressed, can find utterance – before our secret natures can be known? To whom it may concern, I say No, and again I say, No Way. When I was young I used to dream . . . of peeling off my skin plantain-fashion, of going forth naked into the world, like an anatomy illustration from *Encyclopaedia Britannica*, all ganglions, ligaments, nervous pathways and veins, set free from the otherwise inescapable jails of colour, race and clan. . .
>
> So, in writing this, I must peel off history, the prison of the past.' (Rushdie 1995:136)

These words are uttered by 'Moor', Moraes Zogoiby, the narrator of Salman Rushdie's *The Moor's Last Sigh* (1995).[43] The novel, so rich in allusion that it could be seen itself as a kind of palimpsest, tells the story of the Catholic da Gama family, Indian spice merchants with Iberian roots. Moor is the son of Aurora, a talented painter, and Abraham, a Jewish businessman who can trace his lineage back to Boabdil, the Muslim ruler whose legendary 'last sigh' signified the fall of Granada.

Using the da Gama family history and Aurora's artwork, Rushdie weaves the story of medieval Iberia into a fictional account of a family and of Indian history.

The novel is framed by the conceit of Moor's own writing of his personal history while in captivity and, upon his escaping, his nailing of it page by page to trees in the Spanish countryside. Moor has fled India for Spain in search of stolen paintings of his mother's that depict their family history in the context of medieval Spanish history. He ends up being imprisoned by the artist Vasco Miranda, once a protégé and perhaps a lover of Aurora, who has fallen out with her and moved to Spain. Miranda resides in a mansion modelled on the Alhambra, the most famous architectural landmark of al-Andalus and a principal subject of some of Aurora's paintings. Moor's attempt to peel back the layers of his own life, to recover his mother's paintings and learn the identity of her killer, functions as a palimpsest on a literal level (the killer's identity is hidden in a palimpsest in one of her paintings) and also on a figurative one, as Moor wrestles with his own identity. His efforts to discover what lies behind his own 'overneath', however, seem to be in vain (180). Rather than being constituted by an essential core, Moor himself seems to be a composite figure.

Even while it seems to show that for Moor, there may be 'no there there' when all the layers are removed, the novel celebrates the palimpsest and, by extension, the hybrid cultures figured in Aurora's landscapes. Not only characters or artworks are portrayed as palimpsests, but also places: the twin sites of Granada and Bombay. At the novel's end Moor flees a Bombay under siege for the Spain that his mother referred to as 'Palimpstine' or 'Mooristan'. He is off in search of the place 'whence we had been cast out, centuries ago', wondering if in fleeing the place of his birth he is not finally arriving home and asking if Spain might not turn out to be 'my lost home, my resting-place, my promised land? Might it not be my Jerusalem?' (376).

Moor again ponders his own identity as he gazes out upon the Spanish countryside:

> I tried to imagine this landscape as it might have been when our remote ancestors had been here . . . Benengeli, a ribbon of white walls and red roofs, lay above us on its hillside, looking much as it would have looked all those centuries ago. *I am a Jew from Spain, like the philosopher Maimonides*, I told myself, to see if the words rang true. They sounded hollow. Maimonides's ghost laughed at me. *I am like the Catholicised Córdoba mosque*, I experimented. *A piece of Eastern architecture with a Baroque cathedral stuck in the middle of it.* That sounded wrong, too.

> I was a nobody from nowhere, like no-one, belonging to nothing. That sounded better. That felt true. All my ties had loosened. I had reached an anti-Jerusalem: not a home, but an away. A place that did not bind, but dissolved. (388)

This passage is itself a palimpsest of reference and allusion. Benengeli, the fictional town Moor travels to, alludes to the Moorish author from whose work Miguel Cervantes claimed to have created *Don Quixote*. The allusion draws attention to the genre of the novel, which *Don Quixote* is often seen as initiating, and to the framing device of *The Moor's Last Sigh*: the narrative that unfolds is recounted through Moor's own prison manuscript. Alluding to the alleged Moorish roots of Cervantes's classic Spanish text also calls attention to the hybrid roots Cervantes claims for his work, a gesture echoed in reference to Maimonides (1135–1204), the renowned rabbi philosopher of Córdoba who lived at what many consider the end of the 'golden age' of medieval Spanish Jewry.

Like Moor, Maimonides died in exile, having chosen to flee Spain rather than convert to Islam. His scholarship, considered monumental in the Jewish tradition, is steeped in the work of classical Greek and Arabic philosophy and was later influential on the medieval Christian philosophers known as the scholastics, including Thomas Aquinas. Maimonides, revered in so many traditions, seems to scorn Moor, laughing at Moor's attempt at self-comparison. Moor then reflects upon a comparison to the contested Mezquita de Córdoba, figured here less as a palimpsest than as a hodgepodge. In the end, though, Moor finds himself like neither of these Spanish landmarks. He is untethered; he has not found his Jerusalem – that city of palimpsests claimed by so many as home that its very name can represent homecoming – but instead its opposite. Without the lodestar of Bombay, it seems, he has lost his moorings in both time and space, although it is not clear whether this dissolution is positive or negative (383).

Moor's trip west, though, is not quite as random an exile as the above passage might imply. Iberia is a special place for Moor not only because his father's family fled it or because it was his mother who originally gave him the ticket and visa to go there. His mother's family, the da Gamas, take their name from the Portuguese explorer Vasco da Gama (c. 1460–9), known for his establishment of sea routes between Europe and India.[44] The da Gamas' name is also synonymous with exploitation and the beginning of colonialism. At the novel's opening, as Moor begins his story, he says, incongruously, 'And to begin with, pass the pepper', continuing:

I repeat: the pepper, if you please; for if it had not been for peppercorns, then what is ending now in East and West might never have begun. Pepper it was that brought Vasco da Gama's tall ships across the ocean, from Lisbon's Tower of Belém to the Malabar Coast: first to Calicut and later, for its lagoony harbour, to Cochin. English and French sailed in the wake of that first-arrived Portugee, so that in the period called Discovery-of-India – but how could we be discovered when we were not covered before? – we were 'not so much sub-continent as sub-condiment,' as my distinguished mother had it. 'From the beginning, what the world wanted from bloody mother India was daylight-clear,' she'd say. 'They came for the hot stuff, just like any man calling on a tart.' (4–5)

The passage's critique of Eurocentrism ('how could we be discovered when we were not covered before?') plays on the image of a layering that is part of a palimpsest and also reveals the material motivations for voyages of 'discovery', reminding readers of the role these early trade routes played in the beginnings of colonialism.

Moor's concluding trip to Spain inverts Vasco da Gama's original eastward journey. The novel's final section, which recounts this journey, is also entitled 'The Moor's Last Sigh'. The section alludes to works by writers from former Spanish colonies including the Mexican writers Juan Rulfo and Carlos Fuentes.[45] It is through allusion to Bram Stoker's *Dracula*, though, that Moor's passage from East to West is shown as a journey motivated not only by necessity and personal longing, but also by a passage into the West's heart of darkness. Moor finds a region tainted by Francoist repression, empty global capitalism, the lingering legacy of the Reconquista.

There are numerous nods to *Dracula* in this final section, most obviously through the figure of the 'Nazi' Helsing, who alludes to the vampire hunter Van Helsing. The strange cab ride that Moor makes into town parallels the eerie carriage ride that the protagonist Jonathan Harker takes to Dracula's castle, where he soon finds himself a prisoner. At Vasco's mansion, Moor encounters strange female servants who are reminiscent of the young women who mysteriously attempt to attack Harker in Dracula's castle. All of these details create a connection between the journeys that open *Dracula* and close *The Moor's Last Sigh* respectively. Moor's journey, though, is very pointedly in the opposite direction from Harker's. *Dracula* begins with a passage from Harker's journal in which he describes his trip eastward from Munich:

The impression I had was that we were leaving the West and entering the East; the most western of splendid bridges over the Danube, which is here of noble width and depth, took us among the traditions of Turkish rule. (Stoker 1897: 1)

Harker's journey eastward takes him into the Balkans, a region that is, like Spain, so often excluded from definitions of Europe on account of its connection to Muslim rule. Stoker figures the region as the source of an evil menace that spreads westward, much like the Ottoman rule that had attempted to move as far west as Vienna. In *The Moor's Last Sigh*, the evils of imperialism have spread from West to East, from the site of one destroyed golden age to another. Vasco Miranda seems a parallel to Count Dracula, but the real monsters in this scenario are Ferdinand and Isabella, who insisted on monolithic Catholic domination in Spain by expelling Muslims and Jews and whose imperial ventures launched centuries of colonialism.

Aurora's art celebrates Spain's lost golden age and uses it to figure an Indian *convivencia* in the post-colonial period. Moor describes one of her creations:

> Around and about the figure of the Moor in his hybrid fortress she wove her vision, which in fact was a vision of *weaving*, or more accurately interweaving. In a way these were polemical pictures, in a way they were an attempt to create a romantic myth of the plural hybrid nation; she was using Arab Spain to re-imagine India, and this land-sea-scape in which the land could be fluid and the sea stone-dry was her metaphor – idealised? sentimental? probably – of the present, and the future, that she hoped would evolve. (227)

Aurora's utopic visions link past, present and future in Iberia and India, specifically through Granada and Bombay. Depicting Bombay through medieval Granada, she links a 'not-quite-Alhambra' with 'the Mughal palace-fortresses in Dehli and Agra' (226) to create a vision of a 'golden age' *convivencia* in which 'Jews, Christians, Muslims, Parsis, Sikhs, Buddhists, Jains' can mingle together freely; this vision is symbolised by Sultan Boabdil whose 'old skin dropped from him chrysalis-fashion, standing revealed as a glorious butterfly, whose wings were a miraculous composite of all the colours in the world' (227). Revealed in Aurora's painting is that possibility that Moor seeks, freedom 'from the otherwise inescapable jails of colour, race and clan', and, indeed, his own image appears in these paintings.

These idealised hybrids clash with and are threatened by other visions, including those of Raman Fielding, who is also rumoured to be one of Aurora's former lovers. Fielding leads a group of right-wing extremists, the MA, modelled on the group Shiv Sena (Loomba 1998b: 154).

Fielding has a very different vision of a golden age from Aurora; he sees the palimpsestic sites (or imagined layered sites) created by Mughal rule in India as incitements to destruction in the name of restoration. Fielding speaks,

> Of a golden age 'before the invasions' when good Hindu men and women could roam free. Now our freedom, our beloved nation, is buried beneath the things the invaders have built. This true nation is what we must reclaim from beneath the layers of alien empires. (299)

Here we find another view of the palimpsest, one in which a claim to an older layer is seen as a claim to political power justified by temporal priority. Moor relates that it is through Fielding that he

> first heard of the existence of a list of sacred sites at which the country's Muslim conquerors had deliberately built mosques on the birthplaces of various Hindu deities – and not only . . . Where was a deity to go for a decent evening out? All the prime sites had been hogged by minarets and onion domes. It would not do! The gods had rights, too and must be given back their ancient way of life. The invaders would have to be repulsed. (299)

This somewhat comical speech relates to a deadly serious actual event referenced in the novel, the 1992 attack on Babri mosque in Ayodhya, which was destroyed by a crowd that had originally gathered to dedicate a Hindu temple. Moor does not witness this event, but it is in keeping with the increasing violence and chaos in his own life as his own story intertwines with the story of India. He speaks of the destruction of the mosque as having the effect of a 'corrosive acid of the spirit' on the country, an 'adversarial intensity' that destroys a spirit of co-existence in Bombay (351).

A longing for this Bombay that used to co-exist in peace appears throughout chapter 18, with the phrase 'Bombay was central' repeated throughout like a refrain, expressing nostalgia for a city that has fallen as Granada fell:

> Bombay was central; had always been. Just as the fanatical Catholic Kings' had besieged Granada and awaited the Alhambra's fall, so now barbarism was standing at our gates . . . Like Granada – al-Gharnatah of the Arabs – you were the glory of your time. But a darker time came upon you, and just as Boabdil, the last Nasrid Sultan, was too weak to defend his great treasure, so we, too, were proved wanting. For the barbarians were not only at our gates but within our skins. We were our own wooden horses, each one of us full of our doom. (372)

The Reconquista becomes a metaphor for sectarian strife in India, as Bombay becomes like the lost al-Andalus. By alluding throughout the text to the Trojan horse and that other infamous lost city, Troy, Moor lays blame for the destruction of Bombay on himself and his fellow inhabitants. Focusing again on the idea of an elusive inner being beneath an outer layer of skin, Moor implies that that very inner being that he has so long wanted to free is lacking. Like his ancestor Boabdil, Moor is unable to keep his paradise safe and secure.

Moor mourns a lost *convivencia* typified by the story that it was a Muslim worshipper who 'first claimed to see a vision of Lord Ram, and so started the ball rolling; what could be a finer image of religious tolerance and plurality than that?' (363). Here, it seems, the essential being beneath the skin that Moor has fantasised about is a traitor from within dooming any chance for peace. And the belligerence is not uni-directional: Moor describes the torrent of hate and violence unleashed by both Hindus and Muslims upon each other after destruction of the Babri mosque (365).

Using a ticket and travel papers to Spain that his mother had given him, Moor flees a Bombay that is literally exploding with violence. He is also going on the search for his mother's painting, *The Moor's Last Sigh*, which is stolen just after the destruction of the mosque. A member of Raman Fielding's political party

> linked the mosque's fall and the pictures' disappearance 'When such alien artefacts disappear from India's holy soil, let no man mourn,' he said. 'If the new nation is to be born, there is much invader-history that may have to be erased.' (364)

Moor's final words, a confession of his life written out as he is imprisoned by the artist who stole his mother's paintings, serves as a means to prevent the erasure of memory; not only the memory of his mother, the mystery of whose death he has solved, but a memory of the values of co-existence and tolerance that she imagined through her art. Moor's last sigh, his final words, are spoken as he completes the nailing of his 'theses' (3) to trees in the forest, and he then sights, at long last, the actual Alhambra palace.

> And so I left my story nailed to the landscape in my wake . . . Thorns, branches and stones tore at my skin. I paid no attention to these wounds; if my skin was falling from me at last, I was happy to shed that load. And so I sit here in the last light, upon this stone, among these olive-trees, gazing out across a valley towards a distant hill; and there it stands, the glory of the Moors, their triumphant masterpiece and their last redoubt. The Alhambra, Europe's red fort, sister to Delhi's and Agra's – the palace of interlocking forms and secret wisdom, of pleasure-courts and water-gardens, that

monument to a lost possibility that nevertheless has gone on standing, long after its conquerors have fallen; like a testament to lost but sweetest love, to the love that endures beyond defeat, beyond annihilation, beyond despair; to the defeated love that is greater than what defeats it, to that most profound of our needs, to our need for flowing together, for putting an end to frontiers, for the dropping of the boundaries of the self . . . I watch it vanish in the twilight, and in its fading it brings tears to my eyes. (433)

While the novel has not provided any sure answers to questions of self, identity and what truly lies underneath layers of palimpsest on the level of both the individual and of culture, it uses the Alhambra, which is figured as integral to the landscape of Spain, as a place signifying a valued past and perhaps standing for future possibility. The sweetest love mentioned is, at least on one level, the love of Moor for his mother, who rejected him but has now drawn him back to her even in death.

Whether or not Moor's mother is meant to stand for the 'mother India' that her art both captured and challenged is an open question. Since this novel is the first written during Rushdie's own period in hiding after a *fatwa* was issued against him for writing the *Satanic Verses*, critics have also speculated on the personal significance of these images. The novel was banned for a time in India because of its political satire, only adding to Rushdie's controversial status. Because of the focus of this chapter, my reading here focuses on the role of Iberia in the novel, rather than the novel's Indian context or Shakespearean allusion. All of these levels of reading and more are possible. I want to read the pages that Moor nails in the dark wood, pages that recount his story, his family's history and the intertwined stories of India and Iberia, as fragile attempts to resist violent memoricide, the destruction of not only individual, but cultural memories. These memories, through Moor's posting of them in the Spanish forest, become, like Goytisolo's novel, their own landmarks, linking histories of East and West.

The Islam Quintet

Tariq Ali's 'Islam Quintet' consists of five novels that attempt to provide new visions of the relationship between 'Islam and the West'. The four that have already appeared are set in the past, while the fifth, which is to be set in the post-9/11 era, has not been published at the time of writing this.[46] Each of the four historical novels focuses on a specific moment in history of 'Islam and the West', beginning with the fall of Granada to the Reconquista in *Shadows of the Pomegranate Tree* (1993); the Second Crusade in *The Book of Saladin* (1998); Norman Sicily in *A Sultan in*

Palermo (2005); and the decay of the Ottoman empire at the end of the nineteenth century in *The Stone Woman* (2000). Each is narrated by a privileged figure who is also something of an outsider. Through explorations of fictional or fictionalised figures whose lives intersect with important historical developments, Ali challenges monolithic figurations of 'Islamic civilisation'.

The *Shadows of the Pomegranate Tree* opens with the destruction of thousands of manuscripts by the forces of the Reconquista as Granada falls:

> Several thousand copies of the Koran, together with learned commentaries and theological and philosophical reflections on its merits and demerits, all crafted in the most exquisite calligraphy, were carted away indiscriminately by the men in uniform. Rare manuscripts vital to the entire architecture of intellectual life in al-Andalus, were crammed in makeshift bundles on the backs of soldiers. (2)

Some soldiers, however, 'perhaps because they had never been taught to read or write, understood the enormity of the crime they were helping to perpetuate', and they purposely drop 'a few manuscripts in front of tightly sealed doors' (3). Because of their lack of knowledge they leave the books that weigh the most rather than the ones most valued by the learned, but their 'instinctive decency' saves these texts.

I will not provide extended readings of all four novels here but, like this episode, each focuses both on place and on the cultural memory preserved through writing and intellectual and artistic production. *A Sultan in Palermo*, for example, narrates the story of the famous cartographer al-Idrisi and his relationship to Roger of Sicily, the Norman king who was learned in Arabic language and literature. An Arabic version of al-Homa, Homer, plays a crucial role in the story. *The Book of Saladin* is the story of a fictional Jewish writer, Isaac Ibn Yakub, who is friends with Maimonides and who becomes the personal scribe of Saladin as that legendary ruler moves to recapture Jerusalem. *The Stone Woman* presents a family immersed in intellectual debates as their empire decays before their eyes.

Each novel attempts to capture the intellectual and cultural world of a specific time and place and provides a fictionalised fleshing-out of many of the situations and connections explored by scholars of postcolonial medieval studies. The epilogue to *Shadows*, for example, demonstrates in one powerful page the connection between the forces of the Reconquista in Spain and the Conquistadors in the Americas. Within the body of the text, the reader has already encountered the brutal deeds of a leader of the Christian forces in Granada, Cortes. The epilogue finds Cortes in the New World smiling as he embarks on a campaign of exploitation and destruction. In Ali's dramatic shorthand, we find the central idea of scholar Jonathan Boyarin's important new work, *The Unconverted Self* (2009), which demonstrates concretely this connection between how Catholic Spain treated religious Others in its home territories and in ones beyond its shores.

Ali's novels, which are much more traditional in structure than those of Goytisolo and Rushdie do not play on their own status as artifacts that preserve memory, but they nevertheless celebrate texts and works of art: Idrisi's famous map of the world for Roger; Homer's text preserved in Arabic; Ibn Yakub's fictional life of Saladin; and the beloved statue of the Stone Woman. Each of his novels is centred on a specific location and time, the complex and hybrid nature of which can be seen as emblematised in these works of art. The novels themselves attempt to make these worlds accessible in order to demonstrate intimate connections between 'Islam and the West' that neither simplify nor demonise these relationships.

In an Antique Land

I want to conclude by returning to Amitav Ghosh's *In an Antique Land*, a novel in which the main action takes place not in Europe, but in Egypt. Europe plays a more peripheral role, acting as a negative force that, among other things, plays a key part in the dismantling of a repository of cultural memory, the Cairo Geniza. Ghosh's novel, published in 1992, also deals with religious and communal strife, with questions of memory and questions of place.

In an episode near the end of the book, the narrator, Amitav, who is modelled on Ghosh, attempts to visit the shrine of a Jewish holy man in Egypt, Abu-Hasira, whose memory is celebrated annually with a lively festival. He misses the actual festival, the *mowlid*, but is taken to the site by cab. The site is not at all what he expected, not a 'domed tomb, with some candles burning outside perhaps, and a few people gathered outside the grave', but a compound guarded by soldiers ([1992] 1994: 333). The soldiers mistrust Amitav's presence, since he is not Jewish, Muslim or Christian, but Indian. He is then taken to a building that 'seemed very much in the style of colonial offices in India with high ceilings and arched windows: it took no great prescience to tell that it had probably been initiated into its current uses during the British occupation of Egypt' (338). An officer questions him with suspicion; he cannot understand why an

Indian would be visiting the Egyptian tomb of a Jewish holy man. Amitav has been, as I described in Chapter 2, on the historical trail of Bomma and Ben Yiju, an Indian slave and Jewish master from the Middle Ages. Their story appears as a brief reference in the historical record, a fragment of the historical record as fragile as the fictional pages of Moor's tale or the mysterious poems in *State of Siege*. Amitav is tempted to tell the story of his historical detective work in order to provide a link for the officer that makes sense for him of Amitav's presence in Egypt:

> He was not trying to intimidate me; I could tell he was genuinely puzzled. He seemed so reasonable and intelligent, that for an instant I even thought of telling him the story of Bomma and Ben Yiju. But then it struck me, suddenly, that there was nothing I could point to within his world that might give credence to my story – the remains of those small, indistinguishable, intertwined histories, Indian and Egyptian, Muslim and Jewish, Hindu and Muslim, had been partitioned long ago. Nothing remained in Egypt now to effectively challenge his disbelief: not a single one, for instance, of the documents of the Geniza. It was then that I began to realize how much success the partitioning of the past had achieved; that I was sitting at that desk now because the mowlid of Sidi Abu-Hasira was an anomaly within the categories of knowledge represented by those divisions. I had been straddling a border, unaware that the writing of History had predicated its own self-fulfillment. (340)

The stories of Sidi Abu-Hasira and of Bomma, so full of connections across time and across national borders, seem, by virtue of their boundary-crossings, to be too complex to unravel in any clear way. The connections are buried, lying under the weight of heavy and sometimes violently enforced partitions. The officer eventually frees Amitav, who leaves Egypt to return to his work. When he arrives in the United States, he attempts to research Sibi Abu-Hasira. The information he seeks is not, however, readily accessible:

> Looking through libraries, in search of material on Sid Abu-Hasira, I wasted a great deal of time in looking under subject headings such as 'religion' and 'Judaism' – but of course that tomb, and others like it, had long ago been wished away from those shelves, in the process of shaping them to suit the patterns of the Western academy. Then, recollecting what my interrogator had said about the difference between religion and superstition, it occurred to me to turn to the shelves marked 'anthropology' and 'folklore'. Sure enough, it was in those regions that my efforts met with their first rewards. (342)

Amitav learns, first, that Abu Hasira had been revered by both Muslims and Jews, and, second, that not far from where he had been living in

Egypt the local inhabitants had been celebrating this saint 'in defiance of the enforcers of History', that they had kept alive 'a small remnant of Bomma's world' (342). This memory, though, is hidden beneath academic divisions, which make hierarchical distinctions between 'religion' and 'folklore', distinctions that resonate with those made by Egyptians that Amitav has encountered between 'superstition' and 'real religion' (340). The medievalism here takes the form of nostalgia for a time when these distinctions did not exist and when spiritual and cultural connections could flow more freely among different groups.

Ghosh's description captures another instance of resistance against memoricide, the unlikely survival of cultural memory through both the shrine and the fragments of Bomma's history. His description of the Western academy and its potential obscurantist categories and divisions is also extremely illuminating and an important point for us to conclude upon. Postcolonial medieval studies attempts to rethink traditional categories of studies, to question periodisation, challenge the ways that the identity of Europe is conceived, and bring together texts and contexts that might, given traditional categories, seem improbable. New categories and new questions open new possibilities not only for seeing the past, for tracing the traces left by the hand of the dead, but for considering the future of the land of the living. We saw in Chapter 1 the ways in which colonialism and imperialism were related to developments in intellectual and artistic inquiry, and so too, of course, we can now observe similar developments in the postcolonial era. By re-examining 'long memories' with both appreciation and discernment and by trying to understand these memories as themselves palimpsests, postcolonial medievalisms can make new connections and open new possibilities.

Notes

1. For a generalised assessment of demographic projections in Europe, see *www.europarl.europa.eu/news/public/focus_page/047-26504-168-06-25-908-20080414FCS26499-16-06-2008-2008/default_en.htm*, accessed 17 August 2009. For a more negative view of a rising Muslim demographic in Europe, see Timothy Savage (2004). For an excellent overview of the topic, see Jenkins 2007.
2. Kelek (2005: 260). For important readings of Kelek in the context of representations of Muslims, particularly Muslim women in Germany, see Yildiz (2009 and forthcoming).
3. Christopher Caldwell (2009) has also written a book highly critical of the current state of 'Islam in Europe' that provides useful bibliography. I disagree with his conclusions, but would also not categorise the work as a polemic on the order of that by Fallaci.

4. There is a large and growing literature here. For orientation into key issues and bibliography, I have found especially useful Jenkins (2007) and Scott (2007).
5. *http://european-convention.eu.int/docs/Treaty/cv00850.en03.pdfNOTES*, accessed 29 September 2008. See also Fuller (2003) and Sciolino and Fouquet (2004).
6. For links to all of the different translations of the draft treaty, see *european-convention.eu.int/DraftTreaty.asp?lang=FR*, accessed 29 September 2008.
7. For the now classic discussion of medievalisms and 'versions' of the Middle Ages, see Eco ([1986] 2002).
8. On the ideologies of cartography, see Rabasa (1985) and Huggan (2008).
9. Huntington (1993 and 1996). For critical responses see, for example, Said (2001) and O'Hagan (2000: 135–49).
10. Gearóid Ó Tuathail also comments on this map (1996: 172). For a brilliant reading of the significance of 1453, see Lawton (2007).
11. See Menocal ([1987] 2004) and Dainotto (2007).
12. For an outstanding discussion of the 'historiographical challenge' posed by trying to fit Ottoman rule into a narrative of 'the development of European identity and civilisation', see Mazower (2000).
13. On bin Laden's declaration, see Lewis (1998). On al-Qaeda and al-Andalus, see Sennoff (2004) and Socolovsky (2005).
14. There are, of course, contemporary medieval Muslim accounts of the Crusades. See, for example, Maalouf ([1984] 2006) and the anthology by Gabrieli (1969). For an overview of nineteenth- and twentieth-century European traditions of the Crusades, see Siberry (2000).
15. For some similar observations of Muslims as 'Other', see Said (1997: 116).
16. As readily evidenced by headlines such as '*Bundeswehr: Deutsche führen Afghanistan aus dem Mittelalter*' (The Army: Germans lead Afghanistan out of the Middle Ages) (Müller, *Die Welt* online, 12 October 2008).
17. This is the idiomatic equivalent in Spanish of 'Is the coast clear?' but its reference to the coast being clear of Moors hearkens back to the days of the Reconquista, a small reminder of the Reconquista's enduring legacy.
18. The Joan of Arc video can be found at: *www.youtube.com/watch?v=l37EQ GgUszg*, accessed 25 September 2008. The *Front National*, founded in 1972 by Le Pen, began as a fringe party with strong ties to fascist groups and to *L'Algérie Française*, a group supporting French control of Algeria. For an introduction to the history and structure of the FN, see Davies (1999) and Williams (2006). On the FN's showing in the 2002 French elections, mass protests against the FN in response to this success, and the connection to the EU more broadly, see Berezin (2009).
19. On the ideology of Besson's film, see Canitz (2004).
20. *Le Monde*, 4 April 1987, cited in translation in Gross, McMurray and Swedenborg (2002: 198).
21. On ties between Le Pen and Serbian nationalists, see BBC Summary of World Broadcasts (24 January 1997), Borger (1997) and Ward (1998).
22. Njegoš's work, written in the meter of Serbian folk poetry, invokes moments in Serbian military history, including the battle of Kosovo, and celebrates the defeat of Muslim conquerors. It not only has been considered a Serbian text, but has also figured in complex ways in the literary history of Montenegro and at different times in the history of a unified Yugoslavia. For a good summary and judicious assessment of the text, see Wachtel (2003). The Balkans were part of the Byzantine and then Ottoman empires and then went through periods of political division into nationalist and communist regimes; each of these has had influence on recent history. For useful perspectives on the Balkans, see

Aleksic (2007), Bianchini and Dogo (1998), Hupchick (2002), Jelavich (1983), Mazower (2000), Ramet (2006) and Todorova (2004).

23. The pope delivered his address in his native German. The translation of the medieval dialogue that he used reads: 'Zeig mir doch, was Mohammed Neues gebracht hat, und da wirst du nur Schlechtes und Inhumanes finden wie dies, daß er vorgeschrieben hat, den Glauben, den er predigte, durch das Schwert zu verbreiten.' I cite the authorised Vatican English translation in the text. The German version of the address can be found at *www.vatican. va/holy_father/benedict_xvi/speeches/2006/september/documents/hf_ben-xvi_ spe_20060912_university-regensburg_ge.html*. The English version is at *www. vatican.va/holy_father/benedict_xvi/speeches/2006/september/documents/hf_ ben-xvi_spe_20060912_university-regensburg_en.html*. Both were accessed 25 September 2008. The official English translation seems somewhat problematic. Translating 'Schlechtes' as 'evil' rather than as 'bad' is a strong choice. 'Böse' is the usual German equivalent to 'evil'. Arguably, the English translation only heightened the offensive content of the speech for many who accessed it in English.

24. See Kruger (2006) and Maccoby (1982).

25. On Sgorbati, see *news.bbc.co.uk/2/hi/africa/5367972.stm*, accessed 25 September 2008.

26. See *www.unaoc.org*, accessed 20 September 2008.

27. The SVP was formed in 1971; its typical base of support is in German-speaking regions of Switzerland, but it is gaining support in Francophone areas (Hossay 2002: 342–3). The minaret construction ban referendum passed while this book was in production. For a discussion of the use of posters by populist parties across Europe that are engaged in the 'Islam in Europe' debate in light of the referendum's passage, including many images of the posters, see Kimmelman 2010.

28. See the image at *irregulartimes.com/wp-content/uploads/2007/10/sicherheitsch affen.jpg*, accessed 15 October 2008.

29. See Charter (2008), and *http://www.minarette.ch*, accessed 15 July 2009.

30. Pro-Köln was founded in 1996. The article is in *Der Spiegel* online: *http:// www.spiegel.de/international/germany/0,1518,526225,00.html*, accessed 17 August 2009. To see an example of Pro-Köln's political aspirations, view *http:// www.youtube.com/watch?v=kpz1R5ZevLQ* and *http://www.youtube.com/ watch?v=2QQcsSs1HxU*, both accessed 17 August 2009.

31. See *whc.unesco.org/en/list/292*, accessed 15 October 2008.

32. On the DITIP, see Fetzer and Soper (2005: 120).

33. The slogan in German has a catchy feel to it that could be captured less literally through phrasing such as 'everyone . . . live as one'. My thanks go to Helge Weissig, Nancy Nenno and Stephen Della Lana for translation suggestions. The pamphlet can be found at: *http://www.zentralmoschee-koeln.de/*, accessed 19 August 2009.

34. See *http://www.koelner-dom.de/geschichte.html*, accessed 19 August 2009: 'Deshalb ist der Dom "die ewige Baustelle" und wird es hoffentlich noch lange bleiben. Die ständigen Arbeiten am Dom belegen, wie wichtig den Menschen der Dom noch immer ist.'

35. On the mosque, see *http://news.bbc.co.uk/2/hi/europe/6213665.stm*, accessed 1 October 2008. On the issue of mosques in Germany more generally, see Schmitt (2003).

36. Pro-Köln has made a 'German *Fitna*', a propaganda film presenting its viewpoint that not only includes the comparison to the German-Jewish community in Nazi Germany, but also contrasts bucolic German landscapes with what

it labels as scenes of church ruins in Turkey. A poster for Pro-Köln's '*anti-Islamisierung*' (anti-Islamisation) conference is headlined '*Wir Sind Das Volk*' (We are the People), a slogan used during the 'Monday' demonstrations that began in Leipzig against the former East German government and led to the fall of the Berlin Wall in 1989. I would argue that just as Pro-Köln has attempted to co-opt 'victim status' by linking itself to Jews persecuted in Germany, it is also here attempting to cash in on the popularity of the movement against the East German government and connect a fight against this oppressive regime to the fight against 'Islam'. The reference to *Volk* could also be seen as resonating with both East German communist and German fascist rhetorics. The Pro-Köln poster also features a composite of Cologne Cathedral and a mosque. Footage and images can be found through its website at *http://www.pro-koeln-online.de/*, accessed 10 August 2009. On the 'Monday demonstrations' and their slogan, see Schneider (1990: 13).

37. Giordano's remark is part of a conversation in which he opposes the building of the Cologne mosque: *http://www.ksta.de/html/artikel/1176113436263.shtml*, accessed 17 August 2009.

38. The literature on German Jewry is vast. For the study of the Holocaust, a good place to begin is Friedländer (1997). On Jews in Cologne, see Wilhelm (2007).

39. On the medieval Jewish community in York, see Rahtz (1985: 42–5), Dobson ([1974] 1996: 2003). The fullest account of the cemetery at Jewbury is in Lilley et al. (1994), where a picture of the plaque can be found on page 301.

40. The English translation of the essays is included in a larger collection of Goytisolo's work, *Landscapes of War: From Sarajevo to Chechnya* (2000), which appears without the annotations or the photographs. All translations cited are from this edition. My thanks go to Ana Grinberg for her help with this passage.

41. The reference then links backs to the medieval Spanish context of Goytisolo's 1970 novel, *Reivindicación del conde don Julián* (the English translation is entitled *Count Julian*), whose title character is the figure who supposedly permitted the original Moorish invasion of Spain.

42. The similarities between the two books can likely be traced back not only to contemporary events but to Cervante's *Don Quixote*.

43. I have consulted criticism about *The Moor's Last Sigh* by Loomba (1998b), Cantor (1997), Wallhead (1997), Henighan (1998), Greenberg (1999) and Salgado (2007).

44. On malagueta pepper and the Portuguese and Spanish attempts to find routes to India, see Freedman (2008, especially 193–214).

45. Rulfo's *Pedro Páramo* (1955) and Fuentes's *Terra Nostra* (1976). See Henighan (1998).

46. For an interview with Ali about the 'Islam Quintet', see *http://www.socialistreview.org.uk/article.php?articlenumber=9871*, accessed 10 August 2009.

References

Abramczyk, Roland (1903), 'Quellen zu Walter Scotts Roman: "Ivanhoe,"' PhD, University of Leipzig.

Abu-Lughod, Janet L. (1989), *Before European Hegemony: The World System AD 1250–1350*, New York: Oxford University Press.

Abulafia, Anna Sapir (1995), *Christians and Jews in the Twelfth-Century Renaissance*, London, New York: Routledge.

Aers, David (1992), 'A whisper in the ear of early Modernists; or, reflections on literary critics writing the "history of the subject,"' in *Culture and History, 1350–1600: Essays on English Communities, Identities, and Writing*, ed. David Aers, Detroit, MI: Wayne State University Press, pp. 172–202.

Agnani, Sunil, Fernando Coronil, et al. (2007), 'Editor's column: the end of postcolonial theory?' *PMLA* 122: pp. 633–51.

Aidi, Hishaam D. (2006), 'The interference of al-Andalus: Spain, Islam, and the West,' *Social Text* 24: pp. 67–88.

Aizenberg, Edna (1980), 'Raquel y Vidas: myth, stereotype, humor,' *Hispania* 63: pp. 478–86.

Akbari, Suzanne Conklin (2000), 'From Due East to True North: Orientalism and orientation,' in *The Postcolonial Middle Ages*, ed. Jeffrey Jerome Cohen, New York: St Martin's, pp. 19–34.

—— (2004), 'The diversity of mankind in *The Book of John Mandeville*,' in *Eastward Bound: Travel and Travellers, 1050–1550*, ed. Rosamund Allen, Manchester: Manchester University Press, pp. 156–76.

—— (2005), 'Placing the Jews in late medieval English literature,' in *Orientalism and the Jews*, ed. Ivan Davidson Kalmar and Derek J. Penslar, Waltham, MA: Brandeis University Press, pp. 32–51.

Aleksic, Tatjana (2007), *Mythistory and Narratives of the Nation in the Balkans*, Newcastle: Cambridge Scholars.

Alexander, Michael (2007), *Medievalism: The Middle Ages in Modern England*, New Haven: Yale University Press.

Ali, Tariq (1993), *Shadows of the Pomegranate Tree*, London: Verso.

—— (1998), *The Book of Saladin*, London: Verso.

—— (2000), *The Stone Woman*, London: Verso.

—— (2005), *A Sultan in Palermo*. London: Verso.

Alighieri, Dante (1975), *La Divina Commedia*, ed. Giorgio Petrocchi, Torino: G. Einaudi.

—— (1996), *The Divine Comedy of Dante Alighieri*, trans. Robert M. Durling, ed. Robert M. Durling and Ronald L. Martinez, New York: Oxford University Press.

Alonso, Dámaso (1969), 'Menéndez Pidal y la Generación del 98,' *Revista de Letras* 1: pp. 209–28.

Altschul, Nadia (2008), 'Postcolonialism and the study of the Middle Ages,' *History Compass* 6: pp. 588–606.

—— (2009), 'Andrés Bello and the *Poem of the Cid*: Latin America, Occidentalism, and the foundation of Spain's "national philology",' in *Meolievalisms in the Postcolonial World: The idea of the 'Middle Ages' Outside Europe*, ed. Kathleen Davis and Nadia Altschul, Baltimore: The Johns Hopkins University Press, pp. 219–36.

American Anthropological Association (1998), 'AAA statement on race,' *American Anthropologist* 100: pp. 712–13.

Anderson, Andrew Runni (1932), *Alexander's Gate, Gog and Magog, and the Enclosed Nations*, Cambridge, MA: The Medieval Academy of America.

Anderson, Benedict [1983] (2006), *Imagined Communities: Reflections on the Origin and Spread of Nationalism*, rev. edn, New York: Verso.

Appiah, Kwame Anthony (1995), 'Race,' in *Critical Terms for Literary Study*, ed. Frank Lentricchia and Thomas McLaughlin, Chicago: University of Chicago Press, pp. 274–87.

—— (2002), 'History of hatred: George Fredrickson traces the roots of Western racism to Enlightenment beliefs about equality,' *New York Times Book Review*: 11.

'Un arabista estima que el error de traducer cristianos por sionistas en el cartel de alcoi es "intencionado,"' (2004), *El País*, 8 April 2004.

Armistead, Samuel G. (1987), 'A brief history of Kharja Studies,' *Hispania* 70: pp. 8–15.

—— (2001), 'Menéndez Pidal, the epic, and the generation of '98,' *La Corónica* 29: pp. 33–57.

Arrighi, Giovanni (1994), *The Long Twentieth Century: Money, Power, and the Origins of our Times*, London: Verso.

Asad, Talal (2003), *Formations of the Secular: Christianity, Islam, Modernity*, Stanford: Stanford University Press.

Ashcroft, Bill (2001), *Post-colonial Transformation*, London: Routledge.

Ashcroft, Bill, Gareth Griffiths and Helen Tiffin (1995), *The Post-colonial Studies Reader*, London: Routledge.

Asín Palacios, Miguel (1926), *Islam and the Divine Comedy*, trans. Harold Sutherland, London: John Murray.

—— [1919] (1943), *La escatología musulmana en la Divina Comedia; seguida de la historia y crítica de una polémica*, Madrid y Granada: Publicaciones de las escuelas de estudios árabes de Madrid y Granada.

Auerbach, Erich (1968), *Mimesis: The Representation of Reality in Western Literature*, trans. Willard R. Trask, Princeton: Princeton University Press.

'Aznar se pregunta por qué los musulmanes no se disculpan "por haber ocupado España ocho siglos"' (2006), *El Mundo*, 22 September 2006.

Bale, Anthony Paul (2006), *The Jew in the Medieval Book: English Antisemitisms, 1350–1500*, Cambridge: Cambridge University Press.

Balibar, Etienne (1991), 'Is there a "neo-racism"?' in *Race, Nation, Class: Ambiguous Identities*, ed. Etienne Balibar and Immanuel Maurice Wallerstein, London: Verso, pp. 17–28.

Barczewski, Stephanie L. (2000), *Myth and National Identity in Nineteenth Century Britain: The Legends of King Arthur and Robin Hood*, Oxford: Oxford University Press.

Bartal, Israel (2001), 'What's left of the onion? A "post-modernist" tract against "post-Zionism,"' *Israel Studies* 6: pp. 129–38.

Bartlett, Robert (1993), *The Making of Europe: Conquest, Colonization, and Cultural Change, 950–1350*, Princeton: Princeton University Press.

—— (2001), 'Medieval and Modern Concepts of race and ethnicity.' *Journal of Medieval and Early Modern Studies* 31: pp. 39–56.

Bat Ye'or (Gisèle Littman) (2005), *Eurabia: The Euro-Arab Axis*, Madison, WI: Fairleigh Dickinson University Press.

Baumgärtner, Ingrid (2001), 'Die Wahrnehmung Jerusalems auf mittelalterlichen Weltkarten,' in *Jerusalem im Hoch- und Spätmittelalter: Konflikte und Konfliktbewältigung–Vorstellungen und Vergegenwärtigungen*, ed. Dieter R. Bauer, Klaus Herbers and Nikolas Jaspert, Frankfurt: Campus, pp. 271–334.

—— (2006), 'Biblical, mythical, and foreign women in the texts and pictures on medieval world maps,' in *The Hereford World Map: Medieval World Maps and their Context.*, ed. Paul D. A. Harvey, London: British Library, pp. 305–34.

Bawer, Bruce (2006), *While Europe Slept: How Radical Islam Is Destroying the West from within*. New York: Doubleday.

Benjamin of Tudela (1985), *The Itinerary of Benjamin of Tudela*, trans. Marcus Nathan Adler, ed. Marcus Nathan Adler, London: Henry Frowde.

—— (1995), *The World of Benjamin of Tudela: A Medieval Mediterranean Travelogue*, ed. Sandra Benjamin, Madison, WI: Fairleigh Dickinson University Press.

Bennett, Herman L. (2005), '"Sons of Adam": text, context, and the early modern African subject,' *Representations* 92: pp. 16–41.

Bennett, Josephine Waters (1954), *The Rediscovery of Sir John Mandeville*, New York: Modern Language Association of America.

Berezin, Mabel (2009), *Illiberal Politics in Neoliberal Times: Culture, Security and Populism in the New Europe*, Cambridge: Cambridge University Press.

Bernal, Martin (1987), *Black Athena: The Afro-Asian Roots of Classical Civilization*, London: Free Association Press.

Bernáldez, Andrés Diego (1992), *Christopher Columbus's Discoveries in the Testimonials of Diego Alvarez Chanca and Andrés Bernáldes*, trans. Gioacchino Triolo, ed. Anna Unali, Rome: Istituto poligrafico e zecca dello stato, Libreria dello stato.

Bhabha, Homi K. (ed.) (1990), *Nation and Narration*, New York: Routledge.

—— (2004), *The Location of Culture*, London, New York: Routledge.

Bianchini, Stefano, and Marco Dogo (1998), *The Balkans: National Identities in a Historical Perspective*, Ravenna, Italy: Longo.

Biddick, Kathleen (1998a), 'The ABC of Ptolemy: mapping the world with the alphabet,' in *Text and Territory: Geographical Imagination in the European Middle Ages*, ed. Sylvia Tomasch and Sealy Gilles, Philadelphia: University of Pennsylvania Press, pp. 268–94.

—— (1998b), *The Shock of Medievalism*, Durham, NC: Duke University Press.

—— (2000a), 'Coming out of exile: Dante on the Orient Express,' in *The Postcolonial Middle Ages*, ed. Jeffrey Jerome Cohen, New York: St Martin's, pp. 35–52.

—— (2000b), 'Coming out of exile: Dante on the Orient(alism) Express,' *The American Historical Review* 105: pp. 1234–49.

—— (2003), *The Typological Imaginary: Circumcision, Technology, History*, Philadelphia: University of Pennsylvania Press.

Bjork, Robert E. (1997), 'Nineteenth-century Scandinavia and the birth of Anglo-Saxon studies,' in *Anglo-Saxonism and the Construction of Social Identity*, ed. Allen J. Frantzen and John D. Niles, Gainesville: University Press of Florida, pp. 111–32.

Black, Stanley (2004), 'The Author as Hero in the New World Order: The Power of Fictionality in Goytisolo's *El sitio de los sitios*,' in *Heroism and Passion in Literature: Studies in Honour of Moya Longstaffe*, ed. Graham Gargett, Amsterdam: Rodopi, pp. 233–244.

Blackburn, Robin (1997), *The Making of New World Slavery: From the Baroque to the Modern, 1492–1800*, London: Verso.

Blackmore, Josiah (2009), *Moorings: Portuguese Expansion and the Writing of Africa*, Minneapolis: University of Minnesota Press.

Blackmore, Josiah, and Gregory S. Hutcheson (1999), *Queer Iberia: Sexualities, Cultures, and Crossings from the Middle Ages to the Renaissance*, Durham, NC: Duke University Press.

Blamires, David Malcolm (1966), *Characterization and Individuality in Wolfram's 'Parzival,'* Cambridge: Cambridge University Press.

Bloch, R. Howard (1994), '842: The first document and the birth of medieval studies,' in *A New History of French Literature*, ed. Denis Hollier and R. Howard Bloch, Cambridge, MA: Harvard University Press, pp. 6–12.

Bly, Siobhain Montserrat (2002), 'Stereotypical Saracens, the Auchinleck Manuscript, and the problems of imagining Englishness in the early fourteenth century,' PhD, University of Notre Dame.

Borger, Julian (1997), 'Tremors in the Balkans: Belgrade/ Le Pen finds nationalist unity lies in common hatreds,' *The Guardian* (London), 22 January 1997.

Boyarin, Jonathan (2009), *The Unconverted Self*. Chicago: University of Chicago Press.

Braude, Benjamin (1996), 'Mandeville's Jews among Others,' in *Pilgrims and Travelers to the Holy Land*, ed. Bryan F. Le Beau and Menahem Mor, Omaha, NE: Creighton University Press, pp. 133–58.

Braudel, Fernand (1984), *The Perspective of the World*, New York: Harper & Row.

Briggs, Asa (1966), *Saxons, Normans and Victorians*, London: Historical Association Hastings & Bexhill Branch.

Brown, Catherine (1995), 'The Relics of Menéndez Pidal: Mourning and Melancholia in Hispanomedieval Studies,' *La Corónica*: 24: pp. 15–41.

Brown, Gordon S. (2003), *The Norman Conquest of Southern Italy and Sicily*, Jefferson, NC: McFarland.

Bull, Hedley (2002), *The Anarchical Society: A Study of Order in World Politics*, New York: Columbia University Press.

Bunzl, Matti (2007), *Anti-semitism and Islamophobia: Hatreds Old and New in Europe*, Chicago: Prickly Paradigm.

Burgess, Glyn S. (ed.), (1990), *The Song of Roland*, trans. Glyn S. Burgess, New York: Penguin.

Burshatin, Israel (1984), 'The docile image: The Moor as a figure of force, subservience, and nobility in the *Poema de mio Cid*,' *Romance Quarterly* 31: pp. 269–80.

——— (1985), 'The Moor in the text: metaphor, emblem, and silence,' *Critical Inquiry* 12: pp. 98–118.

'Bush's rhetoric fuels violence, critics charge' (2001), *The Toronto Star*, 19 September 2001.

'Bush steps back from word "crusade"' (2003), *St Petersburg Times*, 19 September 2003.

Bustillo, Miguel (2002), 'Ban on gathering racial data on 2004 ballot,' *Los Angeles Times*, 16 July 2002.

Bynum, Caroline Walker (2001), *Metamorphosis and Identity*, New York: Zone Books.

Caldwell, Christopher (2009), *Reflections on the Revolution in Europe: Immigration, Islam, and the West*, New York: Doubleday.

Calkin, Siobhain Bly (2005), 'Marking religion on the body: Saracens, catego-rization, and *The King of Tars*,' *Journal of English and Germanic Philology* 104: pp. 219–38.

Campbell, Kofi O. S. (2006), *Literature and Culture in the Black Atlantic: From Pre- to Postcolonial*, New York: Palgrave Macmillan.

Campbell, Mary B. (1988), *The Witness and the Other World: Exotic European Travel Writing, 400–1600*, Ithaca, NY: Cornell University Press.

Canitz, A. E. Christa (2004), '"Historians . . . will say I am a liar": the ideol-ogy of false truth claims in Mel Gibson's *Braveheart* and Luc Besson's *The Messenger*,' *Studies in Medievalism* 13: pp. 127–42.

Cantor, Paul A. (1997), 'Tales of the Alhambra: Rushdie's use of Spanish history in *The Moor's Last Sigh*,' *Studies in the Novel* 29: pp. 323–41.

Castro, Américo ([1948] 1983), *España en su historia: cristianos, moros y judíos*. Barcelona: Editorial Crítica.

Catlos, Brian (2001), 'Cristians, musulmans i jueus a la Corona d'Aragó medieval: Un cas de conveniència,' *L'Avenç* 236: pp. 8–16.

Cebrian, Juan Luis (2006), 'Barbarie, religión y progreso,' *El País*, 17 September 2006.

'Census, Race and Science' (2000), *Nature Genetics* 24: pp. 97–8.

Chakrabarty, Dipesh (2000), *Provincializing Europe: Postcolonial Thought and Historical Difference*, Princeton: Princeton University Press.

Chandler, Alice (1970), *A Dream of Order: The Medieval Ideal in Nineteenth-Century English Literature*, Lincoln: University of Nebraska Press.

Charter, David (2008), 'Racism row in Switzerland over minaret ban referen-dum,' *Times Online*, 9 July 2008, www.timesonline.co.uk/tol/news/world/europe/article4304838.ece

Chatterjee, Partha (1993), *Nationalist Thought and the Colonial World: A Derivative Discourse?*, Minneapolis: University of Minnesota Press.

Chaucer, Geoffrey (1987), *The Riverside Chaucer*, ed. Larry Dean Benson, Boston: Houghton Mifflin.

Chazan, Robert (1987), *European Jewry and the First Crusade*, Berkeley: University of California Press.

—— (1989), *Daggers of Faith*, Berkeley: University of California Press.

—— (1997), *Medieval Stereotypes and Modern Antisemitism*, Berkeley: University of California Press.

—— (2000), *God, Humanity, and History: The Hebrew First Crusade Narratives*, Berkeley: University of California Press.

Chism, Christine (2002), *Alliterative Revivals*, Philadelphia: University of Pennsylvania Press.

Christoph, Siegfried Richard (1981), *Wolfram von Eschenbach's Couples*, Amsterdam: Rodopi.

Coggeshall, Elizabeth A. (2007), 'Dante, Islam, and Edward Said,' *Telos* 139: pp. 133–51.

Cohen, Jeffrey Jerome (2000), *The Postcolonial Middle Ages*, New York: St Martin's.

—— (2001), 'On Saracen Enjoyment: Some Fantasies of Race in Late Medieval France and England,' *Journal of Medieval and Early Modern Studies* 31: pp. 113–46.

—— (2006), *Hybridity, Identity and Monstrosity in Medieval Britain: On Difficult Middles*, New York: Palgrave Macmillan.

Cohen, Jeremy (1982), *The Friars and the Jews*, Ithaca, NY: Cornell University Press.

—— (1996), 'The Muslim connection; or, on the changing role of the Jew in high medieval theology,' in *From Witness to Witchcraft: Jews and Judaism in Medieval Christian Thought*, ed. Jeremy Cohen, Wiesbaden: Harrassowitz, pp. 141–62.

—— (1999), *Living Letters of the Law: Ideas of the Jew in Medieval Christianity*, Berkeley: University of California Press.

—— (2004), *Sanctifying the Name of God: Jewish Martyrs and Jewish Memories of the First Crusade*, Philadelphia: University of Pennsylvania Press.

—— (2007), *Christ Killers: The Jews and the Passion from the Bible to the Big Screen*, Oxford: Oxford University Press.

Constable, Giles, Kenneth M. Sutton and Hans Eberhard Mayer (1991), 'Memoirs of fellows and corresponding fellows of the Medieval Academy of America: Joshua Prawer,' *Speculum* 66: pp. 727–9.

Corkill, David (2000), 'Race, immigration and multiculturalism in Spain,' in *Contemporary Spanish Cultural Studies*, ed. Barry Jordan and Rikki Morgan-Tamosunas, London: Arnold, pp. 48–57.

Dagenais, John (2004), 'The postcolonial Laura,' *Modern Language Quarterly* 65: pp. 365–89.

Dagenais, John, and Margaret R. Greer (eds) (2000), 'Decolonizing the Middle Ages,' special issue, *Journal of Medieval and Early Modern Studies* 30.3.

Dainotto, Roberto M. (2007), *Europe (In Theory)*, Durham, NC: Duke University Press.

Dalby, Simon (1996), 'The environment as geopolitical threat: reading Robert Kaplan's "Coming Anarchy,"' *Cultural Geographies* 3: pp. 472–96.

Dalché, Patrick Gautier (1995), *Carte marine et portulan au XIIe siècle: Le liber de existencia riveriarum et forma maris nostri Mediterranei (Pise, circa 1200)*, Roma: École Française de Rome.

Daniel, Norman (1997), *Islam and the West: The Making of an Image*, Oxford: Oneworld.

Davenport, Frances G. (1967), *European Treaties Bearing on the History of the United States and Its Dependencies, Vol. 1: To 1648*, Papers of the Department of Historical Research 254, Gloucester, MA: P. Smith.

Davidson, Mary Catherine (2006), 'Remembering our Saxon forefathers: linguistic nationalism in *Ivanhoe*,' in *Memory and Medievalism*, ed. Karl Fugelso, Cambridge: D. S. Brewer, pp. 41–54.

Davies, Peter (1999), *National Front France: Ideology, Discourse, Power*, London: Routledge.

Davies, Rees (2004), 'Nations and national identities in the medieval world: an apologia,' *Revue Belge d'Histoire Contemporaine / Belgisch Tijdschrift voor Nieuwste Geschiedenis* 34: pp. 567–79.

Davis, Kathleen (1998), 'National writing in the ninth century: a reminder for postcolonial thinking about the nation,' *Journal of Medieval and Early Modern Studies* 28: pp. 611–37.

—— (2000), 'Time behind the veil: the Media, the Middle Ages, and Orientalism now,' in *The Postcolonial Middle Ages*, ed. Jeffrey Jerome Cohen, New York, NY: St Martins, pp. 105–22.

—— (2008), *Periodization and Sovereignty: How Ideas of Feudalism and Secularization Govern the Politics of Time*, Philadelphia: University of Pennsylvania Press.

Davis, Kathleen, and Nadia Altschul (eds) (2009), *Medievalisms in the Postcolonial World: The Idea of the 'Middle Ages' Outside Europe*, Baltimore, MD: Johns Hopkins University Press.

Davis, R. H. C. (1976), *The Normans and Their Myth*, London: Thames and Hudson.

Dawson, Christopher (ed.) (1980), *Mission to Asia* [Mongol mission], Medieval Academy Reprints for Teaching 8, Toronto: University of Toronto Press.

de Grazia, Margreta (2007), 'The modern divide: from either side,' *Journal of Medieval and Early Modern Studies* 37: pp. 453–67.

Deibert, Ronald J. (2003), 'Neo-medievalism,' in *Routledge Encyclopedia of International Political Economy* 2: 1114, ed. R. J. Barry Jones, New York: Routledge.

Delany, Sheila (1999), 'Chaucer's Prioress, the Jews, and the Muslims,' *Medieval Encounters* 5: pp. 199–213.

Desai, Gaurav (2004), 'Old World orders: Amitav Ghosh and the writing of nostalgia,' *Representations* 85: 125–48.

Despres, Denise L. (1994), 'Cultic Anti-Judaism and Chaucer's Litel Clergeon,' *Modern Philology* 91: pp. 413–27.

DiMarco, Vincent J. (1991), 'The Amazons and the end of the world,' in *Discovering New Worlds: Essays on Medieval Exploration and Imagination*, ed. Scott D. Westrem, New York: Garland, pp. 69–90.

Dinshaw, Carolyn (1999), *Getting Medieval: Sexualities and Communities, Pre- and Postmodern*, Durham, NC: Duke University Press.

—— (2001), 'Pale faces: race, religion, and affect in Chaucer's texts and their readers,' *Studies in the Age of Chaucer* 23: pp. 19–41.

Dobson, Barrie ([1974] 1996), *The Jews of Medieval York and the Massacre of March 1190*, rev. edn, York: Borthwick Institute of Historical Research, University of York.

———— (2003), 'The Medieval York Jewry reconsidered,' in *The Jews in Medieval Britain: Historical, Literary, and Archaeological Perspectives*, ed. Patricia Skinner, Rochester, NY: Boydell & Brewer, pp. 145–56.

Du Bois, W. E. B. (1924/1925), 'Worlds of Color,' *Foreign Affairs* 3: pp. 423–44.

———— (1999), *The Souls of Black Folk: Authoritative Text, Contexts, Criticism*, ed. Henry Louis Gates and Terri Hume Oliver, New York: W. W. Norton.

Duggan, Joseph J. (1989), 'Franco-German conflict and the history of French scholarship on the *Song of Roland*,' in *Hermeneutics and Medieval Culture*, ed. Patrick J. Gallacher and Helen Damico, Albany: State University of New York Press, pp. 97–106.

Dunn, Charles W. (1960), *The Foundling and the Werewolf: A Literary-Historical Study of Guillaume de Palerne*, Toronto: University of Toronto Press.

Dunn, Ross E. (2005), *The Adventures of Ibn Battuta, a Muslim Traveler of the Fourteenth Century*, Berkeley: University of California Press.

Dussel, Enrique (1993), 'Eurocentrism and modernity (Introduction to the Frankfurt Lectures),' *Boundary 2* 20: pp. 65–76.

Ebenbauer, Alfred (1984), '"Es gibt ain mörynne vil dick susse mynne": Belakenes Landsleute in der deutschen Literatur des Mittelalters,' *Zeitschrift für deutsches Alterthum und deutsche Literatur* 113: pp. 16–42.

Eco, Umberto ([1986] 2002), *Travels in Hyperreality: Essays*, trans. William Weaver, San Diego: Harcourt.

Economou, George (ed.) (1998), *Poem of the Cid: A Modern Translation with Notes*, trans. Paul Blackburn, Norman: University of Oklahoma Press.

Edson, Evelyn (2007), *The World Map, 1300–1492: The Persistence of Tradition and Transformation*, Baltimore, MD: Johns Hopkins University Press.

Erlanger, Steven (2001), 'Italy's premier calls western civilization superior to Islamic world,' *New York Times*, 27 September 2001.

Espósito, Anthony P. (1995), 'Dismemberment of things past: fixing the Jarchas,' *La Corónica* 24: pp. 4–14.

———— (2000), 'The monkey in the *Jarcha*: tradition and canonicity in the early Iberian lyric,' *Journal of Medieval and Early Modern Studies* 30: 463–77.

Fabian, Johannes (1983), *Time and the Other: How Anthropology Makes Its Object*, New York: Columbia University Press.

Faletra, Michael A (2000), 'Narrating the matter of Britain: Geoffrey of Monmouth and the Norman colonization of Wales,' *Chaucer Review* 35: pp. 60–85.

———— (2007), 'The conquest of the past in *The History of the Kings of Britain*,' *Literature Compass* 4: pp. 121–33.

Falk, Richard (2000), 'A "New Medievalism"?' in *Contending Images of World Politics*, ed. Greg Fry and Jacinta O'Hagan, New York: St Martin's, pp. 106–16.

Fallaci, Oriana (2002), *The Rage and the Pride* [Rabbia e l'orgoglio], New York: Rizzoli.

——— (2006), *The Force of Reason* [Forza della ragione], trans. Oriana Fallaci, New York: Rizzoli International.

Fetzer, Joel S. and J. Christopher Soper (2005), *Muslims and the State in Britain, France, and Germany*, Cambridge, New York: Cambridge University Press.

Finke, Laurie, and Martin B. Shichtman (2004), *King Arthur and the Myth of History*, Gainesville: University Press of Florida.

Flesler, Daniela, and Adrián Pérez Melgosa (2003), 'Battles of identity, or playing "guest" and "host": the festivals of Moors and Christians in the context of Moroccan immigration in Spain,' *Journal of Spanish Cultural Studies* 4: pp. 151–68.

Fletcher, C. R. L., and Rudyard Kipling (1911), *A School History of England*, Oxford: Clarendon.

Foster, Morris W. and Richard R. Sharp (2002), 'Race, ethnicity, and genomics: social classifications as proxies of biological heterogeneity,' *Genome Research* 12: pp. 844–50.

Frakes, Jerold C. (1997), 'Race, representation and metamorphosis in Middle High German Literature,' *NOWELE* 31–2: pp. 119–33.

Frantzen, Allen J. (1990), *Desire for Origins: New Language, Old English, and Teaching the Tradition*, New Brunswick, NJ: Rutgers University Press.

Frantzen, Allen J. and John D. Niles (1997), *Anglo-Saxonism and the Construction of Social Identity*, Gainesville: University Press of Florida.

Fredrickson, George M. (2002), *Racism: A Short History*, Princeton: Princeton University Press.

Freedman, Paul H. (2008), *Out of the East: Spices and the Medieval Imagination*, New Haven: Yale University Press.

Freedman, Paul and Gabrielle M. Spiegel (1998), 'Medievalisms old and new: the rediscovery of alterity in North American medieval studies,' *The American Historical Review* 103: pp. 677–704.

Friedländer, Saul (1997), *Nazi Germany and the Jews*, New York: HarperCollins.

Friedman, John Block (2000), *The Monstrous Races in Medieval Art and Thought*, Medieval Studies, Syracuse, NY: Syracuse University Press.

Friedman, John Block and Kristen Mossler Figg (eds) (2000), *Trade, Travel, and Exploration in the Middle Ages: An Encyclopedia*, New York: Garland Publishing.

Fuller, Thomas (2003), 'Europe debates whether to admit god to union,' *New York Times*, 3 February 2003.

Galbraith, V. H. (1941), 'Nationality and language in medieval England,' *Transactions of the Royal Historical Society* 23: pp. 113–28.

Gabrieli, Francesco. 1969. *Arab Historians of the Crusades*, [Storici arabi delle Crociate], London: Routledge & K. Paul.

Ganim, John M. (2000), 'Native Studies: Orientalism and medievalism,' in *The Postcolonial Middle Ages*, ed. Jeffrey Jerome Cohen, New York: St. Martin's, pp. 123–34.

—— (2005), *Medievalism and Orientalism: Three Essays on Literature, Architecture, and Cultural Identity*, New York: Palgrave Macmillan.

Geary, Patrick J. (2002), *The Myth of Nations: The Medieval Origins of Europe*, Princeton: Princeton University Press.

—— (2006), *Women at the Beginning: Origin Myths from the Amazons to the Virgin Mary*, Princeton: Princeton University Press.

Geoffrey of Monmouth(1966), *The History of the Kings of Britain*, ed. Lewis G. M. Thorpe, Baltimore, MD: Penguin Books.

—— (1985), *Historia Regum Britannie*, ed. Neil Wright, Cambridge: D. S. Brewer.

Georgopoulou, Maria (1999), 'Orientalism and Crusader art: constructing a new canon,' *Medieval Encounters* 5: pp. 289–321.

Gerald of Wales (1978), *The Journey through Wales; and, The Description of Wales*, trans. Lewis Thorpe, Harmondsworth: Penguin Books.

Gerli, E. Michael (2001), 'Inventing the Spanish Middle Ages: Ramón Menéndez Pidal, Spanish cultural history, and ideology in philology,' *La Corónica* 30: pp. 111–26.

Ghosh, Amitav, (1993), 'The slave of MS H.6,' *Subaltern Studies: Writings on South Asian History and Society* 7: p. 159.

—— (1994), *In an Antique Land*, New York: Vintage Books.

Gillingham, John (2000), *The English in the Twelfth Century: Imperialism, National Identity, and Political Values*, Woodbridge, UK: Boydell Press.

Gilman, Sander L. (1993), 'Salome, syphilis, Sarah Bernhardt and the "Modern Jewess,"' *German Quarterly* 66: pp. 195–211

Gilroy, Paul (1993), *The Black Atlantic: Modernity and Double Consciousness*, Cambridge, MA: Harvard University Press.

—— (2000), *Against Race: Imagining Political Culture beyond the Color Line*, Cambridge, MA: Belknap Press of Harvard University Press.

Giraldus [Gerald of Wales], J. S. Brewer, James F. Dimock and George F. Warner (1964), *Giraldi Cambrensis Opera*: Kraus Reprint.

Glick, Thomas F. (1992), '*Convivencia*: an introductory note,' in *Convivencia: Jews, Muslims, and Christians in Medieval Spain*, ed. Vivian B. Mann, Jerrilynn Denise Dodds and Thomas F. Glick, New York: G. Braziller in association with the Jewish Museum, pp. 1–10.

GMAP, http://www.laits.utexas.edu/gma/mappamundi/articles.html, accessed 1 October 2008.

Goh, Daniel P. S. (2007), 'States of ethnography: colonialism, resistance, and cultural transcription in Malaya and the Philippines, 1890s–1930s,' *Comparative Studies in Society and History* 49: pp. 109–42.

Gopnik, Adam (1996), 'The First Frenchman,' *The New Yorker*, 6 October 1996.

Gouguenheim, Sylvain (2008), *Aristote au Mont-Saint-Michel: Les Racines Grecques de l'Europe Chrétienne*, Paris: Seuil.

Gow, Andrew Colin (1995), *The Red Jews: Antisemitism in an Apocalyptic Age, 1200–1600*, Studies in Medieval and Reformation Thought 55, Leiden: E. J. Brill.

Goytisolo, Juan (1970), *Reivindicación del conde don Julián*, Mexico: J. Mortiz.

—— (1974), *Count Julián*, trans. Helen R. Lane, New York: Viking Press.

—— (1982), *Paisajes después de la batalla*, Barcelona: Montesinos.

—— (1987), *Landscapes after the Battle*, trans. Helen Lane, New York: Seaver Books.

—— (1993), *Cuaderno de Sarajevo: anotaciones de un viaje a la barbarie*, Madrid: El País/Aguilar.

—— (1995), *El sitio de los sitios*, Madrid: Santillana.

—— (2000), *Landscapes of War: From Sarajevo to Chechnya*, trans. Peter Bush, San Francisco: City Lights Books.

—— (2002), *State of Siege*, trans. Helen Lane, San Francisco: City Lights Books.

—— (2006), ¡Felicitaciones, señor Aznar!, *El País*, 27 September 2006.

Grady, Frank (2005), *Representing Righteous Heathens in Late Medieval England*, New York: Palgrave Macmillan.

Graham, John M. (1996), 'National identity and the politics of publishing the Troubadours,' in *Medievalism and the Modernist Temper*, ed. R. Howard Bloch and Stephen G. Nichols, Baltimore, MD: Johns Hopkins University Press, pp. 57–94.

Granara, William (2005), 'Nostalgia, Arab nationalism, and the Andalusian chronotope in the evolution of the modern Arabic novel,' *Journal of Arabic Literature* 36: pp. 57–73.

Greenberg, Jonathan (1999), '"The Base Indian" or "The Base Judean"?: Othello and the metaphor of the palimpsest in Salman Rushdie's *The Moor's Last Sigh*,' *Modern Language Studies* 29: pp. 93–107.

Greenblatt, Stephen J. (1991), *Marvelous Possessions: The Wonder of the New World*, Chicago: University of Chicago Press.

Greer, Margaret Rich, Walter Mignolo and Maureen Quilligan (eds) (2007), *Rereading the Black Legend: The Discourses of Religious and Racial Difference in the Renaissance Empires*, Chicago: University of Chicago Press.

Groos, Arthur (1995), *Romancing the Grail: Genre, Science, and Quest in Wolfram's 'Parzival'*, Ithaca, NY: Cornell University Press.

Gross, Joan, David McMurray and Ted Swedenburg (1996), 'Arab noise and Ramadan nights: rai, rap, and Franco-Maghrebi identitites,' in *Displacement, Diaspora, and Geographies of Identity*, ed. Smadar Lavie and Ted Swedenburg, Durham, NC: Duke University Press, pp. 119–55.

Gross, John J. (1992), *Shylock: A Legend and Its Legacy*, New York: Simon & Schuster.

Gumbrecht, Hans Ulrich (1986), '"Un souffle d'Allemagne ayant passé": Friedrich Diez, Gaston Paris, and the genesis of national philologies,' *Romance Philology* 40: pp. 1–37.

Hahn, Thomas (2001), 'The difference the Middle Ages makes: color and race before the modern world,' *Journal of Medieval and Early Modern Studies* 31: pp. 1–37.

Hainsworth, Paul (2000), *The Politics of the Extreme Right: From the Margins to the Mainstream*, London: Pinter.

Hall, Stefan Thomas (2007), 'James Macpherson's *Ossian*: forging ancient Highland identity for Scotland,' in *Constructing Nations, Reconstructing Myth: Essays in Honour of T. A. Shippey*, ed. Andrew Wawn, Graham Johnson and John Walter, Turnhout: Brepols, pp. 3–26.

Hamilton, Michelle (2007a), 'The spectral Arab: Rodrigo and the fall of Spain,' paper presented at 'Fables of Faith' workshop, University of California, Irvine, 20 April 2007.

Hamilton, Michelle M. (2007b), *Representing Others in Medieval Iberian Literature*, New Middle Ages, New York: Palgrave Macmillan.

Hannaford, Ivan (1996), *Race: The History of an Idea in the West*, Baltimore, MD: Johns Hopkins University Press.

Hart, Thomas R. (2006), *Studies on the Cantar de mio Cid*, Papers of the Medieval Hispanic Research Seminar 54, London: Queen Mary, University of London, Department of Hispanic Studies.

Harrey, Paul D. A. (1991), *Medieval Maps*, London: British Library.

Heng, Geraldine (2000), 'The romance of England: *Richard Coer de Lyon*, Saracens, Jews, and the politics of race and nation,' in *The Postcolonial Middle Ages*, ed. Jeffrey Jerome Cohen, New York: St Martin's, pp. 135–72.

—— (2003), *Empire of Magic: Medieval Romance and the Politics of Cultural Literacy*, New York: Columbia University Press.

Henighan, Stephen (1998), 'Coming to Benengeli: the genesis of Salman Rushdie's rewriting of Juan Rulfo in *The Moor's Last Sigh*,' *Journal of Commonwealth Literature* 33: pp. 55–74.

Herr, Richard (1958), 'Review: *España, un enigma histórico*, by Claudio Sánchez Albornoz,' *The Hispanic American Historical Review* 38: pp. 553–4.

Higgins, Iain Macleod (1997), *Writing East: The 'Travels' of Sir John Mandeville*, Middle Ages Series, Philadelphia: University of Pennsylvania Press.

Hill, Christopher (1958), *Puritanism and Revolution: Studies in Interpretation of the English Revolution of the 17th Century*, London: Secker & Warburg.

Hillenbrand, Carole (2000), *The Crusades: Islamic Perspectives*, New York: Routledge.

Hirsi Ali, Ayaan (2007), *Infidel*, New York: Free Press.

Hirsi Ali, Ayaan and Theo van Gogh (2005), *Submission, Part I*, Amsterdam: Column Producties.

Holsinger, Bruce W. (1998), 'The color of salvation: desire, death, and the Second Crusade in Bernard of Clairvaux's *Sermons on the Song of Songs*,' in *The Tongue of the Fathers: Gender and Ideology in Twelfth-Century Latin*, ed. David Townsend and Andrew Taylor, Philadelphia: University of Pennsylvania Press, pp. 156–86.

——— (2002), 'Medieval studies, postcolonial studies, and the genealogies of critique,' *Speculum* 77: pp. 1195–227.

——— (2007), *Neomedievalism, Neoconservatism, and the War on Terror*, Paradigm 29, Chicago: Prickly Paradigm.

——— (2008), 'Empire, apocalypse, and the 9/11 premodern,' *Critical Inquiry* 34: pp. 468–90.

Hopkins, Amanda (ed. and trans.) (2005), *Melion and Bisclarel: Two Old French Werwolf Lays*, www.liv.ac.uk/soclas/los/Werwolf.pdf, Liverpool Online Series: Critical Editions of French Texts.

Hossay, Patrick (2002), 'Country profiles,' in *Shadows over Europe: The Development and Impact of the Extreme Right in Western Europe*, ed. Martin Schain, Aristide R. Zolberg and Patrick Hossay, 1st edn, New York: Palgrave Macmillan, pp. 317–45.

Howard, Donald Roy (1980), *Writers and Pilgrims: Medieval Pilgrimage Narratives and Their Posterity*, Berkeley: University of California Press.

Howe, Nicholas (2005), 'Anglo-Saxon England and the postcolonial void,' in *Postcolonial Approaches to the European Middle Ages: Translating Cultures*, ed. Ananya Jahanara Kabir and Deanne Williams, Cambridge: Cambridge University Press, pp. 25–47.

Howe, Stephen (2002), *Empire: A Very Short Introduction*, Oxford: Oxford University Press.

Huggan, Graham (2008), *Interdisciplinary Measures: Literature and the Future of Postcolonial Studies*, Liverpool: Liverpool University Press.

Huizinga, Johan (1959), *Men and Ideas: History, the Middle Ages, the Renaissance*, trans. James S. Holmes and Hans van Marle, New York: Meridian Books.

Hult, David F. (1996), 'Gaston Paris and the invention of courtly love,' in *Medievalism and the Modernist Temper*, ed. R. Howard Bloch and Stephen G. Nichols, Baltimore, MD: Johns Hopkins University Press, pp. 192–224.

Huntington, Samuel P. (1993), 'The Clash of Civilizations?' *Foreign Affairs* 72: pp. 22–49.

—— (1996), *The Clash of Civilizations and the Remaking of World Order*, New York: Simon & Schuster.

Hupchick, Dennis P. (2002), *The Balkans: From Constantinople to Communism*, New York: Palgrave.

Ibn Hazm, Ali ibn Ahmad (1994), *The Ring of the Dove: A Treatise on the Art and Practice of Arab Love* [Tawq Al-hamamah.], trans. A. J. Arberry, London: Luzac Oriental.

—— (1931), *A Book Containing the Risāla Known as The Dove's Neck Ring about Love and Lovers*, ed. A. R. Nykl, Paris: P. Geuthner.

Ibn Jubayr, Muhammad ibn Ahmad (1952), *The Travels of Ibn Jubayr* [al-Rihlah], trans. Ronald J. C. Broadhurst, ed. Ronald J. C. Broadhurst, London: J. Cape.

—— (1964), *Rihlat Ibn Jubayr*, Beirut: Dar Sadir lil-Tibaah wa-al-Nashr.

Ingham, Patricia Clare (2001), *Sovereign Fantasies: Arthurian Romance and the Making of Britain*, Philadelphia: University of Pennsylvania Press.

—— (2003), 'Contrapuntal histories,' in *Postcolonial Moves: Medieval Through Modern*, ed. Patricia Clare Ingham and Michelle R. Warren, New York: Palgrave Macmillan, pp, 47–70.

Jackson, Peter (2005), *The Mongols and the West, 1221–1410*, Medieval World, Harlow: Pearson Longman.

Jelavich, Barbara (1983), *History of the Balkans*, Joint Committee on Eastern Europe Publication Series, Cambridge: Cambridge University Press.

Jenkins, Philip (2007), *God's Continent: Christianity, Islam, and Europe's Religious Crisis*, Oxford: Oxford University Press.

John of Plano Carpini (1929), 'Ystoria Monaglorum,' in *Itinera et relationes fratrum minorum saeculi XIII et XIV*, ed. Anastasius van den Wyngaert, Quaracchi-Firenze: Collegium S. Bonaventurae, pp. 3–130.

Kabir, Ananya Jahanara (2006), '"Oriental Gothic": the medieval past in the colonial encounter,' in *Reorienting Orientalism*, ed. Chandreyee Niyogi, New Delhi: SAGE Publications, pp. 65–88.

Kaplan, Robert D. (1993), *Balkan Ghosts: A Journey through History*, New York: St Martin's.

—— (1994), 'The coming anarchy,' *Atlantic Monthly* 273: pp. 44–77.

Karkov, Catherine E. (2003), 'Tales of the ancients: colonial werewolves and the mapping of postcolonial Ireland,' in *Postcolonial Moves: Medieval through Modern*, ed. Patricia Clare Ingham and Michelle R. Warren, New York: Palgrave Macmillan, pp. 93–109.

Kedar, Benjamin Z. (ed.) (1992), *The Horns of Hattin: Proceedings of the Second Conference of the Society for the Study of the Crusades and the Latin East, Jerusalem and Haifa, 2–6 July 1987*, Jerusalem; Haifa: Israel Exploration Society.

Kelek, Necla (2005), *Die fremde Braut: Ein Bericht aus dem Inneren des türkischen Lebens in Deutschland*, Köln: Kiepenheuer & Witsch.

Kelly, Gary (1989), 'Social conflict, nation and empire: from Gothicism to romantic Orientalism,' *ARIEL* 20: pp. 3–18.

Kennedy, John (2007), *Translating the Sagas: Two Hundred Years of Challenge and Response*, Turnhout: Brepols.

Kimmelman, Michael (2010), 'When fear turns graphic: populist parties in Europe mobilize posters as weapons in their culture wars,' *New York Times*, 17 January 2010.

Kinoshita, Sharon (2001), '"Pagans are wrong and Christians are right": alterity, gender, and nation in the *Chanson de Roland*,' *Journal of Medieval and Early Modern Studies* 31: pp. 79–111.

—— (2004), 'Colonial possessions: Wales and the Anglo-Norman imaginary in the lais of Marie de France,' in *Discourses on Love, Marriage, and Transgression in Medieval and Early Modern Literature*, ed. Albrecht Classen. Tempe: Arizona Center for Medieval and Renaissance Studies, pp. 147–62.

—— (2006a), *Medieval Boundaries: Rethinking Difference in Old French Literature*, Philadelphia: University of Pennsylvania Press.

—— (2006b), 'Political uses and responses: Orientalism, postcolonial theory, and cultural studies,' in *Approaches to Teaching the Song of Roland*, ed. William W. Kibler and Leslie Zarker Morgan, New York: Modern Language Association of America, pp. 269–80.

—— (2007), 'Deprovincializing the Middle Ages,' in *The Worlding Project: Doing Cultural Studies in the Era of Globalization*, ed. Rob Wilson, Berkeley, CA: North Atlantic Books, pp. 61–75.

Kittredge, George Lyman (1966), *Arthur and Gorlagon: Versions of the Werewolf's Tale*, New York: Haskell House.

Kline, Naomi Reed (2001), *Maps of Medieval Thought: The Hereford Paradigm*, Woodbridge, Suffolk: Boydell Press.

Knight, Rhonda (2001), 'Werewolves, monsters, and miracles: representing colonial fantasies in Gerald of Wales's *Topographia Hibernica*,' *Studies in Iconography* 22: pp. 55–86.

Kobrin, Stephen J. (1998), 'Back to the future: neomedievalism and the post-modern digital world economy,' *Journal of International Affairs* 51: pp. 361–86.

Kontje, Todd Curtis (2004), *German Orientalisms*, Ann Arbor: University of Michigan Press.

Kösebalaban, Hasan (2007), 'The permanent "Other"? Turkey and the question of European identity,' *Mediterranean Quarterly* 18: pp. 87–111.

Kristeva, Julia (1982), *Powers of Horror: An Essay on Abjection*, trans. Leon S. Roudiez, European Perspectives, New York: Columbia University Press.

Kruger, Steven F. (1997), 'Conversion and medieval sexual, religious, and racial categories,' in *Constructing Medieval Sexuality*, ed. Karma Lochrie,

Peggy McCracken and James A. Schultz. Minneapolis: University of Minnesota Press, pp. 158–79.

—— (2006), *The Spectral Jew: Conversion and Embodiment in Medieval Europe*, Minneapolis: University of Minnesota Press.

Kupfer, Marcia (2008), '". . . Lectres . . . plus vrayes": Hebrew script and Jewish witness in the Mandeville manuscript of Charles V,' *Speculum* 83: pp. 58–111.

Lachmann, Karl, and Eduard Hartl (eds) (1952), *Wolfram von Eschenbach*, Berlin: W. de Gruyter.

Lampert, Lisa (1998), '"O my daughter!": "Die schöne Jüdin" and "Der neue Jude" in Hermann Sinsheimer's *Maria Nunnez*,' *The German Quarterly* 71: pp. 254–70.

—— (2004), *Gender and Jewish Difference from Paul to Shakespeare*, Philadelphia: University of Pennsylvania Press.

Lampert-Weissig, Lisa (2007), '"Why is this knight different from all other knights?" Jews, anti-semitism, and the old French grail narratives,' *Journal of English and Germanic Philology* 106: pp. 224–47.

Lang, Michael (2006), 'Globalization and its history,' *The Journal of Modern History* 78: pp. 899–931.

Langmuir, Gavin I. (1990a), *History, Religion, and Antisemitism*, Berkeley: University of California Press.

—— (1990b), *Toward a Definition of Antisemitism*, Berkeley: University of California Press.

Laqueur, Walter (2007), *The Last Days of Europe: Epitaph for an Old Continent*, New York: St Martin's Press.

Lasater, Alice E. (1974), *Spain to England: A Comparative Study of Arabic, European, and English Literature of the Middle Ages*, Jackson: University Press of Mississippi.

Lavezzo, Kathy (2004), *Imagining a Medieval English Nation*, Minneapolis: University of Minnesota Press.

—— (2006), *Angels on the Edge of the World: Geography, Literature, and English Community, 1000–1534*, Ithaca, NY: Cornell University Press.

Lawton, David (2001), 'The surveying subject and the "whole world" of belief: three case studies,' *New Medieval Literatures* 4: pp. 9–37.

—— (2007), '1453 and the stream of time,' *Journal of Medieval and Early Modern Studies* 37: pp. 469–91.

Leerssen, Joep (2004), 'Ossian and the rise of literary historicism,' in *The Reception of Ossian in Europe*, ed. Howard Gaskill, London: Thoemmes Continuum, pp. 109–25.

Le Patourel, John (1976), *The Norman Empire*, Oxford: Clarendon Press.

Lerer, Seth (2005), '"*On fagne flor*": the postcolonial *Beowulf*, from Heorot to Heaney,' in *Postcolonial Approaches to the European Middle Ages: Translating Cultures*, ed. Ananya Jahanara Kabir and Deanne Williams, Cambridge: Cambridge University Press, pp. 77–102.

Lewis, Bernard (1990), 'The roots of Muslim rage,' *Atlantic* 266: pp. 47–58.

—— (1998), 'License to kill: Usama bin Laden's declaration of jihad,' *Foreign Affairs* 77: pp. 14–19.

—— (2003), 'I'm right, you're wrong, go to hell,' *Atlantic Monthly* 291: pp. 36–42.

Lilley, J. M., York Archaeological Trust, and Council for British Archaeology (1994), *The Jewish Burial Ground at Jewbury*, York: Council for British Archaeology.

Lincoln, Andrew (2007), *Walter Scott and Modernity*, Edinburgh: Edinburgh University Press.

Lindsay, James E. (2005), *Daily Life in the Medieval Islamic World*, Santa Barbara, CA: Greenwood Press.

Linehan, Peter (1996), 'The court historiographer of Francoism? "La leyenda oscura" of Ramón Menéndez Pidal,' *Bulletin of Hispanic Studies* 73: pp. 437–50.

Lochrie, Karma (2005), *Heterosyncrasies: Female Sexuality When Normal Wasn't*, Minneapolis: University of Minnesota Press.

—— (2009), 'Provincializing medieval Europe: Mandeville's cosmopolitan utopia,' *PMLA* 124: 592–9.

Lomperis, Linda (2001), 'Medieval travel writing and the question of race,' *Journal of Medieval and Early Modern Studies* 31: pp. 147–64.

'Long memories of the crusades overshadow the future' (2003), *Sydney Herald*, 12 April 2003.

Loomba, Ania (1998a), *Colonialism-Postcolonialism*, London: Routledge.

—— (1998b), '"Local-manufacture made-in-India Othello fellows": issues of race, hybridity and location in post-colonial Shakespeares,' In *Post-Colonial Shakespeares*, ed. Ania Loomba and Martin Orkin, London, England: Routledge, pp. 143–63.

—— (2002), *Shakespeare, Race, and Colonialism*, Oxford: Oxford University Press.

Loomba, Ania and Jonathan Burton (2007), *Race in Early Modern England: A Documentary Companion*, New York: Palgrave Macmillan.

López-Morillas, Consuelo (2000), 'Language,' in *The Literature of al-Andalus*, ed. María Rosa Menocal, Raymond P. Scheindlin and Michael Anthony Sells, Cambridge: Cambridge University Press, pp. 33–59.

Maalouf, Amin [1984] (2006), *The Crusades through Arab Eyes*, trans. Jon Rothschild, London: Saqi Essentials.

Macaulay, Thomas Babington (1972), *Selected Writings*, ed. John Leonard Clive and Thomas Pinney, Chicago: University of Chicago Press.

Maccoby, Hyam (1982), *Judaism on Trial: Jewish-Christian Disputations in the Middle Ages*, Rutherford, NJ, London: Fairleigh Dickinson University Press Associated University Presses.

MacDougall, Hugh A. (1982), *Racial Myth in English History: Trojans, Teutons, and Anglo-Saxons*, Hanover, NH: University Press of New England.

Macintyre, Ben (2001), 'Bin Laden hijacks history for his holy war,' *The Times*, 27 October 2001.

Madden, Thomas F. (2005), *The New Concise History of the Crusades*, Lanham, MD: Rowman & Littlefield.

Mallette, Karla (2000), 'Poetries of the Norman courts,' in *The Literature of al-Andalus*, ed. María Rosa Menocal, Raymond P. Scheindlin and Michael Anthony Sells, Cambridge: Cambridge University Press, pp. 377–87.

———— (2003), 'Misunderstood,' *New Literary History: A Journal of Theory and Interpretation* 34: pp. 677–97.

———— (2005a), *The Kingdom of Sicily, 1100–1250: A Literary History*, Philadelphia: University of Pennsylvania Press.

———— (2005b), 'Orientalism and the nineteenth-century nationalist: Michele Amari, Ernest Renan, and 1848,' *Romanic Review* 96: p. 233.

Mandeville, John (1983), *The Travels of Sir John Mandeville*, trans. C. W. R. D. Moseley, New York: Penguin Books.

Margolis, Nadia (2003), 'Rewriting the right: high priests, heroes and hooligans in the portrayal of Joan of Arc (1824–1945),' in *Joan of Arc, a Saint for All Reasons: Studies in Myth and Politics*, ed. Dominique Goy-Blanquet, Aldershot: Ashgate, pp. 59–104.

Marie de France (1966), *Les lais de Marie de France*, ed. Jean Rychner, Les Classiques Français du Moyen Age 93, Paris: Libraire Honore Champion.

———— (1999), *The Lais of Marie de France*, ed. Glyn S. Burgess and Keith Busby, Penguin Classics, 2nd edn, London: Penguin.

Mariscal, Jorge (1998). 'The role of Spain in contemporary race theory,' *Arizona Journal of Hispanic Cultural Studies* 2 (1998).

Mazower, Mark (2000), *The Balkans: A Short History*, New York: Modern Library.

McClintock, Anne (1995), *Imperial Leather: Race, Gender, and Sexuality in the Colonial Contest*, New York: Routledge.

Menocal, María Rosa (2002), *The Ornament of the World: How Muslims, Jews, and Christians Created a Culture of Tolerance in Medieval Spain*, Boston: Little Brown.

———— ([1987] 2004), *The Arabic Role in Medieval Literary History: A Forgotten Heritage*, Philadelphia: University of Pennsylvania Press.

Metcalfe, Alex (2002), 'The Muslims of Sicily under Christian rule,' in *The Society of Norman Italy*, ed. G. A. Loud and Alex Metcalfe, Boston: Brill, pp. 289–317.

———— (2003), *Muslims and Christians in Norman Sicily: Arabic Speakers and the End of Islam*, London: Routledge.

Metlitzki, Dorothee (1977), *The Matter of Araby in Medieval England*, New Haven: Yale University Press.

Micha, Alexandre (ed.) (1990), *Guillaume de Palerne: Roman du XIIIe siècle*, Geneva: Droz.

Mignolo, Walter (2000), 'The many faces of cosmo-polis: border thinking and critical cosmopolitanism,' *Public Culture* 12: pp. 721–48.

Mirrer, Louise (1994), 'Representing 'Other' men: Muslims, Jews, and masculine ideals in medieval Castilian epic and ballad,' in *Medieval Masculinities: Regarding Men in the Middle Ages*, ed. Clare E. Lees, Thelma Fenster and Jo Ann McNamara, Minneapolis: University of Minnesota Press, pp. 169–86.

Mitchell, Jerome (1987), *Scott, Chaucer, and Medieval Romance: A Study in Sir Walter Scott's Indebtedness to the Literature of the Middle Ages*, Lexington: University Press of Kentucky.

Monge, Y. (2006), 'Aznar se pregunta por qué los musulmanes no se disculpan "por haber ocupado España ocho siglos,"' *El País*, 26 September 2006.

Monroe, James T. (ed.) ([1974] 2004), *Hispano-Arabic Poetry: A Student Anthology*, Piscataway: Gorgias Press.

Morrison, Toni (1992), *Playing in the Dark: Whiteness and the Literary Imagination*, Cambridge, MA: Harvard University Press.

Moseley, C. W. R. D. (1974), 'The metamorphoses of Sir John Mandeville,' *The Yearbook of English Studies* 4: pp. 5–25.

Mufti, Aamir (2007), *Enlightenment in the Colony: The Jewish Question and the Crisis of Postcolonial Culture*, Princeton: Princeton University Press.

Müller, Peter (2008), 'Bundeswehr: Deutsche führen Afghanistan aus dem Mittelalter,' *Die Welt online*, 23 June 2008, www.welt.de/politik/article2136097/Deutsche_fuehren_Afghanistan_aus_dem_Mittelalter.html

Müller, Ulrich (1999), 'Wolfram, Wagner, and the Germans,' in *A Companion to Wolfram's Parzival*, ed. Will Hasty, Columbia, SC: Camden House, pp. 245–58.

Navarrete, Rosina D. (1972), 'La Ideología del "Poema de Mío Cid,"' *Hispania* 55: pp. 234–40.

Nichols, Stephen G. (1996), 'Modernism and the politics of medieval studies,' in *Medievalism and the Modernist Temper*, ed. R. Howard Bloch and Stephen G. Nichols, Baltimore, MD: Johns Hopkins University Press, pp. 25–56.

Nirenberg, David (1998), *Communities of Violence: Persecution of Minorities in the Middle Ages*, 2nd edn, Princeton: Princeton University Press.

—— (2007), 'Race and the Middle Ages: the case of Spain and its Jews,' in Margaret Rich Greer, Walter Mignolo and Maureen Quilligan (eds), *Rereading the Black Legend: The Discourses of Religious and Racial Difference in the Renaissance Empires*, Chicago: University of Chicago Press.

Norwich, John Julius (1992), *The Normans in Sicily: The Normans in the South 1016–1130 and the Kingdom in the Sun 1130–1194*, London: Penguin.

Novalis (1978), *Werke, Tagebücher und Briefe Friedrich von Hardenbergs*, vol. 2, Munich: Hanser.

—— (1997), *Philosophical writings*, ed. Margaret Mahony Stoljar, Albany: State University of New York Press.

Nykrog, Per. (1996), 'A warrior scholar at the Collège de France,' in *Medievalism and the Modernist Temper*, ed. R. Howard Bloch and Stephen G. Nichols, Baltimore, MD: Johns Hopkins University Press, pp. 286–307.

Odoric of Pordenone (1929), 'Relatio,' in *Itinera et relationes fratrum minorum saeculi XIII et XIV*, ed. Anastasius van den Wyngaert, Quaracchi-Firenze: Collegium S. Bonaventurae, pp. 381–495.

—— (2002), *The Travels of Friar Odoric*, trans. Henry Yule, Italian Texts and Studies on Religion and Society, Grand Rapids, MI: W. B. Eerdmans.

O'Hagan, Jacinta (2000), 'A "clash of civilizations"?' in *Contending Images of World Politics*, ed. Greg Fry and Jacinta O'Hagan, New York: St Martin's, pp. 135–49.

Olender, Maurice (2002), *The Languages of Paradise: Aryans and Semites, a Match Made in Heaven*, trans. Arthur Goldhammer, New York: Other Press.

Orosius, Paulus (1964), *The Seven Books of History against the Pagans*, trans. Roy J. Deferrari, Washington, DC: Catholic University of America Press.

—— (1966), *Pauli Orosii Historiarum adversum paganos libri VII accedit eiusdem liber apologeticus*, ed. Karl Friedrich Wilhelm Zangemeister, Corpus Scriptorum Ecclesiasticorum Latinorum 5, New York: Johnson Reprint Corp.

Otter, Monika (1996), *Inventiones: Fiction and Referentiality in Twelfth-Century English Historical Writing*, Chapel Hill: University of North Carolina Press.

Ó Tuathail, Gearóid (1996), 'Samuel Huntington and the "civilizing" of global space,' in *Critical Geopolitics: The Politics of Writing Global Space*, Minneapolis: University of Minnesota Press, pp. 240–9.

Patterson, Lee (1987), *Negotiating the Past: The Historical Understanding of Medieval Literature*, Madison: University of Wisconsin Press.

—— (1990), 'On the margin: postmodernism, ironic history, and medieval studies,' *Speculum* 65: pp. 87–108.

Peck, Jeffrey M. (1996), '"In the beginning was the Word": Germany and the origin of German studies,' in *Medievalism and the Modernist Temper*, ed. R. Howard Bloch and Stephen G. Nichols, Baltimore, MD: Johns Hopkins University Press, pp. 127–47.

Perkins, Mary Anne (2004), *Christendom and European Identity: The Legacy of a Grand Narrative since 1789*, Religion and Society, 40, Berlin: Walter de Gruyter.

Perryman, Judith, ed. (1980), *The King of Tars*, Middle English Texts 12, Heidelberg: Winter.

Petar II, Prince Bishop of Montenegro (1970), *The Mountain Wreath of P. P. Nyegosh*, trans. James W. Wiles, Westport, CT: Greenwood Press.

—— (1989), *The Mountain Wreath*, trans. and ed. Vasa D. Mihailovich, Beograd, Serbia: Vajat.

Phillips, Melanie (2006), *Londonistan*, New York: Encounter Books.

Pick, Lucy K. (1999), 'Edward Said, Orientalism and the Middle Ages,' *Medieval Encounters* 5: pp. 265–71.

Piskorski, Jan (2002), 'After Occidentalism: the third Europe writes its own history,' in *Historiographical Approaches to Medieval Colonization of East Central Europe.*, ed. Jan Piskorski, Boulder, CO: Eastern European Monographs.

Pohl, Walter (2004), 'Gender and Ethnicity in the Early Middle Ages,' in *Gender in the Early Medieval World: East and West, 300–900*, ed. Leslie Brubaker and Julia M. H. Smith, Cambridge: Cambridge University Press, pp. 23–43.

Polo, Marco (1975), *Milione*, ed. Valeria Bertolucci Pizzorusso, Milano: Adelphi.

—— (1992), *The Travels of Marco Polo*, trans. Ronald E. Latham, Penguin Classics, New York: Penguin.

Pratt, Mary Louise ([1992] 2008), *Imperial Eyes: Travel Writing and Transculturation*, 2nd edn, New York: Routledge.

Prawer, Joshua (1973), *The Latin Kingdom of Jerusalem: European Colonialism in the Middle Ages*, London: Weidenfeld and Nicolson.

Prendergast, Thomas Augustine, and Stephanie Trigg (2007), 'What is happening to the Middle Ages?' *New Medieval Literatures* 9: pp. 215–30.

Purdum, Todd S. (2001), 'Bush warns of a wrathful, shadowy and inventive war,' *New York Times*, 17 September 2001.

Quayson, Ato (2005), 'Translations and transnationals: pre- and postcolonial,' in *Postcolonial Approaches to the European Middle Ages: Translating Cultures*, ed. Ananya Jahanara Kabir and Deanne Williams, Cambridge: Cambridge University Press, pp. 253–68.

Qureshi, Emran, and Michael Anthony Sells (eds) (2003), *The New Crusades*, New York: Columbia University Press.

Rabasa, José (1985), 'Allegories of the Atlas,' in *Europe and Its Others*, ed. Francis Barker et al., Colchester: University of Essex.

Ragussis, Michael (1995), *Figures of Conversion: 'The Jewish Question' and English National Identity*, Durham, NC: Duke University Press.

Rahtz, Philip A. (1985), *Invitation to Archaeology*, Oxford: Blackwell.

Ramadan, Tariq (2004), *Western Muslims and the Future of Islam*, Oxford: Oxford University Press.

Ramet, Sabrina P. (2006), *The Three Yugoslavias: State-Building and Legitimation, 1918–2005*, Washington, DC; Bloomington, IN: Woodrow Wilson Center Press; Indiana University Press.

Ramey, Lynn Tarte (2001), *Christian, Saracen and Genre in Medieval French Literature*, New York: Routledge.

Reichert, Michelle (2006), *Between Courtly Literature and al-Andalus: Matière d'Orient and the Importance of Spain in the Romances of the*

Twelfth-Century Writer Chrétien de Troyes, Studies in Medieval History and Culture, New York: Routledge.

Reynolds, Susan (1997), *Kingdoms and Communities in Western Europe, 900–1300*, 2nd edn, Oxford: Clarendon Press.

Riley-Smith, Jonathan Simon Christopher (2003), 'Islam and the Crusades in history and imagination, 8 November 1898–11 September 2001,' *Crusades* 2: pp. 151–67.

Risch, Neil, et al. (2002), 'Categorization of humans in biomedical research: genes, race and disease,' *Genome Biology* 3.7.

Robertson, Elizabeth (2001), 'The "Elvyssh" power of Constance: Christian feminism in Geoffrey Chaucer's *The Man of Law's Tale*,' *Studies in the Age of Chaucer* 23: pp. 143–80.

Roe, Harry and Ann Dooley (eds) (1999), *Tales of the Elders of Ireland: Acallam na Senórach*, trans. Harry Roe and Ann Dooley, Oxford: Oxford University Press.

Rogozen-Soltar, Mikaela (2007), 'Al-Andalus in Andalusia: negotiating Moorish history and regional identity in Southern Spain,' *Anthropological Quarterly* 80: pp. 863–86.

Rollo, David (1995), 'Gerald of Wales' *Topographia Hibernica*: sex and the Irish nation,' *Romanic Review* 86: pp. 169–90.

Rosen, Tova (2000), 'The muwashshah,' in *The Literature of Al-Andalus*, ed. María Rosa Menocal, Raymond P. Scheindlin and Michael Sells, Cambridge: Cambridge University Press, pp. 165–89.

Ross, J. J. (1986), 'An English history: Kipling's joint authorship, with C. R. L. Fletcher, of *A School History of England* (1911),' *The Kipling Journal* 60: pp. 31–42.

Rushdie, Salman (1995), *The Moor's Last Sigh*, London: J. Cape.

Said, Edward ([1978] 1994), *Orientalism*, New York: Vintage.

—— (1997), *Covering Islam: How the Media and the Experts Determine How We See the Rest of the World*, New York: Vintage.

—— (2001), 'The clash of ignorance,' *Nation* 273: pp. 11–13.

—— (2004), 'U.S.: a disputed history of identity,' *Le Monde Diplomatique: English Edition*, September.

Salgado, Minoli (2007), 'The politics of the palimpsest in *The Moor's Last Sigh*,' in *Salman Rushdie*, ed. Abdulrazak Gurnah, Cambridge, England: Cambridge University Press, pp. 153–67.

Sánchez-Albornoz, Claudio (1956), *España, un enigma historico*, Buenos Aires: Editorial Sudamericana.

Sanders, Andrew (2000), '"Utter indifference"? The Anglo-Saxons in the nineteenth-century novel,' in *Literary Appropriations of the Anglo-Saxons from the Thirteenth to the Twentieth Century*, ed. Donald Scragg and Carole Weinberg, Cambridge: Cambridge University Press, pp. 157–73.

Sapir Abulafia, Anna (1995), *Christians and Jews in the Twelfth-Century Renaissance*, London: Routledge.

———— (ed.) (2002), *Religious Violence between Christians and Jews: Medieval Roots, Modern Perspectives*, Houndmills: Palgrave.

Savage, Timothy (2004), 'Europe and Islam: crescent waxing/cultures clashing,' *The Washington Quarterly*: pp. 25–50.

Schlauch, Margaret (1939), 'The allegory of church and synagogue,' *Speculum* 14: pp. 448–64.

Schlegel, A. W. (1812), 'Ueber das Lied der Nibelungen,' *Deutsches Museum* 1: pp. 9–36.

Schmitt, Thomas (2003), *Moscheen in Deutschland: Konflikte um ihre Errichtung und Nutzung*, Flensburg: Deutsche Akademie für Landeskunde.

Schneider, Peter (2005), 'The new Berlin wall,' *The New York Times Magazine (NY)*, 4 December 2005.

Schneider, Wolfgang and Peter Förster (1990), *Leipziger Demontagebuch: Demo, Montag, Tagebuch, Demontage*, 2nd edn, Leipzig: Gustav Kiepenheuer.

Schwartz, Robert S. (2001), 'Racial profiling in medical research,' *New England Journal of Medicine* 344 (3 May 2001): pp. 1392–3.

Sciolino, Elaine and Hélène Fouquet (2004), 'God's place in charter is dividing Europeans,' *New York Times*, 26 May 2004.

Sconduto, Leslie A. (2000), 'Rewriting the werewolf in *Guillaume de Palerne*,' *Cygne: Bulletin of the International Marie de France Society* 6: pp. 23–35.

———— (2004), *Guillaume de Palerne: An English Translation of the 12th Century French Verse Romance*, Jefferson, NC: McFarland.

Scott, Joan Wallach (2007), *The Politics of the Veil*, The Public Square Book Series, Princeton, NJ: Princeton University Press.

Scott, Sir Walter (1998), *Ivanhoe*, ed. Graham Tulloch, Edinburgh: Edinburgh University Press.

———— (2005), *Ivanhoe*, ed. Gillen D'Arcy Wood, New York: Barnes & Noble Classics.

Seiferth, Wolfgang S. (1970), *Synagogue and Church in the Middle Ages: Two Symbols in Art and Literature*, trans. Lee Chadeayne and Paul Gottwald, New York: Ungar.

Sells, Michael (1996), *The Bridge Betrayed: Religion and Genocide in Bosnia*, Berkeley: University of California Press.

Sennoff, Charles (2004), 'Seeking Madrid motives in a cradle of Muslim glory,' *Boston Globe*, 28 March 2004.

'Serbian and French nationalist leaders attend friendship rally in Belgrade' (1997), BBC Summary of World Broadcasts, 24 January 1997.

Shakespeare, William (2008), *The Merchant of Venice*, ed. Jay L. Halio, Oxford: Oxford University Press.

Shohat, Ella (1992), 'Notes on the "post-colonial",' *Social Text*: pp. 99–113.

Short, Ian (ed.) (1990), *La chanson de Roland*, Paris: Librairie générale Française.

Siberry, Elizabeth (2000), *The New Crusaders: Images of the Crusades in the Nineteenth and Early Twentieth Centuries*, Aldershot: Ashgate.

Simmons, Clare A. (2006), *Reversing the Conquest: History and Myth in Nineteenth-century British Literature*, New Brunswick, NJ: Rutgers University Press.

Smith, Brendan (1999), *Colonisation and Conquest in Medieval Ireland: The English in Louth, 1170–1330*, Cambridge: Cambridge University Press.

Smith, Colin (ed.) (1985), *Poema de mío Cid*, Madrid: Cátedra.

Smith, Kirby Flower (1894), 'An historical study of the werwolf,' *PMLA* 9: pp. 1–42.

Snowden Jr, Frank M. (1970), *Blacks in Antiquity: Ethiopians in the Greco-Roman Experience*, Cambridge, MA: Harvard University Press.

Socolovsky, Jerome (2005), *Militants Invoke Spain's Andalusian Heritage*, NPR Weekend Edition Sunday, 3 April 2005, radio broadcast.

Sola-Solé, Josep M. (ed.) (1990), *Las Jarchas romances y sus moaxajas*, Persiles 201, Madrid: Taurus.

Southern, R. W. (1962), *Western Views of Islam in the Middle Ages*, Cambridge, MA: Harvard University Press.

Spiegel, Gabrielle M. (2000), 'Épater les Médiévistes,' *History and Theory* 39: pp. 243–50.

Stern, Samuel (1948), 'Les Vers finaux en espagnol dans les *muwaššahs* hispano-hébraïques: une contribution à l'histoire du *muwaššah* et à l'étude du vieux dialecte espagnol "mozarabe,"' *Al-Andalus* 13: pp. 299–248.

——— (1953), *Les chansons mozarabes*, Palermo: U. Manfredi.

Sternsdorff, Jürgen (1979), *Wissenschaftskonstitution und Reichsgründung*. Frankfurt am Main: Lang.

Steyn, Mark (2006), *America Alone: The End of the World as We Know It*, Washington, DC: Regnery.

Stoker, Bram (1897), *Dracula: A Mystery Story*, New York: W. R. Caldwell and Co.

Stow, Kenneth R. (1992), *Alienated Minority: The Jews of Medieval Latin Europe*, Cambridge, MA: Harvard University Press.

——— (2007), *Popes, Church, and Jews in the Middle Ages: Confrontation and Response*, Aldershot: Ashgate.

Strayer, Joseph Reese (1963), 'The historical experience of nation-building in Europe,' in *Nation-Building*, ed. Karl Wolfgang Deutsch and William J. Foltz, New York: Atherton, pp. 17–26.

——— (1970), *On the Medieval Origins of the Modern State*, Princeton: Princeton University Press.

Summit, Jennifer (2000), *Lost Property: The Woman Writer and English Literary History, 1380–1589*, Chicago: University of Chicago Press.

Summit, Jennifer and David Wallace (2007), 'Rethinking periodization,' *Journal of Medieval and Early Modern Studies* 37: pp. 447–51.

Sutcliffe, Adam (2003), *Judaism and Enlightenment*, New York: Cambridge University Press.

Sutherland, John (1995), *The Life of Walter Scott: A Critical Biography*, Oxford: Blackwell.

Todorova, Maria Nikolaeva (2004), *Balkan Identities: Nation and Memory*, New York: New York University Press.

Tofiño-Quesada, Ignacio (2003), 'Spanish Orientalism: uses of the past in Spain's colonization in Africa,' *Comparative Studies of South Asia, Africa and the Middle East* 23.1–2: pp. 141–8.

Tolan, John Victor (2002), *Saracens: Islam in the Medieval European Imagination*, New York: Columbia University Press.

Tomasch, Sylvia (1998), 'Judecca, Dante's Satan, and the *Dis*-placed Jew,' in *Text and Territory: Geographical Imagination in the European Middle Ages*, ed. Sylvia Tomasch and Sealy Gilles, Philadelphia: University of Pennsylvania Press, pp. 247–67.

—— (2000), 'Postcolonial Chaucer and the virtual Jew,' in *The Postcolonial Middle Ages*, ed. Jeffrey Jerome Cohen, New York: St. Martin's, pp. 243–60.

Tremlett, Giles (2003), 'Troops bear "moor killer" badges,' *The Guardian*, 25 July 2003.

Trounson, Rebecca and Nancy Vogel (2003), 'The recall election: Propositions 53 and 54; both ballot measures go down in defeat,' *Los Angeles Times*, 8 October 2003.

Turner, Sharon (1814), *The History of England from the Norman Conquest to the Accession of Edward the First*, London: N.p.

—— (1853), *The History of England during the Middle Ages*, 5th edn, London: Longman, Brown, Green, and Longmans.

Turville-Petre, Thorlac (1996), *England the Nation: Language, Literature, and National Identity, 1290–1340*, Oxford: Clarendon Press.

Uebel, Michael (2005), *Ecstatic Transformations: On the Uses of Alterity in the Middle Ages*, New York: Palgrave Macmillan.

Valman, Nadia. 2007, *The Jewess in Nineteenth-Century British Literary Culture*, Cambridge: Cambridge University Press.

Vauchez, André, R. Barrie Dobson and Michael Lapidge (2000), *Encyclopedia of the Middle Ages*, trans. Adrian Walford, Chicago: Fitzroy Dearborn Publishers.

Verdon, Jean (2003), *Travel in the Middle Ages*, trans. George Holoch, Notre Dame, IN: University of Notre Dame Press.

Verlinden, Charles (1970), *The Beginnings of Modern Colonization*, Ithaca, NY: Cornell University Press.

Vetlesen, Arne (2005), *Evil and Human Agency: Understanding Collective Evildoing*, Cambridge: Cambridge University Press.

Viswanathan, Gauri (1989), *Masks of Conquest: Literary Study and British Rule in India*, Social Foundations of Aesthetic Forms Series, New York: Columbia University Press.

——— (ed.) (2001), *Power, Politics, and Culture: Interviews with Edward W. Said*, New York: Pantheon Books.

Wachtel, Andrew B. (2003), 'How to use a classic: Petar Petrovic Njegos in the twentieth century,' in *Ideologies and National Identities: The Case of Twentieth-Century Southeastern Europe*, ed. John R. Lampe and Mark Mazower, Budapest; New York: Central European University Press, pp. 131–53.

Wade, Nicholas (2002), 'Race is seen as real guide to track roots of disease,' *New York Times*, 30 July 2002.

Wallhead, Celia (1997), 'The subversive sub-text of spices in Salman Rushdie's *The Moor's Last Sigh*,' *Revista Canaria de Estudios Ingleses* 35: pp. 61–76.

Wallace, David (2004), *Premodern Places: Calais to Surinam, Chaucer to Aphra Behn*, Malden, MA: Blackwell.

Ward, Olivia (1998), 'A shudder in those seeking peace: the likely successor to Yugoslavia's Milosevic uses nationalism like a club,' *The Toronto Star*, 13 December 1998.

Warren, Michelle R. (2000), *History on the Edge: Excalibur and the Borders of Britain, 1100–1300*, Medieval Cultures 22, Minneapolis: University of Minnesota Press.

——— (2003), 'Post-philology,' in *Postcolonial Moves: Medieval Through Modern*, ed. Patricia Clare Ingham and Michelle R. Warren, New York: Palgrave Macmillan, pp. 19–45.

——— (2005), '"Au commencement était l'ile": The Colonial Formation of Joseph Bédier's *Chanson de Roland*,' in *Postcolonial Approaches to the European Middle Ages: Translating Cultures*, ed. Ananya Jahanara Kabir and Deanne Williams, Cambridge: Cambridge University Press, pp. 205–26.

Waswo, Richard (1997), *The Founding Legend of Western Civilization: From Virgil to Vietnam*, Hanover, NH: University Press of New England.

Watson, Ritchie Devon (2008), *Normans and Saxons: Southern Race Mythology and the Intellectual History of the American Civil War*, Baton Rouge: Louisiana State University Press.

Wellershoff, Dieter (2007), ' Wofür steht die kölner moschee?' *Frankfurter Allgemeine Zeitung*, 14 June 2007.

West, Francis James (1999), 'The Colonial History of the Norman Conquest?' *History* 84: pp. 119–236.

Westrem, Scott D (1998), 'Against Gog and Magog,' in *Text and Territory: Geographical Imagination in the European Middle Ages*, ed. Sylvia Tomasch and Sealy Gilles, Philadelphia: University of Pennsylvania Press, pp. 54–75.

Wilders, Geert (2008), *Fitna*, www.themoviefitna.com, accessed 8 October 2008.

Willan, Philip (2001), 'Italian PM says sorry for attack on Islam: words that led to uproar had been "twisted,"' *The Guardian*, 29 September 2001.

Wilhelm, Jürgen (2007), *Zwei Jahrtausende Jüdische Kunst und Kultur in Köln*, Köln: Greven.

William of Rubruck (1929), 'Itinerarium,' in *Itinera et relationes fratrum minorum saeculi XIII et XIV*, ed. Anastasius van den Wyngaert, Quaracchi-Firenze: Collegium S. Bonaventurae, pp. 147–332.

—— (1955), *The Mongol Mission: Narratives and Letters of the Franciscan Missionaries in Mongolia and China in the Thirteenth and Fourteenth Centuries*, ed. Christopher Dawson, Makers of Christendom, New York: Sheed & Ward.

—— (1990), *The Mission of Friar William of Rubruck: His Journey to the Court of the Great Khan Möngke, 1253–1255*, trans. Peter Jackson, ed. Peter Jackson and David Morgan, London: Hakluyt Society.

Williams, Michelle Hale (2006), *The Impact of Radical Right-Wing Parties in West European Democracies*, New York: Palgrave Macmillan.

Williamson, George S. (2004), *The Longing for Myth in Germany: Religion and Aesthetic Culture from Romanticism to Nietzsche*, Chicago: University of Chicago Press.

Wilson, H. B. (1960), 'The symbolism of Belakâne and Feirefîz in Wolfram's *Parzival*,' *German Life and Letters* 13: pp. 94–105.

Windisch, Ernst and Whitley Stokes (eds) (1880), 'Acallamh na Senórach,' in *Irische texte* 1, Leipzig: S. Hirzel.

Wolfram von Eschenbach (1961), *Parzival*, trans. Helen M. Mustard and Charles E. Passage, New York: Vintage.

Yildiz, Yasemin (2009), 'Turkish girls, Allah's daughters, and the contemporary German subject: itinerary of a figure,' *German Life and Letters* 62.3: pp. 465–81.

—— (forthcoming), 'Governing European subjects: tolerance and guilt in the discourse of "Muslim women",' *Cultural Critique*.

Young, Robert (1995), *Colonial Desire: Hybridity in Theory, Culture, and Race*, London: Routledge.

—— (2008), *The Idea of English Ethnicity*, Malden, MA: Blackwell.

Further Reading

This suggested further reading, especially the monographs section, is intended primarily to point scholars and students to texts not already cited, including work that has appeared too recently to be discussed in the body of the text.

Anthologies

Akbari, Suzanne, and Amilcare Iannucci (eds) (2008), *Marco Polo and the Encounter of East and West*, Toronto: University of Toronto Press. Wide-ranging essays on Marco Polo and on texts such as Mandeville's *Travels*, including modern takes on Marco Polo in fiction and film.

Allen, Rosamund (ed.) (2004), *Eastward Bound: Travel and Travelers: 1050–1550*, Manchester: Manchester University Press. Essays on medieval travellers from the Jewish, Christian and Muslim traditions.

Bullón-Fernández, María, ed. (2007), *England and Iberia in the Middle Ages, 12th–15th Century: Cultural, Literary, and Political Exchanges*, New York: Palgrave Macmillan. Historically informed essays on the often overlooked relationship between England and Iberia in the medieval period.

Doubleday, Simon R. and David Coleman (eds) (2008), *In the Light of Medieval Spain: Islam, the West, and the Relevance of the Past*. New York: Palgrave. Provocative essays on the role of medieval Iberia in contemporary global politics.

Tomasch, Sylvia and Sealy Gilles (eds) (1998), *Text and Territory: Geographical Imagination in the European Middle Ages*. The Middle Ages series. Philadelphia: University of Pennsylvania Press. Includes essays on Brut, Chaucer, Dante and Orosius.

Journals: Articles and Special Issues

Altschul, Nadia (2008), 'Postcolonialism and the study of the Middle Ages,' *History Compass* 6. 2: pp. 588–606. Lucid and perceptive review of the field.

Braude, Benjamin (1997), 'The sons of Noah and the construction of ethnic and geographical identities in the medieval and early modern periods,' *The William and Mary Quarterly* 54. 1 (January): pp. 103–42. Important discussion of the role of this biblical model in medieval understandings of human difference. Part of a special issue of the journal on medieval and early modern race.

Dagenais, John and Margaret R. Greer (eds and intro.) (2000), 'Decolonizing the Middle Ages,' special issue, *Journal of Medieval and Early Modern Studies* 30. 3 (October). Introduction to a special issue that includes essays both on medieval texts and modern medievalisms.

Fuchs, Barbara and David J. Baker (2004), 'The Postcolonial Past,' special issue, *Modern Language Quarterly: A Journal of Literary History* 65. 3 (September 1): pp. 329–40. Introduction to a special issue that includes essays on ancient Greece, Petrarch and *La Celestina*.

Hahn, Thomas (ed.) (2001), 'Race and ethnicity in the Middle Ages,' special issue, *Journal of Medieval and Early Modern Studies* 31. 1 (Winter). Special issue with numerous excellent essays on questions of race in the medieval period.

Summit, Jennifer and David Wallace (eds) (2007), 'Medieval/Renaissance: after periodization,' special issue, *Journal of Medieval and Early Modern Studies* 37. 3 (Fall). Special issue on periodisation, including essays by Jóse Rabasa and Ania Loomba.

'Theories and methologies' cluster: (2009), 'Medieval studies in the twenty-first century,' *PMLA* 124. 2: (March): 576–646. Articles especially relevant to postcolonial medieval studies by McCracken, Mallette, Lochrie, Kinoshita, Chism and Blackmore.

Monographs

Akbari, Suzanne (2009), *Idols of the East: European Representations of Islam and the Orient, 1100–1450*, Ithaca, New York: Cornell University Press. Important study of representations of Muslims and Islam and of the development of Orientalism in the medieval period.

Barrett, Robert W. Jr (2009), *Against All England: Regional Identity and Chesire Writing, 1195–1656*. Notre Dame, Indiana: University of Notre Dame Press. Study of Chesire that engages issues of regionalism and periodisation.

Blurton, Heather (2007), *Cannibalism in High Medieval English Literature*, New York: Palgrave Macmillan. Examines cannibalism as a political metaphor and includes readings of *Andreas*, *Beowulf*, Matthew of Paris and *Richard Coer de Lyon*.

Finke, Laurie and Martin B. Shichtman (2004), *King Arthur and the Myth of History*, Gainesville: University Press of Florida. Important and stimulating essays on medieval Arthurian narrative from a critical historicist perspective.

Grieve, Patricia (2009), *The Eve of Spain: Myths of Origins in the History of Christian, Muslim, and Jewish Conflict*, Baltimore: Johns Hopkins University Press. Examines, with an emphasis on the importance of gender and sexuality, the role of the myth of King Rodrigo and his rape of La Cava on the 'founding myth' of the fall of Visigothic Spain to Muslim invaders.

Hiatt, Alfred (2008), *Terra Incognita: Mapping the Antipodes before 1600*, Chicago: University of Chicago Press. Explores the impact of the idea of 'unknown lands' on medieval European literary and political expression.

Holsinger, Bruce (2007), *Neomedievalism, Neoconservatism, and the War on Terror*, Paradigm, vol. 29, Chicago: Prickly Paradigm. Important critique of post-9/11 medievalisms, including their role in justifications of torture by the US government.

Huot, Sylvia (2007), *Postcolonial Fictions in the 'Roman de Perceforest': Cultural Identities and Hybridities*, Gallica, vol. 1, Woodbridge: D. S. Brewer. Reading informed by postcolonial theory of the important, but little-studied, fourteenth-century French prose romance.

Lalla, Barbara (2008), *Postcolonialisms: Caribbean Rereading of Medieval English Discourse*, Kingston, Jamaica: University of the West Indies Press. Critical readings of Old and Middle English literature through contemporary Caribbean texts.

Schildgen, Brenda Deen (2002), *Dante and the Orient*, Urbana: University of Illinois Press. Traces the themes of the Orient and Islam in Dante, including useful discussions and explanations of contemporary texts and materials.

Strickland, Deborah Higgs (2003), *Saracens, Demons, and Jews: Making Monsters in Medieval Art*, Princeton, NJ: Princeton University Press. Art historical exploration of medieval Christian representations of non-Christians and of the so-called monstrous races. Excellent visual resource.

Web Resources

www.inthemedievalmiddle.com: An engaging medieval studies group blog begun by Jeffrey Jerome Cohen. Very useful resource for reviews and information on events and recent or forthcoming materials related to postcolonial medieval studies.

www.laits.utexas.edu/gma/portal: Portal to three essential sites for postcolonial medieval studies: Mappamundi, the Global Middle Ages Project, and the Scholarly Community the Globalization of the Middle Ages. Project created and organized by Susan Noakes and Geraldine Heng.

Index